Guatemala

INSIDE

Guatemala

Tom Barry

The Inter-Hemispheric Education Resource Center
Albuquerque, New Mexico

Published by the Inter-Hemispheric Education Resource Center

**The Inter-Hemispheric Education Resource Center
Box 4506 / Albuquerque, New Mexico 87196**

Library of Congress Cataloging-in-Publication Data

Barry, Tom, 1950–
Inside Guatemala / Tom Barry. — 1st ed.
p.   cm.
Includes bibliographical references.
ISBN 0-911213-40-6 : $9.95
1. Guatemala—Politics and government—1985– 2. Guatemala—Economic conditions—1985– 3. Guatemala—Social conditions.
I. Title. II. Title: Guatemala.
F1466.7.B37   1992
972.8105'3—dc20   92-71797

Acknowledgments

Acknowledgments are not a simple matter when they concern people and organizations in Guatemala, a nation long characterized by its pervasive repression and state terrorism. This book would not have been possible without the advice, information, and hospitality offered by many friends and acquaintances in Guatemala whose names are left unmentioned for fear of further endangering their safety. In the United States, the book benefited from comments and critiques given by Bonnie Tenneriello, David Loeb, and Michael Willis. Like all publications of the Resource Center, Inside Guatemala is a collective effort of the staff: Steve Whitman, Rose Hansen, Felipe Montoya, and Debra Preusch provided valuable research assistance; Chuck Hosking edited and proofread the text; John Hawley designed the book and managed the word-processing. I would also like to thank the financial assistance generously provided by the Threshold Foundation, United Church of Christ, and the Maryknoll Fathers and Brothers.

Contents

Contents

Part 8: U.S. Influence

Reference Notes

Bibliography

Chronology

For More Information

List of Figures

Introduction

Guatemala, the most populated country in Central America, stuns visitors with its natural and human beauty. From black-sand beaches and fertile plains along the Pacific Coast, the land sweeps up into the rugged highland region. Marking this dramatic division between the coastal lowlands and the western highlands is a wall of 23 majestic volcanoes, some of them still fuming, skirting the central heights. Like most of Central America, Guatemala is located in a zone of extreme geological instability. Guatemala City and the old capital city of Antigua have been severely damaged by earthquakes at least 15 times since the 16th century.[1]

On a clear day one can witness both topographical worlds from the peak of the extinct Volcán de Agua. Looking toward the Pacific Ocean, the country's economic heartland fans out before you. In the distance, vast agroexport plantations extend to the sea. Closer in, as the terrain rises, the folds of the hills and the volcano itself are covered with the deep green of coffee bushes. Antigua, which lies in the shadow of Agua, was the colonial capital and produces some of the world's finest coffee. Looking east toward Guatemala City, there appear occasional flashes of fire and brimstone from the fitful Pacaya volcano.

Turning away from the sea are the western highlands or *altiplano*. Throughout these mountains live the indigenous peoples of Guatemala. For centuries, they have survived tending their corn and beans on small mountain plots. Market days announce themselves with an explosion of color and community as indian families trickle out of the mountains to buy and sell in the plaza of the local municipality.

Poverty and hunger stalk these mountains. From the youngest to the oldest, the focus of daily life is survival. Young girls walk for miles carrying heavy jars of water. By the side of the road, old men, like pack animals, carry impossibly heavy burdens of firewood and agricultural produce.

The *altiplano* is stained with the blood of massacres from a counterinsurgency campaign that swept through the mountains in the early 1980s. It is a region whose sad story is told by the proliferation of army outposts and the scorched remains of indian villages. For the most part, the voices of its indian inhabitants have been silenced by terror and trauma.

Beyond the highlands lies the Northern Transverse Strip (FTN), a band of jungle that spans the top of the departments of Alta Verapaz, Quiché, and Huehuetenango. Settled only during the last twenty years, the FTN has become known as the Zone of Generals, owing to the wholesale land-grabbing by military officers. Like the *altiplano*, it has been one of the country's main conflictive zones. The army has attempted to assert control over the FTN with road-building projects and counterinsurgency sweeps, but elusive guerrillas have largely managed to check the advance of the roads and disappear into the jungle in the face of army offensives and bombing raids.

Jutting out like some unnatural appendage is the department of Petén, a vast expanse of tropical forest and once a center for the Mayan civilization. From the heights of the Tikal pyramids, the Petén seems a never-ending carpet of tropical green. But flying over the region, it is not the tropical forests that draw your attention but the spreading deforestation by timber companies, cattle ranchers, and slash-and-burn peasant farmers. It is here in the Petén where the Kaibiles, an elite counterinsurgency battalion, hold sway.

In the northeast, the Caribbean laps the shores of the steamy department of Izabal, the center of the Del Monte banana enclave. Stretching south along the eastern border is Guatemala's *oriente*, an arid, often desolate region populated by a *ladino* (non-indian) peasant class. The torrid departments of Zacapa, Chiquimula, Progreso, Jalapa, Santa Rosa, and Jutiapa provide the country with its police and military officers.

Population Growth and Environmental Crisis

The imbalanced geographic distribution of wealth and economic infrastructure is dramatic. The department (province) of Guatemala—home to the nation's capital, Guatemala City—accommodates 26 percent of the population but produces 46 percent of the national income. In contrast, the largely indian departments of northwestern Guatemala, Quiché and Huehuetenango, house 12 percent of the population but produce only 4 percent of national income.

Guatemala is still a mostly rural society, and its pace of urbanization is slow when compared with many other Latin American nations. In 1950, 30 percent of Guatemalans lived in the cities, a proportion that jumped to 42 percent by 1990. It is projected that 55 percent of Guatemalans will be urban dwellers by the year 2010.[2]

Population is expanding at an annual rate of 2.9 percent, although in large urban centers, particularly Guatemala City, the population swells 4 percent annually due to migration from rural areas. It is an exceedingly young population—46 percent under the age of 15 years. As landlessness, joblessness, and environmental problems intensify, Guatemala is slowly waking up to its population problem. In 1950 the nation numbered 2.9 million people, soaring to 6.9 million by 1980 and to an estimated 9.6 million in 1992. It is projected that by the year 2000 there will be more than 12 million Guatemalans, rising to 16 million by 2010. Population density per square kilometer jumped from 27.3 in 1950 to 84.5 in 1990, and is projected to rise to 112.2 by the year 2000—a four-fold increase in 50 years.[3] Still, many Guatemalans believe the old adages that "Children are the treasure of the poor" and that "Each child is born with a loaf of bread under his arm."

The country's rapid population growth is a major factor in its dramatic environmental deterioration in recent years. Not only is the enchanting beauty of Guatemala vanishing but the land base is also weary from overuse. Such structural obstacles as skewed land-tenure patterns, military dominance, the absence of a well-developed civil society (social development and organizing outside the traditional political, military, and religious institutions), and repression of workers and peasants have stalled political and economic development in Guatemala. The environmental crisis now threatens to restrict the development options of future generations. Even in the unlikely event that other major impediments to broadly shared development are overcome, the ever-worsening tension between population growth and conservation of land resources may condemn Guatemala to deepening impoverishment and destitution. Some social commentators predict that in the absence of radical economic and social reforms and due to continuing environmental deterioration there will be a gradual "Africanization" of Guatemala, meaning that widespread malnutrition will turn to starvation. In the Ixil Triangle in northern Quiché, indian farmers, recognizing the impending environmental crisis, complain: "The land no longer gives."[4]

A Land of Contrasts

Guatemala is a country rife with contrasts. In Antigua, an international tourist class escapes the industrialized world in a fantasyland of colonial churches, cobblestoned streets, an indigenous culture, pastry shops, and vegetarian pizza. The stone walls of the city, however, mask a brutal economy exploiting indian laborers who toil for a dollar or two a day picking coffee for local oligarchs. Tourists flock to Guatemala to dip into the past and savor the beauty of native artisans, blind to the economic cruelty that pervades the society.

Deep in the country's interior, army psychological-operations teams show videos about the threat of communist "delinquents" and "terrorists" to indians who, having never seen television before, are more mesmerized by the medium than the message. Civil Affairs promoters from the army initiate patriotic educational campaigns and organize beauty contests of teenage indian girls dressed in their traditional *traje* to inaugurate government infrastructure projects and "model villages" in an attempt to integrate indian communities into the "national life." In the cities, indian men cut mansion lawns with their machetes, while pentecostal preachers trudge through the city dumps, salvaging the souls of those who contend for scraps of garbage alongside legions of vultures.

Guatemala is an armed camp, from the countryside where local military garrisons preside over political and social life to the cities where armed power is shared by the security forces and criminal bands. Agroexport oligarchs and military-linked death squads round out the diverse power blocs that enforce their concept of law and order with weapons and terror. Although the poor bear the brunt of this culture of violence, even the elite are engulfed in an environment of fear as the result of frequent political feuds, threats of extortion, and factional rivalries.

Life, commonly lived on the edge in Guatemala, is becoming increasingly precarious. For most Guatemalans, rising human rights violations and mounting repression are a lesser concern than the daily death and suffering inflicted by society's inequitable economic structures. More Guatemalans die of preventable diseases than from political violence. Although Guatemala has shifted politically, it remains entrenched in its benighted systems of land tenure and labor exploitation.

Tourists are lured to Guatemala by promotions touting the land of "eternal spring." Characteristic of the black humor of the country, students joke that their country is the land of "eternal repression." Indeed, repression seems an almost natural part of the climate in Guatemala. So final is the repression that the country has no political prisoners—there are just bodies and disappearances. So pervasive is the repression that the army has infiltrated even remote communities with so-called "voluntary civil-defense patrols."

Fear, suspicion, and paranoia are almost endemic to Guatemalans. Politics is a subject of conversation between only the most trusted of friends. Personal information—where one works or lives— is closely guarded in Guatemala. Despite the institution of civilian government, many Guatemalans still go about their daily life looking over their shoulders to see if they are being followed or watched. Yet, for lack of alternatives, many Guatemalans would support a return to the era of dictators, yearning for someone who could check the forces of anarchy, crime, and social disintegration.

Political and Economic Modernization

Modern history in Guatemala dates back to 1944, the year when longtime dictator General Jorge Ubico retired and a successor regime was overthrown by a reformist alliance of military officers, students, professionals, businessmen, and politicians.[5] For ten years Guatemala experimented with democracy, social reforms, and economic modernization. A violent coup in 1954—supported by the CIA, rightwing politicians, the Catholic hierarchy, and the oligarchy—brought that period to an abrupt end.[6] For nearly four decades, the country has suffered the legacy of that abortion of democracy and reform.[7]

The coup, engineered by Colonel Carlos Castillo Armas and his CIA backers, reinstalled oligarchic and military control in Guatemala, melded now with the ideology of anticommunism and national security. Many hoped that the 1985 elections that brought Vinicio Cerezo into the National Palace would return the light of reason and progress to a country darkened by decades of rightwing extremism, military rule, and oligarchic conservatism. Some even dared to dream that a civilian Christian Democratic government might return Guatemala to the path optimistically initiated in 1944 by Juan José Arévalo and the October Revolution.

Political modernization has come to Guatemala in the form of elections and the institution of civilian rule. Guatemala is also undergoing a process of economic modernization ushered in by structural adjustment programs guided by neoliberal principles. The changes since 1985 have been dramatic. With the inauguration of Jorge Serrano in January 1991, Guatemalans experienced the first transfer of power between elected civilians in four decades. The new government boasts an aggressive Human Rights Ombudsman and even asserts a degree of control over the military. On the economic front, the influence of the diehard reactionaries of the agroexport oligarchy is fading as neoliberal modernizers wrest control over economic policy.

Though political and economic structures have been adjusted or modernized, the future for most Guatemalans still looks grim. The remedies proffered never seem to address the nation's deepest structural weaknesses: the concentration of land and wealth, the unwillingness of the private sector to risk its money in long-term investments, the weak state of the domestic market, overreliance on the international market, the marginalization of the indian and rural population, and the unresponsiveness of the state to the basic needs of its citizenry.

In an attempt to remedy the ills resulting from a model predicated on agroexport production and exploitation of labor, more of the same is being tried. Since 1985 the nation's president has been freely elected, but repression and economic deprivation bind civil society in a state of atrophy. Popular organizations have braved the wrath of both the state and the economic power structure to demand their basic economic and human rights, while providing a forum for indian communities. But grassroots groups have largely been ignored by the political parties and targeted for repression by the nation's many reactionary forces. The hope cherished by some within the popular movement that armed revolutionary forces would usher in a progressive state have long since faded.

For the neoliberal modernizers, the future may look bright. But for most Guatemalans the future barely exists. Instead, they are worried about day-to-day survival, perhaps even occasionally pining for a time when families could count on having at least a small plot of land, steady work, and the expectation that the future might be better for their children.

The tragic plight of Guatemala is largely a product of its many internal troubles—including ethnic divisions, decades of military control, and an unusually reactionary economic elite. Yet Guatemala is hardly alone in its misery and hopelessness. Together with other third world nations, Guatemala is being shaped by a world market and an international political environment that marginalizes peasant societies, promotes unsustainable development practices, and offers crass capitalism as the only course toward the future.

PART 1

Government and Politics

© Derrill Bazzy

Institution of Civilian Rule

Jorge Serrano received the blue and white presidential sash from Vinicio Cerezo on January 14, 1991—marking the first time in 51 years that one elected civilian government had succeeded another. But the hope and joy that had greeted the inauguration of Cerezo in January 1986 had (after five years of "democratic" rule) given way to despair and cynicism. The election of Serrano (like that of Cerezo) was fair and free of fraud, but its credibility was undermined by the high rate of abstention.

In the January 6 run-off election between Serrano and Jorge Carpio Nicolle, 55 percent of the registered electorate did not even bother to go to the polls. Serrano won the contest with 68 percent of the vote, but because of the high abstention rate those voting for Serrano represented only about 30 percent of the registered electorate.[1]

The peaceful transfer of power from Cerezo to Serrano seemed to indicate the success of the democratization process launched in the mid-1980s and heralded the nation's move away from direct military rule. The Guatemalan citizenry, however, were less than enthusiastic about the type of democracy they were experiencing. Their hopes for economic and social progress had been dashed by the Cerezo administration. It was true that the economy was growing again, but macroeconomic indicators meant little to a population assaulted by unprecedented inflation, cuts in social services, eroding purchasing power, and amplified concentration of wealth and resources (see State of Poverty). Since the 1960s Cerezo's Christian Democratic Party of Guatemala (DCG) had been regarded as a voice for reform and social progress. By the end of his term, however, the Guatemalan people perceived the DCG as the embodiment of the traditional vices of national politics: corruption, collaboration with the military, and disregard for the demands of popular organizations. Continued human rights violations, military and police impunity, a surge in strikes by public-sector employees, and an explosion in street crime inclined many Guatemalans to equate democracy and civilian rule with lawlessness and anarchy.

In 1989-90 widespread disenchantment with Cerezo resulted in a surge in popularity for ex-dictator General Efraín Ríos Montt (previously in power from 1982-83), whose blend of moral authoritarianism and political iconoclasm appealed to a populace rocked by economic crisis, crime, and social disintegration. When the Ríos Montt candidacy was ruled unconstitutional (because he had led a coup d'état), the electorate responded by voting for dark-horse candidate Jorge Serrano. Although not a political newcomer, Serrano and his Solidarity Action Party (MAS) were regarded as challengers to the world of traditional party politics. Besides enjoying this outsider image, Serrano benefited more than the other candidates from the prohibition of the Ríos Montt bid. Like Ríos Montt, Serrano is a neopentecostal evangelical, viewed as possessing the same kind of moral righteousness that many found so appealing in Ríos Montt. The election of Serrano surprised most political pundits but was in keeping with Latin American trends of installing conservative (and in the case of Peru, also evangelical) candidates advocating neoliberal economic reforms into high political office.

Though Serrano won the presidency, he faced the prospect of running the country with little political support. His party won less than 5 percent of the mayoral elections and only 18 of the 116 seats in the Congress. He also faced immediate opposition from the popular movement, which would have little to do with his offers of establishing a "social pact." In marked contrast to Cerezo, Serrano assumed office with few assurances of international financial or diplomatic support from the industrial nations.

Democracy Born of Counterinsurgency

Until 1986 the military loomed unquestionably as the nation's supreme political institution, having governed the country continuously (with one exception) since 1954 when a U.S.-directed military coup d'état overthrew the democratically elected government of Jacobo Arbenz. The coup plunged the "land of the eternal spring" into a political winter. Anticommunism became the official ideology, and counterinsurgency the mode of governance. The economic, social, and political modernization begun during the 1944-54 period of reform was retracted, leaving a mix of reactionary oligarchs and foreign investors in charge of the nation's economy. Center to extreme right defined the accepted political arena. Those attempting to broaden the level of political debate were classified as subversives and targeted by the military's repressive apparatus.

The guerrilla forces that emerged in the early 1960s were roundly defeated by the end of the decade, but a new insurgent movement took hold in the late 1970s, paralleling an expanding popular movement (see Popular Organizing). As the guerrilla threat intensified, the nation's already restrictive climate of repression worsened. A major counterinsurgency campaign was launched in 1980-81 to eliminate the guerrilla threat by decimating their popular base of support. Hundreds of indian villages were destroyed and tens of thousands of peasants died at the hands of the army. The steadfast determination of the army combined with extremist political parties and sectors of the business elite to wipe out all traces of leftist dissidence and popular rebellion, oblivious to the cost in lives. This effort became infamous throughout Latin America as the "Guatemalan solution."

After quelling the popular rebellion, the army launched a pacification campaign in the western highlands designed to control the indian population by isolating it from the guerrillas. The military undertook an ambitious program of "development poles" directed by army psychological-operations teams in conflict zones. At the center of this effort were "model villages" where displaced indians were corralled and subjected to military indoctrination. Key to the scheme were the civil patrols operating in most villages under military supervision (see Paramilitary Groups).[2]

The army's "security and development" plan proved successful in breaking most links between the highlands population and the guerrilla forces. Borrowing maoist jargon about guerrilla warfare, the army was boasting by 1984 that it had separated the fish from the sea. Whereas the army succeeded in its security objectives, it failed to make much progress on the "development" side of its counterinsurgency plan. In the absence of any real economic development, the residents of the army's development poles were "pacified" with food handout programs sponsored by foreign agencies.[3]

The 1980-83 counterinsurgency campaign seriously crippled the leftist revolution in Guatemala. But the military high command, under the direction of General Oscar Mejía Víctores in the 1983-85 period, recognized that a return to civilian rule was essential to guarantee national stability. It realized that a transfer to civilian hands would not only undermine the credibility of the guerrilla forces but would also open channels for increased foreign aid. Ríos Montt's resistance to facilitating this transfer to civilian rule may have been one of the reasons why he was deposed. Rather than an outgrowth of popular pressure, the democratization process of the mid-1980s was at its heart an element of the military's strategy to achieve national political and economic stability (see Armed Forces). As President

Cerezo himself observed: "If anyone is responsible for this democratizing process and willing to consolidate it, it is the army."[4]

The democratization process—confined by the military to the transfer of government into civilian hands—has assumed its own dynamic. Successful as part of a strategy of counterinsurgency and national stability, democratization has resulted in the creation of such governmental institutions as the Human Rights Ombudsman and the Court of Constitutionality, which increasingly challenged military influence. The institutionalization of civilian governance and attempts to enforce the rule of law in Guatemala have also been boosted by the forces of neoliberalism, both domestic and international. In the search for a new model of development, conservative economic modernizers recognize the need for efficient governmental administration independent of military control. This process of economic structural adjustment is also creating pressure for demilitarization and the restructuring of the army and police forces.

Legacy of the Cerezo Years

The critical role of the military in directing the democratization process was never in doubt. There was, however, widespread hope that the Cerezo government would take measures to build popular support for government and would seek more independence from the military. Yet Cerezo did not avail himself of the considerable popular support he enjoyed at the beginning of his term to widen the political space by asserting civilian authority over the military and establishing a true rule of law (estado de derecho) in Guatemala. Instead, as the bases of support for his Christian Democratic government contracted Cerezo became increasingly dependent on the continued goodwill of the military high command.

Through his inaction Cerezo quickly revealed that he was not the reformist that most of the electorate assumed him to be. His five-year administration committed itself to the "state stability" model of government, struggling to balance the need for social stability with the demands of the private sector. By 1990, however, it had largely adopted the neoliberal option. To Cerezo's credit, his administration did help create space for popular organizing. But social justice activists were not protected from the security forces. The local press reported some 2,000 extrajudicial killings and 500 kidnappings during his presidency—without a single conviction of the police and army officials primarily responsible for this political violence. With the support of the military high command, Cerezo did try to institute a social investment fund during his term. In the end, however, all attempts to improve social welfare through government intervention were blocked by the business elite and hard-line elements in the armed forces. Cerezo left the nation in economic shambles, with his own image reduced to that of a corrupt and opportunistic playboy.

The 1990 elections offered little reason for hope, with contending parties blaring slogans about law, order, and honesty while differing little from one another in terms of their conservative economic principles and allegiance to the military-controlled state. So disgusted were many people (particularly among the urban middle class) that there was surprising support for military candidates, including General Ríos Montt. The controversial general had headed the 1974 Christian Democratic ticket, and in March 1982 had led a successful military coup of young army officers. Among many Guatemalans he had the reputation as a reformist, individualist, and moral crusader. He was seen as an old-fashioned *caudillo* (strongman) who could single-handedly whip the country back into shape.[5] The 1990 electoral campaign was played out against a frightening backdrop of escalating human rights violations, a downsliding economy, exacerbating poverty, and expanded guerrilla activity.

At the end of his administration, Cerezo was hard put to boast of any positive legacy. Local and regional development plans had fallen flat, health ministry officials were discovered to have lined their pockets with U.S. economic aid, and social services were cut to the bone. Unlike preceding regimes, the Cerezo government could not even proclaim any large infrastructure projects as its own, and by 1990 the government was virtually broke as international lenders had cut off further loans. Although the Christian Democratic Party could claim that it had retained government in civilian hands for five years, the continued existence of a civilian government was due more to the commitment of the military high command than to the resolve of the Christian Democrats.

The Serrano Administration

Jorge Serrano Elías won a landslide election against his opponent Jorge Carpio Nicolle in the run-off elections of January 1991. Serrano, the leader of the Solidarity Action Party (MAS), took office on January 14, 1991, forming a minority government initially in alliance with the National Advancement Party (PAN). Recognizing the minority position of MAS in Congress, Serrano has sought to achieve a broad political consensus for his government. The two major parties in Congress and at the local level are the DCG and the National Union Center (UCN) (Figure 1a). Besides welcoming a representative of PAN, Serrano in a conciliatory—some say cooptive—gesture toward the popular bloc and the left-of-center political forces also incorporated a representative of the Democratic Socialist Party (PSD) into his first cabinet. Most of these appointees were from the private sector, however. In Congress, the administration has struggled to form alliances with other parties, but the composition of these alliances has continually shifted as each party jockeys for more power and a better position from which to contest future elections.

The economic policies of the Serrano administration represent no radical departure from those of the previous government. At the urging of foreign lenders and leading elements within the private sector, Serrano has deepened the structural adjustment program already undertaken by the Cerezo administration, although still falling short of what its ardent promoters have advocated. The most significant measures instituted by the new government have been trade liberalization guidelines, the implementation of a tax reform program, removal of most remaining price controls on basic goods, and the opening of new lines of foreign lending through debt renegotiation and the reduction of overdue debt payments. During his first year in office Serrano balanced the government's budget, reduced inflation, and dramatically bolstered the nation's foreign exchange reserves. But not all economic indicators were so propitious. Productive eco-

Figure 1a

Congressional and Municipal Party Representation, 1991

	Congressional	Municipal
National Union Center (UCN)	41	132
Christian Democratic Party of Guatemala (DCG)	27	86
Solidarity Action Party (MAS)	18	13
National Advancement Party (PAN)	12	16
Guatemalan Republican Front (FRG)- Democratic Institutional Party (PID)- National Unity Front (FUN)	12	18
National Liberation Movement (MLN)/ National Advancement Front (FAN)	4	10
Revolutionary Party (PR)	1	4
Democratic Socialist Party (PSD)/AP-5	1	9
Others	0	12
Total	116	300

SOURCE: Supreme Electoral Court of Guatemala.

nomic investment remained stagnant, and the trade balance still tipped dangerously negative (see Economy).

In a move typical of governments undergoing structural adjustment, Serrano soon after his inauguration sought to achieve a social consensus for his economic policies. Despite some conciliatory gestures (such as withholding electricity rate increases and the appointment of the PSD's Mario Solórzano as labor minister), Serrano failed to achieve the social pact he wanted. Whereas the government enjoyed the firm backing of the private sector in most matters, it was met with suspicion by the labor movement. Due to the weakened state of labor unions, however, no explosion of worker unrest arose during the first 18 months of the Serrano presidency.

At the outset of his administration Serrano promised that 1992 would be the year of "social investment." But this government commitment to renew deteriorating social services proved easier said than done. The government was counting on an influx of foreign funding for social programs, which as of mid-1992 was not forthcoming. Bilateral and multilateral sources were reluctant to commit large sums while the guerrilla conflict persisted. They also expressed some dissatisfaction that the government was attempting to exercise full control over social-investment funding rather than allowing it to be distributed and managed with some independence by nongovernmental organizations (NGOs). For the government's part, the 1992 tax reform did institute fiscal measures that would generate some revenue for social services but fell far short of what was needed. Congress also had conflicting ideas about how government revenues should be spent, with many favoring added spending on crime prevention.

What most distinguished the early part of the Serrano administration was his shake-up of the military command structure and his support for direct peace talks with the Guatemalan National Revolutionary Unity (URNG) guerrillas. Nonetheless, the extent of the government's control over the military remained in doubt. Several surges in human rights violations, bombings, and death threats served as reminders of the degree to which political violence still ruled the country. Despite some significant human rights initiatives, Serrano's inability to abolish military and police impunity undermined his claim to be supervising the security forces. The president's failure to aggressively pursue peace negotiations, to agree to the immediate implementation of measures to protect human rights, and to accept international mediation of the peace talks also cast doubt on his commitment to negotiate an end to the conflict (see The Peace Process).

Government corruption and the rise of narcotrafficking arose as major issues during Serrano's first two years. Fueled more by hatred

ity requirement necessitates two rounds in most presidential elections, the second round pitting the winner against the runner-up. The president appoints a 15-member Cabinet, including the key ministers of defense, economy, finance, and interior along with the director of the Central Bank.[6] The vice-president, also elected to a five-year term, presides over the National Congress and participates in Cabinet meetings (known as the Council of Ministers).

Figure 1c

Political Departments of Guatemala

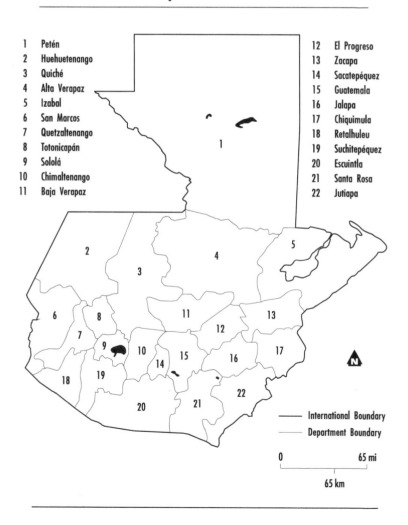

1 Petén	12 El Progreso
2 Huehuetenango	13 Zacapa
3 Quiché	14 Sacatepéquez
4 Alta Verapaz	15 Guatemala
5 Izabal	16 Jalapa
6 San Marcos	17 Chiquimula
7 Quetzaltenango	18 Retalhuleu
8 Totonicapán	19 Suchitepéquez
9 Sololá	20 Escuintla
10 Chimaltenango	21 Santa Rosa
11 Baja Verapaz	22 Jutiapa

International Boundary

Department Boundary

0   65 mi

65 km

Legislative power resides in the Congress, composed of 116 deputies, 87 of whom are elected directly by universal suffrage, with the other 29 elected on the basis of proportional representation. Deputies serve five-year terms consecutive with the president, and may be reelected for one additional term.

Members of the Supreme Court are elected by Congress to four-year terms. Judges of the Court of Appeal, the Administrative Disputes Tribunal, and other lower courts are, in turn, nominated by the Supreme Court and approved by Congress. In addition, there is a Court of Constitutionality headed by the President of the Supreme Court.

Department governors are appointed by the president, but the mayors of the municipalities are elected every three years. Municipal elections are scheduled for 1993.

Discussion of establishing a new National Constituent Assembly to reform the constitution began as part of the National Dialogue sponsored by the National Reconciliation Commission. Among the items mentioned for possible reform have been the definition of the military's role in society, the social function of property as set forth in the constitution, and the rights of indian communities. Suggestions that the constitution be revised to accommodate guerrilla demands were, however, strongly resisted by the government and the military. There was also widespread concern that an open-ended constitutional convention could result in a new round of political instability as myriad reform proposals are introduced. Anticipating numerous changes, the Christian Democratic Party introduced a proposal to convert the government to a parliamentary system. Such major constitutional reforms require two-thirds approval by Congress and assent by a national plebiscite.

Political Parties and Elections

A casual visitor might conclude from the roadside display of political artifacts that Guatemala must be a vibrant democracy. Whenever one turns a bend in the road, the colors, acronyms, or flags of one or more political parties are painted on the exposed rocks and cliffs. Bridges, bus stops, and even the highways themselves bear these emblems. In Guatemala, political parties are not accustomed to paying for billboard space—instead they simply take advantage of any exposed surface as an outlet for their political fervor.

Electioneering is not a new fad in Guatemala. Political campaigning occurred throughout the long succession of military regimes that date back to 1954, reflecting the jockeying for power by different sectors of the military and oligarchy. The National Liberation Movement (MLN), the self-denominated "party of organized violence," has a long tradition of political campaigning and of proliferating its red-white-and-blue colors. In some areas of the country, there is scarcely a bus stand or large roadside rock without a painted MLN flag.

Political parties also have a tradition of taking their campaigns to the people. They do this in a party atmosphere of car caravans filled with party faithful waving party flags and scattering party propaganda leaflets about the villages through which they pass. Another tradition is the political violence that precedes and accompanies electoral campaigns. Kidnappings, death threats, and beatings are as much a part of campaigning in Guatemala as bullhorns and posters.

Along with the traditions of elections and political parties in Guatemala, there is also a heritage of electoral fraud, military control, and a decided lack of pluralism. This latter trait has proved costly to the country's international image and its ability to attract foreign aid. In 1983, the military high command embarked the country on a tentative process of democratization, having decided that the political and economic stability of Guatemala would be better served by a civilian government chosen in pluralistic elections. In 1984, elections were held for the Constituent Assembly, and a year later Guatemalans went to the polls to elect their next president.

Compared with previous presidential elections, the 1985 balloting was free of fraud and relatively open. For many Guatemalans, the election was viewed as a chance to set Guatemala on a new path that would liberate the country from the terror of the past. Others, however, were less hopeful, pointing out that the last civilian president, Julio César Méndez Montenegro (1966-1970), was completely controlled by the military.

The installation of a civilian government did significantly enhance the country's reputation in international circles and gave rise to important political maneuvering room within the country as well. But many basic characteristics of the political world in Guatemala did not change. The guerrilla opposition continued to be excluded from the political process, and the military continued to be the final arbiter of political and economic change. As in the past, political parties remained largely divorced from the popular movement, each catering to its own narrow base of financial and citizen support.

For three decades the country's political spectrum has ranged from the ultraright to the armed left. Both political poles have traditionally defended the need for political violence: the right, to defend the country's institutions; the left, to change them. However, whereas the ultraright participates in the political process, the armed left has been excluded and repressed, with most of the legal political parties being clustered on the right. Peace initiatives by the guerrillas have demonstrated their willingness to give up the armed struggle, but the extreme right has shown no similar interest in resolving differences peacefully.

Since the mid-1980s the political arena has been altered by the transfer to civilian rule and the rise of neoliberalism. Both processes caught the traditional actors of the political left and right off balance, enabling a "new right" of political and economic modernizers to enter the ideological vacuum. Lack of experience, disinclination, and continuing repression—as well as the conviction that the military and oligarchy would never permit their significant participation in national politics—have been among the factors that dissuaded the left-leaning popular bloc from directly entering the political fray. On the right, extremists have been increasingly marginalized by newcomers closely linked to a modernizing private sector that seeks a more direct role in running the government (see The Business Lobby). Despite its declining influence, the extreme right still exerts considerable influence through its continued support of terrorism directed against social reformers.

If the health of a representative democracy was measured solely by the number of political parties, Guatemala would be considered a thriving democratic state. In 1992 the government's Supreme Election Tribunal reported that there were 18 registered parties and 27 provisional parties awaiting government recognition. Guatemala has a National Women's Party (run by a man), an Ecology Party, a Catholic Union party, an Orthodox Liberal Party, and numerous other political entities unknown to the general public and consisting of little more than their founders.

The Left and Center-Left

The **Guatemalan Workers Party (PGT)**, the country's official communist party, has functioned clandestinely since 1954. Two tendencies of the party—the PGT Central Committee and PGT Nucleus—have at various times been associated with the URNG guerrilla coalition. The PGT Nucleus was a founding member of the Guatemalan National Revolutionary Unity (URNG) in 1982 but eventually left. The URNG was later joined by the PGT Central Committee. In early 1989, a reformist offshoot of the party, PGT-6th of January, demanded the incorporation of *glasnost* into the Guatemalan communist party and sought to join in coalition with another leftist group called Revolutionary October (OR). The OR, composed primarily of former members of the Guatemalan Army of the Poor (EGP) guerrillas, placed strong emphasis on women's, ethnic, and environmental issues,[7] believing the URNG focus on armed struggle to be too narrow.

The **Democratic Socialist Party (PSD)**, which disbanded following the assassination of its founder Alberto Fuentes Mohr and 15 other party activists during the Lucas García regime, reestablished itself in 1985 in time to take advantage of the political opening afforded by the democratization process.[8] Affiliated with the Socialist International, the PSD is more a social-democratic party than a socialist one. It stands to the right of the National Revolutionary Movement (MNR) in El Salvador and to the left of the National Liberation Party (PLN) in Costa Rica, both also members of the Socialist International.

The PSD's leader is Mario Solórzano, who represents the more conservative or centrist faction of the party. Articulating a reformist rather than a socialist political philosophy, Solórzano claims the party promotes the "full development of capitalism, a modern not exploitative capitalism, to replace the feudalism that currently imprisons Guatemala." The PSD originated the "social pact" between government, the private sector, political parties, and labor. In 1988, this reformist vision split the party when its secretary general, Luis Zurita, left the PSD, charging that Solórzano was catering to elites rather than organizing the masses, and that the party should be socialist, not social democratic.[9]

Typical of the opportunism that characterizes centrist politics in Guatemala, the PSD proclaimed René de León Schlotter as its presidential candidate. Nominated as a presidential candidate by a dissident faction of the DCG called the Popular Alliance (AP-5), de León was regarded by the PSD as their best chance to win enough votes in the elections to guarantee the party's national registry and its representation in Congress. De León, long a leader of the DCG's conservative wing, adopted a left-leaning discourse to criticize the government after having failed to capture the DCG's nomination. Along with other dissident Social Democrats, Luis Zurita was forced to leave the country after the 1990 assassination of Dinora Perez. Perez and Zurita were among the co-founders of a preparty, left-center grouping that may have been viewed by hard-line elements within the military as an attempt to integrate the URNG into electoral politics.

The announcement in early 1992 of the formation of the Revolutionary Movement 3rd of November by ex-political strategist of the Armed Revolutionary Forces (FAR) Danilo Rodríguez was greeted with some distrust by the popular movement. Rodríguez had been a school friend of Serrano and had played a divisive role in the labor movement and within FAR itself. Despite his continuing criticism of the Serrano government, it was suspected that the two had arranged a deal whereby Rodríguez would be accepted into political life with his security ensured so as to undermine the credibility of the URNG's claims that it could not safely participate in national politics.

The Center and Center-Right

The **Christian Democratic Party of Guatemala (DCG)** is the only major political party that can be considered centrist. The DCG was founded as a rightist party in 1955, in the shadow of the 1954 coup. Since the 1960s, however, the party has cultivated a reformist image, posing as the moderate route between revolutionary change and extreme rightwing reaction. It is the product of the Christian Democratic movement in Europe, which emerged as an alternative to the more communist and social-democratic parties that sought power in post-World War II Europe. The movement was grounded in the social teachings of the Catholic Church, expounded for the first time in the late 19th century by Pope Leo XIII in his *Rerum Novarum* encyclical. This Christian social philosophy proclaimed that economic classes could work in harmony. To achieve this goal, socialism, with its philosophy of inevitable class conflict, had to be opposed, while capitalism needed to be reformed to insure social justice.[10]

Despite its support for social reforms, the DCG has remained strictly an electoral party, eschewing coalitions with the popular movement. In contrast to the other political parties, however, the DCG did develop an extensive national infrastructure with a wide base of popular support, which was reinforced by patronage and public-works programs during the Cerezo administration. Although it has lost dozens of party activists to political repression, the DCG has been steadfast in its commitment to the electoral path. In fact, pursuit of political power gradually distanced the party from the popular movement, shifting it ever closer to the very elements of society responsible for the country's main social ills.

The party rode into power on a wave of popular enthusiasm for the prospects of civilian rule and peaceful change. Instead of trying to shape this mandate into a broad base of popular support, the Cerezo government sought to establish stronger links with the military and private sector, alienating those who had swept the party into office. When the party occasionally did attempt to answer popular demands, it inevitably withdrew its offers in the face of warnings by the military and the private sector.

The successful ascent to power of the DCG and Vinicio Cerezo was due largely to its opportunistic alliance with the military and sectors of the right wing. From its earliest years, the DCG formed alliances with such ultraright parties as the Anti-Communist Unification Party (PUA) and has a long tradition of backing military candidates for president. In 1974, General Efraín Ríos Montt, the presidential candidate of a reformist coalition including the DCG and the social-democratic parties of Fuentes Mohr and Manuel Colom Argueta, was denied the presidency in a fraudulent election. Despite this experience, the DCG persisted in its quest for political power, fielding candidates again in 1978 and 1982, thereby lending a continued credibility to the electoral process.

Through its support of active and retired military candidates, the DCG gradually came to regard the military as a natural ally in the democratization and modernization process. This sentiment was articulated by DCG Secretary General Vinicio Cerezo in his 1977 essay entitled *The Army: An Alternative*:

> We must tear down the barriers that impede communication between two of the national forces that can rely on organization, discipline, and progressive ideology. They are the Army and the Christian Democratic Party. . . . The present social, economic, and political conditions suggest that there will be no positive so-

lution unless the two sectors UNITE and make a gigantic and combined effort to reorganize and reorient the country.[11]

The party's cardinal figures have been Vinicio Cerezo, René de León Schlotter, Alfonso Cabrera, and Rodolfo Paiz Andrade. A fifth leader, Danilo Barillas, was assassinated by unidentified assailants in August 1989 after it was rumored that he was on the verge of revealing the penetration of narcotraffickers into party politics. Cerezo, previously head of the party's more progressive wing, adopted a more conservative political posture after inheriting the presidential sash. He assumed control of the party from DCG patriarch René de León Schlotter, who represented the more conservative faction and had served as president of the Christian Democratic International for eight years. Cerezo's decision to promote the candidacy of Alfonso Cabrera Hidalgo, who served as minister of foreign relations and as the party's secretary general, embittered de León supporters. De León subsequently attempted (without success) to establish a new base of political power through the Ministry of Development and the General Confederation of Guatemalan Workers (CGTG). The final key player within the DCG, Rodolfo Paiz Andrade, a personal friend of Cerezo's and a member of the powerful Paiz Ayala family, served as a contact between the party and the private sector.

As in El Salvador, the Christian Democrats in Guatemala began to splinter before the end of their first term in office. Most of the infighting resulted from Cerezo's efforts to engineer the candidacy of Alfonso Cabrera for the 1990 elections. Cabrera, a former school teacher, has accumulated a personal fortune through his political career. In his bid for office, he relied solely on the party machine, the only political infrastructure with a national reach and an organization capable of drumming up national grassroots support. But a reputation of corruption and association with narcotraffickers, including his two brothers, handicapped the Cabrera candidacy as did his uncharismatic, party-hack image. Supporters of de León complained that the nominating process was fraudulent and refused to recognize the legitimacy of the Cabrera candidacy. Cabrera supporters struck back, brutalizing the supporters and family of de León. Besides the bitter dispute between the Cabrera and de León factions, the party also suffered from the emergence or resuscitation of party offshoots, including both the Popular Alliance (AP-5), whose secretary general was forced into exile by death threats, and the Movement for the Recuperation of the Christian Democrat's Ideological Identity. Government corruption, economic chaos, worsening socioeconomic conditions, and escalating political violence helped defeat the party's bid for a second term.

Hoping to attract the progressive and anti-right vote, the Cabrera campaign integrated such center-left figures as Andrés Girón and Luis Zurita, formerly of the PSD, into the DCG slate and even adopted a populist discourse. Cabrera placed third in the November 1991 presidential election, but the party won 27 congressional seats and 86 municipalities. Once out of power, the DCG and Cerezo became the main targets of an anticorruption campaign mounted by the private sector and competing political parties. Cerezo continued to be a key figure in the party, serving as a broker of alliances between the MAS and the two main opposition parties. But his political future was irrevocably damaged by his legacy of corruption.

With its extensive party infrastructure and the experience it gained as a ruling party, the DCG can not be completely discounted as a strong future political contender despite its corrupt image. Though it continues to be dominated by its right-of-center leadership, the DCG could decide in an opportunistic fashion to enter the next presidential election as the leader of a centrist or even left-of-center political coalition with a social-democratic character, seeking to capitalize on popular rejection of the conservative economic policies of the Serrano government.

The **Revolutionary Party (PR)**, founded in 1957 (after the death of Castillo Armas) by former militants of the revolutionary parties of the 1944-54 era, has been directed since its debut by its most conservative elements (members of the Popular Liberation Front). In 1959 the party even expelled its leftists—seven years later it won national office with Julio César Méndez Montenegro as its presidential candidate. The unrelenting repression that has characterized political life in Guatemala for the last two and half decades began during the Montenegro government. In 1978 the PR allied itself with the rightwing Democratic Institutional Party (PID) to win (fraudulently) with candidate Romeo Lucas, ushering in the most corrupt and bloody government the country had yet known. In 1990 the PR initially hoped to regain a share of power through the candidacy of Fernando Andrade Díaz Durán, who withdrew from the race even before it had officially begun. Also initially backing the Andrade candidacy were the center-right Democratic Party of National Cooperation (PDCN) and the National Renewal Party (PNR).

By Guatemala standards, the PR and Andrade are located at the center-right of the political spectrum. Both have strong connections with the military and oligarchy. Andrade co-founded the Bank of the Quetzal and married into the wealthy Falla coffee family. He was at first a DCG party member and has worked closely with the party and the Social Christian Student Front (FESC). While a key adviser under the military regimes of Lucas García and Mejía Víctores (for whom he served as minister of foreign relations), Andrade designed the army's foreign policy of active neutrality. During the Cerezo government he represented the country at the United Nations. According to one political commentator, "Andrade speaks with leftist language, meets with the right, is an excellent intermediary between prominent military groups, and has important international connections."[12] He is regarded as a member of the "informed right."

The loss of Andrade further split the party, which then nominated José Angel Lee Duarte in March 1990. Interparty negotiations and intraparty squabbles intensified before the official campaign period began in June 1990. Three other small parties that held talks with the PSD and PR concerning coalition party tickets were the United Revolutionary Front (FUR), Democratic Revolutionary Union (URD), and the United Guatemala Movement (MGU).

The Right

Most political parties in Guatemala are situated on the right side of the political spectrum. They range from the National Liberation Movement (MLN), the traditional standard-bearer of anticommunist politics, to the National Union Center (UCN), which poses as a centrist party but leans decidedly to the right. In between are a jumble of other rightist parties that are commonly little more than platforms for their current leaders.

The right wing in Guatemala can be divided roughly into a segment that is organized politically and one that is not. Suffering its worst crisis in 35 years, the organized right has found itself dangling without a popular base and out of touch with the political thinking of both the army and private sector. In a quandary of both ideology and organization, the traditional right wing has proven unable to adapt to the political changes brought on by the challenge of democratization and the advent of neoliberalism.

Since the late 1940s anticommunism, more visceral than rational, has been the driving force of the political right in Guatemala. The right wing has been characterized by its reactionary response—first to the Arévalo and Arbenz governments and later to all forms of popular dissidence—rather than by any coherent political program for change. It has also historically allied with the Catholic Church and with U.S. foreign policy.

With the dissolution of the Soviet Union, anticommunism as an ideology does not stir the blood of the party faithful as it had in the past. In the new political rhetoric adopted by the army and government, terrorism is posed as the main threat to democracy. But unlike the military, rightist parties have failed to modernize their political tactics. Like a defective phonograph needle, the extreme right remains stuck in its decades-old rut expounding on the communist threat to national security.

A major weakness of the right wing has been its division into two sectors: political and economic. This split became apparent in the 1970s when a younger business class emerged that no longer identified with the antediluvian politics of the traditional oligarchy. Many of these new entrepreneurs embraced the economics of neoliberalism with its enshrinement of both the free market and the private sector. Reflecting this trend, in 1971 Francisco Marroquín University was founded to train the country's future economic power structure in the conservative principles of neoliberalism.

The Chicago School's economics of free enterprise did not automatically find a home among the political right. For two decades, rightwing parties had participated in the development of a corporative state economic sector and had not objected as the military itself moved into the economic arena. It was, for example, during the MLN-PID government of Carlos Arana Osorio that the state infiltrated the economy through such public-sector corporations as INDECA, INAFOR, and BANDESA.

In mid-1989, elements of the private sector formed the **National Unity Movement** with the intention of rallying behind one candidate who could win the election. The strategy of this clique and of a subsequent one called the **Pyramid Group** was to select a candidate representing the remodeled right wing, similar to Cristiani in El Salvador and Callejas in Honduras.[13] In 1990 the Pyramid Group selected the UCN's Jorge Carpio Nicolle as the private-sector candidate, but it was not displeased when the less favored Serrano won the popular vote.

The notorious old guard of the extreme right, the **National Liberation Movement (MLN)** is directed by Mario Sandoval Alarcón, alleged godfather of Guatemala's death squads. As the party whose coup ousted the Arbenz government, the MLN has long been viewed favorably by the traditional agroexport oligarchy and by rightist factions within the military. Only once, however, has the MLN tasted political power—during the regime of Carlos Arana Osorio (1970-74), president by virtue of an MLN-PID coalition. Since that heyday the MLN has waned, marginalized in the political arena by the rise of neoliberalism and the dissolution of the communist bloc. A member of the World Anti-Communist League (WACL), the MLN claims to be revitalizing the party, while remaining firm in its ideology of "total and absolute unity against communism."

Founded in 1983 by *El Gráfico* publisher Jorge Carpio Nicolle, the **National Union Center (UCN)** is legislatively the country's most powerful party, ahead of the DCG. Benefiting from its ability to influence public opinion through the country's second-largest newspaper, the UCN quickly achieved the national prominence and outreach that other rightist parties lacked. Associated with the International Liberal Party based in Spain, the UCN poses publicly as a centrist party but is clearly in the conservative political camp. It is characterized both by its political pragmatism and its rightwing populism. The party suffers from constant desertions and splinterings, usually over complaints that it is little more than a vehicle for the personal political ambitions of Carpio Nicolle. The UCN sustained a major loss in 1988 with the departure of Ramiro de León Carpio, Jorge's cousin and key political adviser.[14]

Jorge Carpio Nicolle, while an adept politician, is not widely regarded as a statesman or intellectual. His defeat in the 1991 run-off election weakened him as a serious presidential contender in the future, although he may still harbor presidential aspirations. The electoral defeat coupled with the Serrano government's attempts to build alliances with the UCN and its various factions have opened up the party to increased factionalism. The most serious split occurred in early 1992 when party stalwart Jorge Arenas refused to back the nomination of Edmund Mulet for president of the Congress. Arenas, who functioned as the link between UCN and the private sector's Pyramid Group, subsequently left the party with some other UCN deputies. Among the various interpretations of the split were that Jorge Carpio wanted to check the rise of Arenas as a contender for party leadership, that the private sector engineered the split as part of its conspiracy to undermine the traditional political sector, or that Arenas and his supporters were really voicing their opposition to the heightened influence of drug traffickers (who supported the Mulet nomination).

Edmund Mulet, elected as president of the Congress in 1992, is one of Guatemala's most able and articulate rising stars, but like most politicians he is not well-known outside the capital. Although he has strong roots within rightwing political parties (including the MLN and PNR), Mulet is acknowledged as a strong proponent of establishing a rule of law and introducing political modernization in Guatemala.[15]

The **Authentic Nationalist Central (CAN)** is an extreme right party dating back to the Arana Osorio regime and now led by his son, Tito Arana. Originated in 1964 by chief-of-state Enrique Peralta Azurdia, the **Democratic Institutional Party (PID)** was billed as the "army's party." The PID's candidate Aníbal Guevara, the handpicked successor of Lucas García, was ousted in a military coup within days of taking office in 1982. In 1985, through political alliance with the MLN, the PID won one congressional seat. In the 1990 elections the PID allied with the **National Unity Front (FUN)** to support the controversial candidacy of Ríos Montt, whose campaign slogan was "Security, Well-Being, and Justice."

Among the newer conservative parties are the **Solidarity Action Party (MAS)** and the **National Advancement Party (PAN)**. MAS formalized the "Solidarity" citizen's committee that backed Serrano in the 1985 presidential election. It lacks a national party infrastructure, but boasts an associated political institute that has served as a training center for conservative Latin American politicians. As president, Serrano angered MAS stalwarts by replacing party members in the presidential cabinet during a shake-up of ministers in May 1992. MAS is a member of the International Democratic Union, a conservative political association that includes the U.S. Republican Party.

Initially PAN joined the MAS government coalition but a year later defected to the opposition. Alvaro Arzú, the former mayor of Guatemala City and a 1990 presidential candidate, is the leading figure in the party and served as Serrano's first foreign affairs minister, resigning in mid-1991 over Guatemala's recognition of Belizean independence. Party functionaries have little experience in politics but hope to catapult PAN into a strong position to contest the 1995 elections as the political vehicle of the private sector.

The superficial nature of Guatemalan democratization became ever more apparent during the 1990 campaign. The political parties revolved around personal ambitions rather than ideas or any serious commitment to democracy. Despite the country's debilitated state, there was no substantive debate about the nation's economic direction, military control, or social reforms. Neither was there any link between the political parties and the rising chorus of demands from popular organizations. Hence, democracy born of counterinsurgency has thus far failed as a vehicle for realizing the aspirations of the vast majority of the Guatemalan people.

Lawlessness and Human Rights

Personal violence pervades Guatemalan society. Until the mid-1980s most of this violence was politically motivated—to eliminate dissidents, repress workers and peasants, terrorize communities suspected of supporting the guerrillas, and rid the country of all threats to established elites. A trademark of Guatemalan society, political violence has persisted despite the transfer of government to civilian rule in 1986 (Figure 1d).

In recent years, the rise of "common crime" has rendered Guatemala an even more violent society. Common crime represents both a physical and economic threat. All are affected: the poor worker who loses what few possessions he has, the small businessperson who has her cashbox robbed for the third time, women who are raped, and the wealthy who are assaulted in their cars. Accompanying the sense of physical insecurity caused by increasing crime is the economic threat it represents—personal savings and hard-earned possessions vanish. In 1989 the United States and some European governments began issuing travel advisories warning tourists about the Guatemalan crime wave. These advisories endangered the tourism industry, Guatemala's second largest source of foreign exchange.

The proliferation of guns has greatly contributed to the high incidence of serious crime. In 1992 the rate of homicides per 100,000 people reached 34—compared with 10 in Panama, 5 in Costa Rica, and 10 in the United States. Only 2,000 firearms are legally registered by civilians in Guatemala, although the government's arms-registration office estimates that there are some 300,000 guns in individual hands—not counting the army and police arsenal.[16]

The surge in muggings, gang violence, vehicle hijacking, and armed robberies has (particularly in the cities) largely overshadowed concerns about repression and selective political violence. In many quarters such human rights concerns as proper penal and judicial procedures are regarded as obstacles in the fight against crime. Merchants, street vendors, and homeowners have demanded that the state's security forces crack down on the crime sector. So widespread and uncontrolled was this crime epidemic by early 1992 that newspaper columnists and politicians asserted that the Serrano government was placing too much emphasis on human rights and controlling political violence while not giving adequate attention to common crime—which, they claimed, was a greater human rights problem.[17]

Figure 1d

Human Rights Chronology

1966: Guatemalan military and associated death squads introduce use of "disappearances" as a repressive tactic in Latin America during 1966-68 counterinsurgency war in which an estimated 8,000 civilians are killed.

1967: United Nations Human Rights Commission creates position of Human Rights Rapporteur to study countries where there has been a consistent pattern of gross human rights violations, choosing Guatemala as one of six countries recommended for such scrutiny.

1970-74: Dubbed by his critics the "Jackal of Zacapa" for leading brutal counterinsurgency campaign in 1966-68 period, Colonel Arana Osorio becomes president in 1970 and institutes a climate of repression. During his first three years in office, an estimated 15,000 die at the hands of security forces and death squads.

1978-82: Repression of dissidents during Lucas García regime is highly centralized, with president and senior ministers selecting those targeted for torture, disappearance, or assassination in meetings held in National Palace annex. In 1978-80 period popular movement is crushed. During next two years army unleashes wave of terror in highlands to eliminate actual and potential base of popular support for guerrillas. In 1982 United Nations assigns permanent human rights observer to Guatemala and keeps country on list of most serious offenders (Category 12) through 1986. An amnesty edict, Decree Law 33-82, exempts from prosecution "members of the Security Forces of the State who in fulfilling their duty participated in counter-subversion activities during the Lucas García regime."

1982-83: Scorched-earth counterinsurgency campaign continues in countryside during 16 months of Ríos Montt regime, which also instituted civil patrols (PACs), development poles, and model villages in counterinsurgency zones.

This widely shared concern about crime and spreading lawlessness was one reason why there was such popular support for the Ríos Montt candidacy in 1990. Out of desperation many Guatemalans called for the return of the *caudillo*, in the mode of Estrada Cabrera or Ubico, who would (by force, if necessary) restore order to the country. In early 1992 the government responded to this widespread anxiety about crime by assigning army troops to patrol streets with the police—a measure that apparently met with the approval of most of

---

1984: Mutual Support Group (GAM) founded as association of relatives of the disappeared and as human rights group, marking beginning of national human rights movement.

1986: Days before ceding office to civilian government, Mejía Víctores regime promulgates Decree Law 8-86 granting amnesty for "political crimes and related common crimes" during 1982-86 (his regime and that of his predecessor Ríos Montt).

1987: United Nations upgrades Guatemala's human rights status to Category 21, removing permanent observer but maintaining yearly monitoring. Cerezo and Serrano governments consider less serious categorization a political victory.

1989-90: Human rights violations multiply during last two years of Cerezo administration. 1989 killings of 11 University of San Carlos students, 1990 murders of U.S. citizen Michael Devine, anthropologist Myrna Mack, social democrats Héctor Oquelí and Gilda Flores, and Christian Democrat Danilo Barrillas, together with Santiago Atitlán massacre in December 1990, spark new international pressure to end system of impunity in Guatemala.

1991-92: Despite Serrano's promise to establish rule of law in Guatemala, human rights violations continue during his presidency, with all sectors of popular movement targeted by death threats. In apparent expression of their displeasure with peace talks and increasing discussion of ending impunity of military and police, elements of security forces occasionally escalate level of human rights abuses. Peace talks with leftist guerrillas stall over URNG demands to have human rights guarantees (including international supervision) implemented before negotiations are concluded. Rising crime levels, especially in Guatemala City, provoke new citizen concern for country's climate of lawlessness and impunity of security forces. By mid-1992 mixed human rights climate prevails, with human rights investigations and prosecutions by government's Human Rights Ombudsman and attorney general increasing, but overall impunity of security forces remaining in force and all dissident sectors still subject to death threats and direct human rights abuses.

---

the frightened populace. There were, for example, no loud protests from the popular organizations or opposition politicians about the increased militarization of Guatemalan society.

Related Problems

The categories of human rights violations and common crime are by no means unrelated. Police and army officers are frequently involved in bank holdups, drug smuggling, and burglaries. And when those responsible are not current members of the security forces, they are frequently ex-members or operate under official protection. Death threats and hired killers have become a way of life in Guatemala. Not only are political dissidents victims, but personal feuds and disputes over business deals are often also resolved in this cheap and efficient way.

The crime problem cannot be isolated from the climate of political violence that has characterized Guatemala for at least four decades. Nor can it be considered apart from the impunity with which the police and military have historically operated. In their repression of popular threats to wealth and privilege, the armed agents of the government have been given free rein. This atmosphere of officially sanctioned lawlessness has not been confined to politically motivated human rights violations. It has bred corruption, crime, and violence at all levels of society.

Crime is largely the product of a deepening economic and social crisis. Economic deprivation and the lack of alternatives help explain the rise in petty crime—such as pickpocketing, muggings, and the theft of car parts common in Guatemala City. But there does not exist a one-to-one correlation between poverty and crime. Guatemala has always been a poor country, yet common crime was rare until the 1980s. Other social factors—such as the breakdown of rural communities and cultures, massive dislocation caused by the war, and an assault by the mass media on traditional values—also help explain crime and lawlessness. Even among the poorest communities, individualism and consumerism have weakened long-held communitarian and humanistic values.

The penetration of narcotrafficking in Guatemalan society since the late 1980s is another factor. The drug business has bred an organized crime sector, while at the same time drawing in government officials, police, and army officers at all levels. Drug consumption and smuggling permeate both the highest and lowest social strata. Among poor and unemployed youth, crack consumption is increasing, propelling the users into a life of crime to support their habits. Cocaine consumption is likewise expanding among the wealthy, who have also seized the opportunities for easy income through drug smuggling and trafficking. Looking at the drug culture in a wider social context, a member of the government's drug and alcohol prevention program sarcastically commented, "Miguel Angel Asturias [the country's most famous literary figure] said that the only way to endure the tragedy of Guatemala was by being drunk. Drugs also help kill the pain." It is likely that as the competition for narcodollars increases in coming years the level of drug-related violence in Guatemalan society will rise dramatically.

Establishing the Rule of Law

The violence in Guatemalan society is palpable. If by chance you have not directly encountered it, all you have to do is read the morning papers—or just glance at the display of carnage in the news photos. Next to grisly accounts of the latest robbery or personal vendetta are reports of new death threats and disappearances, or the discovery of more unmarked graves and mutilated corpses. Most of the political violence never makes the papers but enough of it does to keep the citizenry reminded that speaking out or protesting can often lead to bloody reprisals. Even as peace talks advanced in 1991-92, the climate of terror in Guatemala thickened. Many labor leaders, reformist politicians, journalists, human rights activists, and peasants, none of whom were associated with the guerrillas, were the victims of a wave of death threats and harassment during Serrano's first year and a half in office.

The dual threat of political violence and common crime has fostered a new popular sentiment—crossing class and social boundaries—calling for an end to lawlessness. Throughout society demands have arisen that the "rule of law" (estado de derecho) be established in Guatemala and that the impunity traditionally enjoyed by politicians and the security forces be terminated. Some feel the priority should be to intensify the war against crime. Others say the key element is addressing human rights violations and punishing those responsible. Once the army and police are brought under control, they contend, social and political stability will follow. In some cases the campaign against impunity has been opportunistically embraced by politicians eager to bring their rivals to court. With differing intentions, both police and criminals have seized the issue of proper legal process and legal rights to enhance their position—the police claiming that they cannot solve the crime problem because of all the legal procedures they have to follow.

Establishing a rule of law in Guatemala involves everyone—no one is blameless. Lawlessness spans the spectrum of society. At the upper echelons, the country's top officials—army commanders, government officials, congressional members, judges, political candidates, and mayors—enjoy an exemption from normal criminal procedure called *antejuicio*. Military officers can only be tried in military courts, even for crimes not related to military operations. Demanding and offering bribes is a social norm that raises few eyebrows. Bus drivers regularly pay police a bribe for allowing them to carry more than the legal—or safe—limit of passengers. Tax evasion is widespread, and laws regulating everything from vehicle emissions and garbage dumping to minimum wages and traffic rules are routinely ignored. Respect for and enforcement of the law is simply not integral to Guatemalan culture and society. Instead, fear and money rule the country in the most blatant ways.

A World-Class Violator of Human Rights

Systematic human rights violations have been a constant factor in Guatemala for nearly four decades. Historically, violations tend to surge as the intensity of political reformism, popular organizing, and guerrilla insurgency increases. Politically motivated deaths and disappearances also commonly accompany election campaigns. The lack of consistent human rights monitoring obscures the exact number of human rights violations, but all observers agree that Guatemala ranks among the top nations in the world in its level of gross human rights abuses. It is one of the most dangerous places in the world to be a human rights activist, topping the list of murdered human rights monitors in 1990. For the past ten years the United Nations Working Group on Forced or Involuntary Disappearances has listed Guatemala third among the 19 countries where such disappearances are common. Guatemala also has the dubious distinction of being the Latin American country where the practice of "disappearances" originated.

It is estimated that since 1980 political violence in Guatemala has resulted in 100,000 civilian deaths, 40,000 disappearances, 440 villages destroyed, 250,000 orphans, more than 100,000 refugees, and as many as one million internally displaced persons. The massive violence that characterized the early 1980s subsided by mid-decade. Nonetheless, human rights violations against all those suspected of challenging the established order continued in ebbs and flows through the early 1990s.

Perhaps the best indicator of the severity and finality of repression in Guatemala is that there are no political prisoners in the country's jails or military bases. Both the police and the military do, however, maintain clandestine detention centers where victims are tortured and mutilated during interrogation before their inevitable death.[18] Dissidence is treated in three ways: death threats warning a person to leave the country, disappearances in which the corpse is often never found, and torture and assassinations where the mutilated body leaves a clear warning to other dissidents or would-be activists. During torture, captured guerrillas are often given the option of cooperating with the military as members of its intelligence unit (G-2).

International human rights monitors such as Americas Watch and Amnesty International have undertaken the discouraging task of assessing the improvement or worsening of violations in a country where the level and type of violations can only be described as horrific or more horrific. Amnesty International titled their 1981 report *Guatemala: A Government Program of Political Murder* while Americas Watch called their 1988-90 report *Messengers of Death*. Summing up the state of abuses during the first six months of the Serrano administration, Americas Watch in its *Getting Away with Murder* report concluded: "Getting away with murder is easy in Guatemala not only because of the lack of skills, equipment, and training on the part of forensic doctors and the archaic system of death investigation under which they work, but because the entire system is subverted by the involvement of government forces in the same crimes they are supposed to investigate."[19]

Civilian Government Lacks Will to End Impunity

Although human rights violations decreased after the height of the counterinsurgency war of the early 1980s, they remained at high levels by international standards. Even after the inauguration of the civilian government headed by Cerezo, Amnesty International and Americas Watch continued to express grave concern about human rights violations on the part of the security forces. Americas Watch concluded in its 1988 report, "While the numbers of political killings are lower than in the early 1980s—a time of great carnage—the apparatus of state terror remains intact and undiminished in strength."[20]

From the beginning of his administration President Cerezo dismissed charges by international and local monitors of continuing human rights abuses. The president labeled the reports of continued disappearances "pure fiction," claiming that most were the result of family problems where children and fathers were running away to leave a bad "family situation."[21] Until the last year of his administration Cerezo counted on favored treatment by the official international community. Eager to support the new civilian government, international lenders such as the United States downplayed continuing human rights violations. Rather than assessing the actual state of abuses, the international community seemed content to observe that human rights violations had declined since the early 1980s. Willing to give Cerezo the benefit of the doubt, economic and military aid again began to flow into Guatemala. Ironically, the United States and West Germany demonstrated their support for the "democratization" process by dramatically increasing police and military assistance.

In its pre-1990 reporting the U.S. State Department distinguished between the "government" and the "military," tacitly recognizing that the government had little control over the military. It noted that the government regularly condemned violations that did occur and that the judiciary was attempting to improve the investigation of these cases. The State Department also emphasized that the government itself was not to blame for the "infrequent" and "isolated" violations that did occur. Similarly, the United Nations Human Rights Commission took Guatemala off its list of most serious human rights offenders after 1986. In 1989 the United Nations concluded that "the violation of civil and political rights of Guatemalans is not the product of government policy, but the actions of powerful groups and can be linked to a climate of violence that still escapes control by the government."[22] In keeping with its progovernment tone, the UN report included only violations confirmed by the government and presented only the government's version of the Aguacate massacre of 22 peasants in November 1988.

By the fifth year of the Cerezo administration the deteriorating human rights climate was causing increasing problems for the government. The August 1989 assassinations of Christian Democratic leader Danilo Barillas and banker Ramiro Castillo—followed by a wave of disappearances and deaths of student leaders—signaled an escalation in the level of death squad terror and resulted in condemnations of the political violence from all quarters. Shocked by the Barillas and Castillo killings, private-sector leaders began to complain that the deepening climate of terror was undermining their ability to do business.

Accusations by the U.S. embassy in early 1990 that the government was doing little to clamp down on human rights abuses shocked the Cerezo administration. Throughout his term Cerezo had devoted considerable effort in international forums to shielding Guatemala from condemnations of its human rights abuses. The government and the military had been largely successful in blaming the increasing violations on the guerrillas, rightwing extremists, and narcotraffickers. But the U.S. State Department indicated that it was no longer accepting the official story. The January 1990 murder of Salvadoran socialist leader Héctor Oquelí and Guatemalan lawyer Gilda Flores of the Democratic Socialist Party sparked strong international rebuke of the country's human rights climate. The case was immediately compared to the massacre of six Jesuit priests in El Salvador two months before. Throughout 1990 the human rights climate continued to worsen. Internationally respected anthropologist Myrna Mack was murdered, U.S. hotel owner Michael Devine was tortured and murdered, U.S. Ursuline Sister Diana Ortiz was kidnapped and tortured, and the army massacred 13 residents of Santiago Atitlán.[23]

During his tenure Cerezo demonstrated little political will to halt human rights violations by the armed forces. There were some superficial advances such as the establishment of a congressional Human Rights Commission and the creation of a Human Rights Ombudsman as well as several foreign-financed programs to improve the judicial system. In 1989 the Supreme Court named the square in front of the Palace of Justice "Human Rights Square." But Cerezo, while personally uncomfortable with the continuing human rights violations, did not use the power of his office to ensure that rights violations were investigated and prosecuted. With respect to the security forces, a policy of impunity remained in force.

In fact, before taking power Cerezo brokered a deal with the military that retained its unaccountability to law. Four days before Cerezo's inauguration, the military passed an amnesty decree that exempted members of the security forces from prosecution for political or related common crimes. Cerezo supported this measure, explaining, "We are not going to be able to investigate the past. We would have to put the entire army in jail."[24] Reassuring the voters, candidate Cerezo promised that he would become very "heavy-handed" if repression continued under his administration. Yet Cerezo's heavy hand was never seen.

Not only did President Cerezo uphold the military's impunity for past offenses, he even declined to push for the conviction of security officials for gross abuses committed during his own government. During his tenure no member of the security forces was convicted and imprisoned for a politically motivated violent crime. In the one case where police officials were convicted of killing two university students in 1987, they were later released by higher courts.

Other civilian governments, such as those in Argentina, Bolivia, and Chile, have sought an accounting for the human rights abuses of past military regimes. But Cerezo decided to let bygones be bygones. In doing so he effectively authorized the military and police to continue meting out their own form of justice. In 1990 Americas Watch branded the response of the Cerezo administration to the expanding human rights crisis a "triumph of form over substance," and concluded that President Cerezo acted as an "army apologist."[25]

Violations Continue Under Serrano

Serrano came to the presidency with promises to establish the rule of law in Guatemala and to ensure respect for human rights. As part of his inaugural address, Serrano affirmed his "solemn commitment to make every possible effort to fully reestablish human rights in Guatemala." Addressing the sensitive issue of the impunity of the security forces, the new president asserted that "hierarchies will not be able to go against the majesty of the law. . . . He who breaks the law will be punished without exception."[26]

Despite these promises human rights violations continued unabated. In fact, the human rights situation deteriorated in many respects in 1991. In just five months, four human rights activists were murdered, one disappeared, and three sons of human rights activists were also murdered. The human rights group hit the hardest was the Runujel Junam Council of Ethnic Communities (CERJ), which Serrano called a "parallel organization" to the guerrilla movement and whose president, Amílcar Méndez "is working with the insurrection."[27] Indicative of the repressive political climate that persisted under Serrano was the April 1991 killing of social-democratic leader Dinora Peréz Valdez, who had recently helped create a new reformist political grouping called United Guatemala. In early 1992 the directors of the Labor and Popular Action Unity (UASP) received written death threats signed by the "Anti-Communist Unity," warning that the UASP directorate would "die en masse in the coming slaughter of the country's last communist leaders."

Like Cerezo, Serrano exhibited his concern by establishing new institutions such as the presidential Human Rights Commission and by instituting formal civilian control over the Interior Ministry (which oversees the police). Investigations were accelerated in several of the most prominent human rights cases but few convictions were immediately forthcoming. A military court did convict two officers for the December 1990 massacre in Santiago Atitlán, but in light of their meager sentences Human Rights Watch called the case a "parody of justice."[28] In response to increasing criticism of its treatment of the internally displaced, the military disbanded its detention and relocation center and desisted bombing the "communities in resistance" in northern Quiché. Two measures pending congressional approval in early 1992—a new labor code and a revised and greatly improved penal code—hold some hope for a better foundation for the respect of human rights in Guatemala.

In spite of these and other measures, human rights abuses reached such alarming levels that Human Rights Ombudsman Ramiro de León Carpio warned that the "selective violence" against labor leaders, reporters, human rights activists, and peasants resembled that experienced during the Lucas García regime.[29] Harassment of the press, beating and killing of street children by police, repression of human rights activists, and violence by civil patrol members were among the main human rights issues that surfaced in 1991. Despite Serrano's promise to use an "iron fist" to stem the rise in violence and some important human rights initiatives on the part of the government, most human rights violations went uninvestigated. At the end of Serrano's first year, Archbishop Penados denounced the mounting "culture of death" that was enveloping the country.[30]

In its 1992 report the U.S. State Department concluded that during Serrano's first year in office "the military, civil patrols, and the police continued to commit the majority of serious abuses against human rights including assassinations, extrajudicial killings, torture and disappearances of, among others, human rights activists, union members, indigenous people, and street children."[31] Simultaneously the United Nations Human Rights Commission issued a strong denunciation of human rights violations occurring early in Serrano's second year, but once again failed to include the country among the ranks of the world's most serious human rights violators. Instead, Guatemala was categorized as a nation with serious human rights violations but one in which the government was taking significant steps to correct the situation. The distinction was an important break for the Serrano government, since being castigated would have made it all the more difficult for Guatemala to obtain foreign aid.

As human rights violations continued unabated into the Serrano administration the government faced rising domestic and international pressure to end the impunity of the security forces. The Serrano government, unlike its predecessors, pursued the prosecution of members of the armed forces in several key cases, although in no case has a superior officer been convicted.[32] The end to impunity became a rallying cry of many popular organizations as they joined with foreign donors to demand that human rights violators be prosecuted and convicted. Once a forbidden subject, human rights violations became part of the daily vocabulary in Guatemala as politicians and businessmen alike included mention of human rights concerns in their rhetoric. Human Rights Ombudsman Ramiro de León, once an isolated figure, suddenly became one of the country's most popular politicians. Yet even as impunity and human rights violations were coming to the forefront in discussions of foreign aid and the credibility of the government, there were those who once again questioned the motives of human rights critics. In an effort to stir up nationalist sentiments, the weekly newsmagazine *Crónica* echoed government statements suggesting that the human rights issue was an international "conspiracy" promoted by the guerrillas.[33] Other opinionmakers suggested that de León was using the human rights issue to further his own political ambitions, and that the real human rights issue confronting Guatemala was crime.[34]

Local Human Rights Monitors

Perhaps one of the greatest indicators of the depth of the repression in Guatemala has been the tragic history of efforts to establish human rights groups. Time and again, harassment, killings, disappearances, and the overwhelming aura of fear they engender have thwarted the longevity of domestic monitoring groups. The absence of established groups, which could chronicle, investigate, and assign blame for the daily violations of the most fundamental rights, has worked to the tremendous advantage of successive Guatemalan regimes, allowing them to deny responsibility for innumerable tortured bodies found on countless roadsides.[35]

Among the early groups that focused on human rights violations in Guatemala were the Committee of Relatives of the Disappeared of the University Student Association (AEU) and the National Commission for Human Rights. The organizer of the AEU committee was shot at the university legal aid center in 1974, and the founder of the human rights commission was "disappeared" by security forces in 1980. Military and death squad violence extinguished these and other early efforts to establish human rights monitoring in Guatemala.

It was not until after the counterinsurgency campaign of the early 1980s had subsided that enough political space opened up to permit the emergence of human rights organizing. During the military regime of Mejía Víctores the Mutual Support Group (GAM) was founded in June 1984 as a support and advocacy organization for the disappeared.[36] Besides publicly raising the issue of government responsibility for the tens of thousands of disappeared, GAM helped lay the foundation for the resurgence of the popular movement after 1985 by leading demonstrations in front of the National Palace. The death of a GAM founder in 1985 was attributed by the army to a "lamentable accident." President Cerezo advised the group, 90 percent of whom are rural indian women, to "stop acting *macho*" and "forget the past."

During the second year of the Cerezo administration, in 1987, the Center for Investigation, Study, and Promotion of Human Rights (CIEPRODH) was established. Unlike GAM, it was not an activist group but focused on sponsoring seminars, producing bulletins, and providing legal assistance. Another popular-based human rights group that arose in the 1980s was CERJ, founded in 1988 to assist peasants wishing to resign from civil patrol duty. CERJ not only voices the demands of its members but also documents human rights abuses.[37] Other groups highlighting human rights issues are the National Coordinator of Guatemalan Widows (CONAVIGUA) and Peace Brigades International. In early 1990 two human rights offices were established within the Catholic Church, one by the archdiocese and a second by an organization of Catholic religious orders called CONFREGUA. One monitoring group considered by the army to be a political front for the guerrillas is the Mexico-based Guatemala Human Rights Commission, whose limited impact is due to its location outside the country.

In Human Rights Watch's 1990 survey of the persecution of human rights monitors around the world, Guatemala was singled out as the country where the largest number of monitors had been murdered or disappeared.[38] During the Cerezo years, 19 human rights activists were either killed or disappeared in circumstances implicating government forces or their agents. In none of the cases were the killers or kidnappers brought to justice.[39] Disappearances, killings, and death threats continued to victimize members of the country's besieged human rights groups under the Serrano government. Despite the administration's rhetoric about instituting the "rule of law," GAM and CERJ activists continued to be victimized with impunity by members of the civil patrols and security forces. Between 1974 and 1991, 27 human rights activists were murdered in Guatemala—23 of them since 1986.[40]

Through the persistence of the beleaguered Guatemalan groups and thanks to continued monitoring work by international organizations, human rights became a central issue in national reconciliation talks, electoral politics, and the peace negotiations by 1991. Changing world politics and reduced U.S. preoccupation with leftist challenges to its hegemony in Central America also opened up new space for such human rights concerns as the impunity of the security forces.

The nongovernmental human rights sector is constrained not only by repression but also by lack of resources and investigative capacity. The governmental human rights sector—comprising the Human Rights Ombudsman and the Human Rights Commission—has also been handicapped by financial limitations, as well as the government's lack of political will to pursue human rights convictions. During the Cerezo administration governmental initiatives to investigate human rights violations served more to polish the image of the government than to seriously address the issues. This began to change with the appointment of Ramiro de León in late 1989. Beginning in 1990 major international support, including help from the United States, bolstered the position of the Human Rights Ombudsman by increasing its investigative capability, thereby breaking the police monopoly on criminal investigations.

A major obstacle to human rights prosecution is the country's corrupt and inefficient judicial system.[41] As Americas Watch described it: "The Guatemalan judiciary remains crippled by a combination of sloth, corruption, and perhaps most decisive, fear of the consequences should it seek to touch the military's impunity in matters of human rights."[42]

But beyond Guatemala's faulty investigative process and corrupt judiciary, the major obstacle to improving the human rights climate is the lack of political will on the part of the government. Having just concluded a three-year program to improve the country's judiciary, the Harvard University professor directing the university's Center for Criminal Justice told a U.S. congressional committee in 1990: "It was too late in the day for the highest authorities in Guatemala to claim that the incompetence of the criminal justice system prevented effective investigation."[43] Instead he blamed the government for its lack of political will to bring to justice those responsible for the 1988 Aguacate massacre of 22 peasants, the 1989 murder of 11 university students, and other gross violations of human rights.

Main Human Rights Issues Unresolved

In the early 1990s concerns about impunity, lawlessness, and institutionalized human rights violations came to the fore in both the international and national arenas. No longer could the government or military count on the good faith of the international community. If Guatemala did not want to be cast as an international pariah, as it was in the 1978-83 period, it would have to demonstrate its ability to institute a state of law.

Human rights concerns were proving to be major stumbling blocks on several fronts: in peace talks with the URNG, in the repatriation of refugees living in Mexico, and in access to foreign aid and loans. Among the most prominent issues Guatemala will need to resolve if it is to transform the climate of lawlessness into a state of law are the following:

– Lack of convictions in the most prominent human rights cases, such as the deaths of Myrna Mack, Danilo Barrillas, Michael Devine, Héctor Oquelí, Dinora Peréz Valdez, and the University of San Carlos students.

– Existence of the civil patrols, development poles, and military commissioners.

– Forced military conscription.

– Military control over the police.[44]

— Existence of a clandestine repressive apparatus, including plainclothes military units and vehicles without license plates.

— Exemption of military personnel from prosecution by military courts, and the amnesty decree pardoning the military for human rights violations prior to 1986.

— Lack of respect for wartime humanitarian law.

— Need for investigation into responsibility for the tens of thousands of deaths and disappearances since the 1970s, exhumation of corpses found in unmarked graves, and indemnification of families of victims of human rights violations.

Many of these issues were introduced without resolution in the 1991-92 peace negotiations. Critical to the eventual solution of any of these concerns will be the existence of some type of impartial investigating organization and verification commission as well as a foreign presence to ensure that rhetorical commitments become reality.

PART 2

Military and Insurgency

© Derrill Bazzy

Armed Forces

The military's paramount status in Guatemala has long gone unquestioned. It is, after all, the institution that ran the government almost without interruption between 1954 and 1985. Even the country's leaders during the 1944-54 reformist period, Arévalo and Arbenz, were army officers. Following the 1954 coup the military became the nation's central institution, and by the mid-1960s it was considered to be the strongest and most nationalistic military force in the region.[1] Even the transfer to civilian government in 1986—the highly touted "democratization" of Guatemala—was a process engineered by the military itself as part of its National Security and Development Plan. As expected, placing elected civilian presidents in the National Palace did not end the armed forces' impunity from prosecution nor its central role in the nation's political scene. Neither has civilian rule brought about a decline in human rights abuses or a reduction in the army's considerable presence in rural Guatemala.

The armed forces have long assumed for themselves the role of society's guardian—protecting the established order against communists, socialists, rebellious workers and peasants, and all other left-of-center dissident groups and individuals. Its political-security apparatus relies on the systematic use of torture, death threats, and assassination to check opposition groups.[2] In the military's view, its long traditions of nationalism, patriotism, and anticommunism qualify it as society's ultimate arbiter and most honorable defender. Justifying the pervasive army presence in both external and internal affairs, the military high command cites the national constitution, which charges the army with maintaining Guatemala's "independence, sovereignty, and territorial integrity" and enforcing "internal peace and security."

Before the 1944-54 reform period the army was simply an instrument of dictators; with the 1954 coup it became the bride of the oligarchy.[3] In its campaign against the guerrillas in the 1960s the army evolved a fearsome image, or as one observer noted, it "gradually grew whiskers and developed strong muscles."[4] By the mid-1970s the army not only controlled the countryside but had also cemented its control of Guatemala's political institutions and acquired an economic profile through new military-managed enterprises.

It is still too early to downplay the Guatemalan military's unchallenged supremacy. But changes in international politics and new economic imperatives, as well as tensions and problems within the institution itself, currently threaten the military's position and prestige. The specter of international communism, paraded for so long to justify military control, has lost its shock value. And rather than being appreciated for maintaining political and economic stability, the military apparatus is increasingly viewed as a destabilizing element by many politicians, investors, and international lenders.

For decades, the military has defined the terms of political discourse in Guatemala—generally with the approval of the oligarchy. No longer. Public-policy issues such as demilitarization, challenges to traditional military impunity, and the importance of establishing a "rule of law" have achieved unexpected prominence. Having watched the value of its traditional ideology erode and with its theories about "national stability" contested by the politics of neoliberalism, the military has grown uneasy about its future.

The Dimensions of Counterinsurgency

The Guatemalan armed forces—incorporating the accumulated wisdom and experience of Argentinean, Israeli, Taiwanese, and U.S. advisers—decimated the guerrilla insurgency of the early 1980s with ruthless violence and sophisticated pacification techniques. Notably, the military conducted this multifaceted campaign without large infusions of foreign assistance—in marked contrast to neighboring El Salvador.

As successful as counterinsurgency and nation-building have been in Guatemala, the stability and security of the Guatemalan state remain precarious. Despite massive butchering of dissidents and the militarization of society, the army has failed over the last three decades to rid the country of the guerrilla threat. The army's apparent success in gaining control over the rural population has been more a function of its use of terror than of the performance of its civic-action and psychological-operations teams. Since 1954 the security forces have eliminated successive generations of community leaders, activists, and educators, rendering communities largely unorganized and deprived of social and political foundations. Although the army successfully pacified what was becoming a widespread popular rebellion, it failed in its broader goal of constructing a unified nation.

Since the April 1982 release of the National Security and Development Plan, the military has been committed to pursuing what could be called the "soft" side of counterinsurgency. This is not to imply that it has shirked from military offensives designed to defeat the insurgency while keeping the rural population terrified and passive. Massacres, torture, random terror, and aerial bombardments continue as part of a campaign to guarantee national security. These "hard" tactics, however, are often combined with measures designed to pacify the guerrillas' rural base of support. As the military began to achieve a firmer grip on the conflictive highlands in 1982 and 1983, this other side of counterinsurgency received added attention.

The army's pacification strategy functions in conflictive zones through civic-action projects, model villages, re-education and psychological operations, food distribution, and development projects. In the interests of national stability, the military high command has also backed limited reforms designed to broaden the financial base of government (tax increases) and pacify popular organizations (wage hikes, land-sales programs, expanded social services).

Counterinsurgency theorists generally recognize that deteriorating socioeconomic conditions create a seedbed for rebellion. Yet despite a widespread commitment to a developmentalist facet of counterinsurgency, the military has been unable to conceptualize and implement the kind of development projects that would indeed alter the socioeconomic circumstances of the countryside.

The military high command has guided a nation-building project designed to create a modernized state capable of responding politically, socially, and economically to revolutionary insurgence. Although successful in establishing the structure of such a state, the army's nation-building efforts in the 1980s failed to achieve the kind of national-unity pact needed to support its broad vision of security. Continued repression, military impunity, and the army's continuing influence in the National Palace undermine the credibility of the government while at the same time dashing hopes that political modernization will bring peace, stability, and progress. There also always remains the possibility that the military would return to a central place in government, perhaps even with the assent of the civilian administration, if the nation's fragile stability seemed in danger of collapsing.

Structure of the Armed Forces

The Guatemalan armed forces consist of some 46,000 troops in land, sea, and air branches. Unlike in many countries, the navy and the air force are not autonomous, but are dependencies of the army. The navy has only 1,000 sailors (including 600 marines) and the air force only numbers 1,300.

The High Command (Estado Mayor) serves as the central authority for the military, and it is here that the politics and overall strategy of the armed forces are formulated. Subordinate to the High Command are the tactical commands: Personnel, Intelligence, Operations, Logistics, and Civil Affairs. The commands of the navy and the air force are not included within these national divisions, falling instead under the jurisdiction of the 22 individual army zone commanders. The main tactical formation within the armed forces is the brigade. Two of the brigades, the Mariscal Zavala and Guardia de Honor, are based in Guatemala City. A third brigade is based in San José on the Pacific Coast, a fourth at Puerto Barrios on the Atlantic.[5] During the early 1980s military garrisons were established in virtually all municipalities of over 10,000 people with smaller outposts in many surrounding villages.

The Civil Affairs division is responsible for pacification efforts. Civil Affairs, created as a military command in 1982, is an outgrowth of the army's civic-action programs, formerly a branch of the intelligence division. Civic action and nation building have been components of military operations since the early 1960s, when the U.S. army began civic-action training and activities in Guatemala in response to the birth of an armed resistance. Guatemala, in fact, was the first Latin American country to receive this kind of military assistance from the United States.

There is a Civil Affairs section (S-5) associated with each of the military zones, although the main focus of Civil Affairs operations is the conflictive areas. According to the army, S-5 teams "act as advisors to the Military Zone Commanders on the political, economic, social, and social-psychological aspects of military operations." These teams are composed of soldiers specially trained in the areas of social services, psychological techniques, and ideological indoctrination. Usually nonuniformed, they function as a fifth column for the military in conflictive zones. Their work includes: intelligence gathering, re-education of the displaced and refugees, coordination of the projects of government ministries in targeted areas, and in general implementation of the "development" side of counterinsurgency.

In addition to coordinating development, Civil Affairs also manages the army's extensive psychological operations. It is called upon to "create an efficient leadership, which permits the formation of local leaders to spread the doctrinal elements of counterinsurgency strategy. The leadership must incorporate social promotion and community organization to arrive at integral community development."[6]

As part of its general public relations effort, the army has mounted a nationwide campaign about the values of military life. Officially, a military stint is required of all Guatemalan males. In fact, men trying to obtain a passport must show their military enlistment card. But universal compliance is a myth, as is voluntary recruitment. Generally, only sons of the rural poor enter the ranks of the army, and for the most part they are recruited forcibly. Typically, army trucks arrive in a village on market days and the feast days of patron saints with the local military commissioner signaling which youth should be recruited. In fact, the forcible roundup of over 900 poor youth during an unprecedented urban "recruiting" campaign by military commissioners was defended by the army as its "normal practice." Forced recruitment campaigns, which occur about every three months, have come under mounting criticism by the church, politicians, and the popular movement. An end to forced recruitment also ranked as one of the URNG (guerrilla coalition) demands at the peace talks, and there are signs that the military may be ready to concede on this point. Beginning in 1992 the army began to send conscription notices through the mail, although its forcible recruitment practices still continued in some areas.

With the reduced intensity of the counterinsurgency war after 1983 and the widening economic crisis, some rural youth have voluntarily enlisted, attracted by the $35 monthly pay and another $20 for their parents. Good food, shelter, and military privileges have also increasingly attracted poor Guatemalan youth. Officers come generally from middle-class *ladino* stock. To the rank of colonel, promotions are tied to tenure and performance, having little to do with personal connections.

Among the most important military institutions are the following:

– *Polytechnical School*: This is the officer training school (like West Point) from which students graduate with the rank of sublieutenant.

– *School of Military Studies (CEM)*: Officers (majors and above) receive advanced training here.

– *Military Social Welfare Institute (IPM)*: Officially, the IPM is the military's pension and investment fund, but unofficially it is a source of capital for investments on the part of both the armed forces and individual officers. This tax-exempt corporation manages numerous economic concerns, including the army commissary, an insurance company, a multi-level parking lot in the center of Guatemala City, and several urban properties. The IPM's most lucrative concern is the Army Bank, which it created in 1972.[7]

— *Army Bank*: The nation's tenth-largest bank, capitalized by the IPM and tax revenues, has military officers as its major stockholders and advertises that it provides "the safest place for your money."

— *Adolfo Hall*: This school is known for its military-style education. Not all graduates, however, enroll in the armed forces; many parents send their children to Adolfo Hall for its disciplinary reputation.

Police Divisions

Closely associated with the military structure are the nation's various police units. The National Police, with 7,500 members, is the principal police organization and is a dependency of the Ministry of Interior. Until 1991 it was thought that the National Police had more than 10,000 members, but a close count by the Serrano administration revealed that more than 2,000 ghost employees had been on the roles collecting wages for corrupt department chiefs. There is only one National Police officer for every 1,280 Guatemalans, with a much greater ratio in rural areas such as in the Quiché department where only 18 officers patrol. The Treasury Police (Guardia de Hacienda), which includes some 2,100 members, is adjunct to the Ministry of Finance and is limited to special service, border patrol, and contraband control.[8] Although smaller than the National Police, the Treasury Policy multiplies its influence by working closely with the army's G-2 intelligence command.[9] The third police unit, the Mobile Military Police (Policía Militar Ambulante), is actually part of the military and is directly controlled by the Ministry of Defense. In addition, there is also a Military Police.

Despite police training and assistance programs launched during the Cerezo presidency, the nation's security forces are in shambles due to a lack of adequate personnel and equipment. A West German police-assistance program boosted the number of police cars to 262, but by 1991 only 158 were functioning and, owing to budget restraints, each car was allocated only five gallons of gasoline each day. The Guatemalan police lack investigative skills, relying instead on torture and circumstantial evidence to elicit charges against those they arrest. Eventually all but a small percentage of those arrested are freed for lack of hard evidence. One newspaper report cited confidential police files showing that of the 7,000 arrested by the National Police during the first three months of 1991, all but 20 were later released. There are only 300 police detectives in the entire country, another reason why only 40 of every 100 serious crimes are investigated.

One proposal would merge all police forces into a single unit, possibly called the Civilian Guard, and separate the police from military control. But given how corrupt and inefficient the police are, any modernization would take at least several years.

Proposals to expand and modernize police units while curtailing the military have driven a wedge between these two security forces. These tensions surfaced during the Cerezo administration when the National Police became the recipient of considerable foreign training and supplies from the United States, Spain, West Germany, and other European countries. This aid raised concerns among sectors of the military that the Cerezo government was creating a source of armed power independent of them. Adding to this concern was the creation by Cerezo of the Presidential Security Department, which answered to the Estado Mayor Presidencial (a type of presidential security council). Also concerned with the new balance of police power was the Treasury Police, given its growing reputation as a center of organized political violence and common crime.

The creation of SIPROCI (Civil Protection System) in 1988 allayed fears that the government was crossing over into the security business. This police unit, placed directly under the army's high command, coordinated the Mobile Military Police, civil patrols, National Police, and Treasury Police. Aside from asserting military control over the country's various police forces, SIPROCI was apparently created in an effort to avoid internecine conflicts between the various units. Its formation came in the wake of an ongoing dispute between the National Police and the Treasury Police over an incident in which the former arrested members of the latter who were linked to death squad killings.

One objective of SIPROCI was to present a common police front to rising street crime in Guatemala City. As it turns out, the new SIPROCI coordinated unit has done little to check crime waves but has proved effective in breaking strikes and removing workers from occupied workplaces. The launching of SIPROCI also coincided with a wave of violence directed against media outlets such as the progressive *La Epoca* newsweekly.[10]

By 1992 the government was no longer highlighting SIPROCI in its proclamations about clamping down on the spiraling crime problem. Instead, it announced a new campaign called Immediate Tranquility for the Citizenry (TIP), which promoted joint police-military operations through the Hunapú anticrime force established by Serrano in March 1992. The Hunapú task force coordinated operations of the National Police, Treasury Police, Mobile Military Police, and the

Military Police based in Guatemala city. Yet despite all these maneuverings, killings and beatings of student demonstrators and the involvement of police and military officials in a wave of bank assaults in 1992 offered new evidence that the nation's security forces were themselves integral to the infrastructure of crime.

Paramilitary Groups

Although most death squad activity is directly sponsored by the security forces, the country also has a history of private rightwing paramilitary cadres. Military-sanctioned paramilitary violence was responsible for much of the repression inflicted on the left and the popular movement arising from the 1954 coup. A second surge of paramilitary violence, coordinated largely by the National Liberation Movement (MLN), arose as part of the counterinsurgency campaigns of the 1960s. The two major death squads of this period were the White Hand and the New Anti-Communist Organization. Some sources report that death squads killed between 30,000 and 40,000 people during the 1966-1973 period.[11]

Paramilitary killings and disappearances revived in the late 1970s and early 1980s. Although their activities remained an undercurrent of life in Guatemala, it was not until 1988 that death squads again began publicly identifying themselves. In May 1988, while dissident elements in the military were mounting a coup attempt, the White Hand took credit for death threats to a Cuban correspondent for Prensa Latina, while the Secret Anti-Communist Army (ESA) claimed responsibility for firebombing the home of the Tass correspondent. In 1989, a new death squad known as Jaguar of Justice (JJ) emerged. "We will bring to justice thieves, murderers, youth gang members, child abusers, corrupt bureaucrats, and political gangsters—both left and right," pledged JJ in its first press release. In reaction to the peace talks with the URNG, another rightwing group called the New Guatemalan Revolutionary Movement (NGRM) arose with the apparent objective of disrupting the negotiations. Another vigilante group that surfaced in 1991 was the Anti-Communist Unity, exploding on the scene with a barrage of death threats against most of the country's popular leaders and warning that the entire UASP directorate would "die en masse in the coming slaughter of the country's last communist leaders."

Civil patrols have been the army's main instrument in maintaining the militarization of the Guatemalan countryside. The Civilian Defense Patrols (PAC), first formed in Alta Verapaz in 1976 and expanded in mid-1981 by the Lucas García regime, became a central element in the counterinsurgency strategy of the Ríos Montt government aimed at breaking guerrilla links with the population. By late 1984 there were more than 900,000 members of the civil patrol system.

Supposedly a voluntary movement, the civil patrols are effectively obligatory. In municipalities selected by the army, all males above 16 years are required to "volunteer" to "serve" in these military-directed patrols. Failure to volunteer leads to being branded a guerrilla sympathizer and sometimes results in imprisonment and torture at the local army base. Beginning in 1982 civil patrols became an ubiquitous facet of rural life. At every entrance to most villages, civil patrols maintained guard posts to monitor the movement of visitors and villagers alike. According to a 1985 army publication acclaiming its rural pacification strategy, the civil patrols "have doubled the efficiency of the security forces in creating the conditions of peace basic to the integrated development of these communities."[12]

The main function of the civil patrols is population control—functioning as the eyes and ears of the military. The patrols also fulfill a certain political or administrative role, superimposed by the army over traditional community organizational structure. In conflictive areas the civil patrols have served as combat auxiliaries, often accompanying the army in military sweeps and capturing displaced families eluding military control. The patrols also fulfill a propaganda function by spreading an antileftist message among their communities and accusing those who resist joining the patrols of being proguerrilla.[13] Not uncommonly, civil patrol members also perform unpaid construction and maintenance work for the local army commander.

The failure of President Cerezo to honor his promise to disband the patrols sparked the formation of a daring popular organization called the Runujel Junam Council of Ethnic Communities (CERJ), which means "all are equal" in the Quiché dialect. Since 1988 this Santa Cruz del Quiché-based group has struggled for an end to the civil patrol system. Condemning the civil patrols as a form of military conscription, CERJ exhorts the rural male population to exercise their constitutional rights not to capitulate before the most extensive civil-patrol network in the world.

Although civil patrols are no longer as extensive and numerous as they were in the early 1980s, they remain an important mechanism for population control. In 1992 there were an estimated 450,000 boys and men incorporated into PAC units. Organized by local military commissioners (retired army officers who enjoy impunity and other military privileges), the civil patrols function as part of the nation's repressive apparatus by keeping tabs on popular movements. In some areas of the highlands, they have turned into vigilante units operating under the protection of the local base commander. Although unpaid, more zealous participants relish being considered special friends of the army and take advantage of their privileged status to wage personal vendettas. Rightwing parties and elements within the army have suggested that the system be extended to the cities, particularly in the light of heightened urban activity by the URNG. Human rights activists, the Catholic Church, and the popular bloc, together with the URNG negotiating team and the UN Human Rights Commission, have instead demanded that the patrols be abolished countrywide because of their repressive nature.

The Privatization of the Military

It used to be that the army was considered to be the *cholero de la burguesía* (half-breed servant of the wealthy). Though elements of this relationship persist, since the early 1970s the military and its officers have acquired a degree of economic power and respect in their own right. This trend, conceived during the Arana regime in 1970, has been called the "Somocization of Guatemala," referring to the way the Somoza family once manipulated the Nicaraguan National Guard for personal and political benefit. Anastasio Somoza, in fact, is reputed to have personally advised Arana on tips for acquiring wealth.

The IPM and the Army Bank constitute the financial heart of the military octopus, but the tentacles of martial economic power extend to all sectors of the economy and into the most isolated regions of Guatemala. Since the 1970s, the juiciest plums of economic aggrandizement for colonels and generals have been the Northern Transverse Strip, the Petén territory, and the department of Alta Verapaz. It became common practice during the Arana, Laugerud, and Lucas García regimes for high-ranking officers to receive large plots of land in these frontier regions slated for peasant colonization projects.[14] Among the public-sector corporations capitulating to military control in the 1970s and early 1980s were INDE (National Electricity Institute), the National Geographic Institute, the Aviateca national airline, Aurora international airport, GUATEL (national telephone company), and Channel 5 television station. The military has also gobbled up such state agencies as the National Reconstruction Committee (CRN), National Emergency Committee, and FYDEP (Petén development directorate—currently being dismantled). Yet another dimension of the military's economic reach is the weapons industry it operates, including an armored-vehicle plant in Santa Ana Berlín and a munitions factory in Cobán.

Active and retired military officers have sashayed in and out of these corporations and agencies always in the name of improving efficiency and accountability, but inevitably advancing them to new levels of depravity. Military corruption, though below the exorbitant levels attained during the Lucas García regime, continues to be a fact of life in Guatemala, ranging from cases of major graft to low-level plundering, such as vehicle-importing deals and other customs fraud. The army's past record of intervening in the economy and in the administration of public services (supposedly for the public good) undermines the credibility, especially among the private sector, of its nation-building pretensions.

Trade liberalization and the private sector's campaign against government corruption have not yet curtailed the extensive smuggling and customs-fraud operations of military officers. But if structural-adjustment measures were to be fully and honestly implemented, among those most adversely affected would be members of the officer corps, who routinely supplement their low salaries by selling tax-exempt vehicles, liquor, and domestic appliances imported through the military commissary. The army's ability to skirt customs regulations through its control of the commissary and the national customs office has long frustrated the private sector, yet many businessmen use their contacts with military officers to arrange their own special trade deals. An early indication of the army's resistance to proposals to reduce their domain was its refusal to comply with a law passed by the National Congress in 1990 returning the National Geographic Institute to the Ministry of Public Works.

Saving the Nation

The National Palace, official center of government in Guatemala, has for most of its history been largely an adjunct of the military high command. From 1954 to 1986 only one civilian president (Julio César Méndez Montenegro) occupied the palace. Yet even his regime (1966-1970) was guided by the dictates of the military.

Just as military rule is a tradition in Guatemala, so are "elections."[15] Every four years, the military would select its candidate, hold an election, and declare its candidate the winner. By the early 1980s this system began disintegrating as elements within the military started to question the validity and wisdom of government by direct military rule. In 1982 a group of dissident officers, led by General Efraín Ríos Montt (retired), seized the National Palace and ousted the handpicked successor of former president General Fernando Romeo Lucas García.

A month after the coup, the military government took a decidedly new approach to the counterinsurgency war. While continuing the scorched-earth tactics of the predecessor regime, the Ríos Montt government began to incorporate a developmentalist and nation-building aspect into the military effort. This new vision was outlined in the National Security and Development Plan (PNSD), decreed as law in April 1982. According to this plan: "The war is to be combated on all fronts: on the military and the political, but above all on the socioeconomic. The minds of the population are the principal objective." The PNSD addressed four problem areas undermining national stability:

– 1. Political Stability: the need to legitimize the government on both local and international levels. To return government to a legal framework, the military consented to a new constitution, elections, and the revival of political parties.

– 2. Economic Stability: the need to pull the country out of economic recession and to address the severe poverty of the rural population.

– 3. Psycho-Social Stability: the need to subvert the advances of the guerrillas among peasants, indians, and the illiterate.

– 4. Military Stability: the need to defeat the armed subversion.[16]

The PNSD set the guidelines for the evolution of government in the 1980s. It established politics as an extension of war, and government as an instrument of a national-stability project defined by the military. The plan for security and development veered Guatemala from a military-controlled "national-security state" to a national-security civilian government, managed by the military.[17] The course of this evolution of war and politics was evident in the military's annual designation of objectives, gradually siphoning its priority from the war effort into an enhanced focus on politics and the stabilization of government (Figure 2a).[18]

The coup injected a new dynamism into the military's response to the guerrilla threat and the popular rebellion in the highlands. As president, Ríos Montt also injected a new legitimacy into government through the creation of a Council of State, with representatives from various social sectors. He was not, however, the ideal coordinator for the military's stabilization efforts. His evangelical religious convictions alienated many vital elements of Guatemalan society and did little to dispel the country's international isolation.

In August 1983, a year and a half after the coup that installed Ríos Montt as president, the National Palace was the scene of another military coup, this time replacing Ríos Montt with his minister of defense, General Oscar Humberto Mejía Víctores. The Mejía Víctores coup simultaneously restored to government the traditional military hierarchy and initiated the evolution to civilian rule—according to the principles of the PNSD. Elections for the Constituent Assembly were held in 1984, and a new constitution was approved. In late 1985 the military sponsored fraud-free elections for the presidency and for seats in the new National Congress.

Thus, as originally set forth in the PNSD, civilian rule was reinstituted in Guatemala. A formal democracy was established whose limits were clear from the beginning: there would be no room for the revolutionary left, and the army would be its guardian and final arbiter. The military also remained in direct administrative control over all conflictive areas in the country.

Splits within the Military

The Guatemalan armed forces have long been torn by tactical differences and divisions between the ranks. A longstanding source of tensions has been the rift between those favoring developmental and nation-building programs and those committed to a strictly military approach to maintaining national stability. The National Reconstruction Committee (CRN), created in 1976, was, for example, largely a project of the army developmentalists. In the early 1980s the adoption of the PNSD represented a fusion of the two approaches to counterinsurgency and a moderation of tensions between the two camps. But as the guerrillas began to recuperate their former strength and the civilian government grew less capable of forging a national consensus in the late 1980s, earlier differences between the reformist and hard-line approaches resurfaced.

The unity of the Guatemalan military has also been weakened at times by splits between junior and senior officers, with the former backing a reformist agenda. This was the case in the 1960 rebellion by junior officers, which led to the founding of Guatemala's first guerrilla force, as well as the March 1982 coup led by Ríos Montt. Similar fractioning erupted again in the late 1980s as younger officers on the frontlines of the counterinsurgency war grew embittered with the military high command. They resented the luxuries available to these senior officers, who were not directly involved in the increasingly dangerous counterinsurgency campaigns. In many cases, the internal divisions within the military assumed an ideological character when in fact the disputes stemmed more from disparity in privileges and perks.[19]

Since the switch to civilian rule the army has been wracked by a disagreement over the best strategy for ensuring national security and stability. While Defense Minister Gramajo touted the democratization process as the best way to defeat the leftist insurgency and to ensure economic stability, hard-liners contended that the political opening had grown dangerously wide and that the more repressive tactics of the pre-1982 years needed to be reinstated.

The "national stability" strategy popularized by Defense Minister Gramajo during the Cerezo administration interwove the military's role in maintaining internal security with its "historic task of saving the nation." As the vanguard of its nation-saving project, the military invited all sectors to participate "within an integrated concept of the Guatemalan State." Closely related to this integrated nation-building effort was a military initiative in the political realm embodied in the September 1988 creation of the Center for Strategic Studies for National Stability (ESTNA). According to Gramajo, the objective of ESTNA is to "promote better understanding among the different elements of Guatemala's leadership circles, and to give these leaders a better understanding of the global strategic concept the army has conceived as the most adequate for the current situation in Guatemala." At a September 1989 roundtable sponsored by ESTNA, Gramajo charged that stability is threatened by those military and business figures who hold to the "iron hand" national-security policy in vogue prior to 1982. Instead, he declared, the emphasis should be on national stability that seeks harmony between various power blocs.

Figure 2a

From Victory in the Mountains to National Stability

— *Victory 82:* The army continued the scorched-earth campaign of terror and massacres initiated during the Lucas García regime in 1981, while forming Civilian Defense Patrols (PAC) to tighten its grip on the rural population.

— *Firmness 83:* The development component of counterinsurgency swung into action this year with the creation of development poles, model villages, and interinstitutional coordinators (which brought the representatives of all government agencies under the direction of the local army commander). According to the army, this campaign commenced "integrating public service institutions in the struggle against terrorism to vitalize the work and accelerate the task of pacification of the country."

— *Institutional Re-encounter 84:* The army expanded the concept of "security and development" to include political stabilization. Recognizing the need for a legal framework for the counterinsurgency war, the army sponsored elections for a Constituent Assembly whose function was to formulate a new constitution. Additionally, the military assigned itself the task of leading the reconstruction of the country and started to address the problem of the displaced population.

— *National Stability 85:* The army described this year's goals as follows: "During the development of the [1985] campaign plan, military operations were intensified. Governmental institutions directed their activities toward the support of the socioeconomic

ESTNA aims at building a consensus for the state, as conceived by the army and its civilian advisors, and at creating a political establishment to defend that conception of the state. The center is directed by and receives its financing from the military-spawned Foundation for the Institutional Development of Guatemala (DIG), a nongovernmental organization whose board of directors includes both civilian and military members (including Gramajo himself). ESTNA is but one element in the military high command's efforts to establish a common definition of national stability. General Juan Leonel Bolaños, who succeeded Gramajo as defense minister in 1990, described the process this way: "To counteract the occurrence of those elements which oppose the strategy of the military and other centers of power, the Guatemalan Army deems necessary the establishment of an educational process oriented toward all strata in the nation, with the object of learning to live within a system of democratic life and maintaining in this manner the constitutional order."[20]

In May 1987 a military faction, calling itself the "Officers of the Mountain," began publishing clandestine communiques critically analyzing the government and the Gramajo faction. These internal

---

programs and paid close attention to the political developments, motivating the active forces in the country to achieve massive participation in the upcoming elections." This "return to constitutionality" was designed "to consolidate the democratic system of life, to develop the nation's economy, strengthen government institutions, create a feeling of security in the population, and attempt to gain international recognition and support for the nation and its government."

— *National Consolidation 86:* The election of a civilian president and increasing international respect and assistance marked the success of the army's democratization strategy. Now the army moved to consolidate the Guatemalan state. Defense Minister General Héctor Alejandro Gramajo exhorted: "In Guatemala, politics ought to be the extension of war. We are still ready for battle, only we are fighting on a broader horizon within a democratic framework, and we are renovating fighting methods."

— Campaign Plan 87 was followed by Determination 88. New military and political strategies were adopted, always guided by the principle that "politics ought to be the extension of war." Campaigns were launched in the late 1980s to assert military control over the entire displaced population and to defeat the URNG forces, both militarily and strategically. The army also spearheaded the creation of multisectoral teams to spur development projects in conflictive zones.

critics represented the most rightwing elements within the army, most being veterans of the 1978-1983 counterinsurgency war. Many, in fact, were still commanding troops involved in counterinsurgency efforts. Their dissatisfaction had both economic and political dimensions. The emergence of the "Officers of the Mountain" faction also reflected a longstanding rift between field commanders and desk officers.

The Officers of the Mountain challenged Gramajo's contention that the counterinsurgency war had been reduced to a police action against isolated bands of terrorists. From their battlefront perspective, these military dissidents knew that the guerrilla offensive was still generating large numbers of casualties. The re-emergence of the CUC peasant group irked the Officers of the Mountain, who felt that the fighting forces were getting the short shrift in this pretentious new democracy. While members of the high command and officers in the city were living high, the dissidents charged that the combatants were not getting the logistical support they needed to fight the war successfully.

Limited at first to grumbling in the barracks, the internal tensions exploded into the open on May 11, 1988. Dissident officers, supported by ultraright political parties and sectors of the oligarchy, attempted a coup. Among the immediate factors that precipitated this break in the ranks were the following:

– The August 1987 signing of the Esquipulas II peace accords, which called for negotiations with the URNG and the beginning of a national dialogue.

– The November 1987 meeting in Madrid between government and URNG representatives.

– The embarrassing failure of the "Year's End" offensive in late 1987, finally abandoned in March 1988 after major casualties and an obvious failure to stamp out the tenacious guerrilla forces. The effort, which involved over 6,000 military combatants, was proclaimed the "final battle against the insurgency" by General Gramajo, but it ended without even so much as a final report.

– A March 1988 government pact with the UASP popular coalition that the oligarchy and rightwing officers regarded as a compromise with leftists.

– The arrival in the country in April 1988 of a Unity Representation of the Guatemalan Opposition (RUOG) delegation, a commission of the political opposition closely associated with the URNG.

– The success of the Christian Democratic Party and the rout of the rightwing parties in the April 1988 municipal elections, which signaled to the country's hard-liners the futility of the electoral option as a path to power.

— The failure of the government and military high command to secure substantially higher levels of military aid from the United States.

From the perspective of the perpetrators of the May 1988 and subsequent coup attempts (August 1988 and May 1989), the political and military situation had gone awry. While always ideologically opposed to the foreign policy of "active neutrality" owing to their support of the contras, this opposition crescendoed to new levels as it became apparent the Esquipulas II peace accords were having repercussions at home. The URNG took full advantage of this political opening to the chagrin of the government, the military, and the oligarchy. Not only was the URNG gaining strength on the diplomatic front, but it also showed increased vitality and durability on the battlefield.

Although not claiming full responsibility for the various 1988-89 coup attempts, the clandestine Officers of the Mountain were certainly among the rebel ranks. The coups appeared more to be negotiating maneuvers than serious attempts to seize state power. They succeeded in nudging the government more to the right, as well as rendering the civilian government yet more dependent on the Gramajo faction. While Cerezo and Gramajo survived the rebellions, many of the demands of the rebel officers were granted, including: the cancellation of the agreement with UASP, the closing of the political opening for the URNG, extra spending for military supplies, the reinsertion of military officers into key positions in the public administration, tightened military control over police forces, and maintenance of civil patrols.

The Officers of the Mountain and other rightwing elements within the armed forces have received direct backing and encouragement from ultraright political and economic factions. Significantly, the coup attempts and threats of 1988-89 were not condemned by the leading voices of the private sector. Instead, the destabilizing impact of the attempted coups served immediate business interests in that both the government and the army hardened their position against popular demands for wage hikes and price freezes.

The maneuverings of the Officers of the Mountain and the degree to which coup-mongering was accepted by the private sector demonstrated just how fragile and unsubstantial the democratization process really was. It became apparent that sizable factions of the military and the private sector were not prepared to accept the full significance of the "institutional re-encounter" as outlined by the military's leading political strategists.

Future of the Military

The divisions that surfaced within the military during the Cerezo presidency continued into the Serrano administration. Aggravating the fragmentation within the ranks were new sources of tension arising from the advancing peace talks, the breakdown of internal discipline, and international pressures to demilitarize.

Upon becoming president, Serrano selected as his defense minister General Luis Enrique Mendoza. But Mendoza soon began voicing his opposition to the peace talks, thereby undermining Serrano's unprecedented initiatives to negotiate an end to the civil war. The talks with the URNG were paralleled in 1991 by a rise in human rights abuses. Observers agreed that the perpetrators of these waves of political violence during Serrano's first year were members of the armed forces. In May 1991 the secretive Officers of the Mountain released a communique lashing out at the military hierarchy, charging that the dialogue with the URNG was "high treason against the noble goals of the military institution." Although some attributed the outbreak of human rights violations and death threats to extreme rightwing elements within the military, there was also widespread speculation that the military command itself unleashed the violence either in dissatisfaction with the government's willingness to consider guerrilla demands or to remind the popular bloc that the arena for left-of-center organizing remained tightly constricted.

Angered that his peace and human rights initiatives were so blatantly thwarted by the military high command, Serrano reshaped the military power structure, replacing key officers with those more loyal to his policies. In December 1991 Serrano named José Domingo García Samayoa as his new defense minister and Jorge Alberto Perussina as the new army chief of staff. The reshuffle also included 16 rotations in base commander positions, while six colonels were promoted to general. The shake-up in the military command demonstrated Serrano's ability to assert his own presidential authority over the military, and by violating normal rotational procedures it illustrated the lack of cohesion within the institution.

Ideological differences over the peace talks (or "national stability" project) were not the only factors in the army's internal fragmentation. Mounting international pressure to demilitarize, together with an institutional economic crisis encouraged officers at all levels to seek with renewed vigor personal financial security through illegal means. In the interests of maintaining a strong, nationalist institution, the military high command has discouraged collusion between the army and nacrotraffickers, but military corruption generally thwarts any reform efforts. The existence of several crime and smuggling rings within the army involved in car theft, gun running, and highway banditry has appreciably weakened the authority of the military command. Some within the military lament the moral disintegration of the ranks, citing the emergence of virtually autonomous internal cliques—some organized by type of crime or contraband, others arranged geographically by area commanders.

An August 1991 communique from the Officers of the Mountain focused a spotlight on tensions between older and younger commanders. The dissident officers complained that top military brass was increasingly scapegoating younger officials to protect senior authorities from corruption charges and prosecution for human rights abuses.

Further fractionalization within the ranks is likely in coming years in reaction to peace talks and demilitarization proposals. Long opposed to any direct talks with the URNG, the military high command finally agreed in 1991 to face-to-face negotiations with guerrilla commanders. But rather than an indication that the military had softened its stance, the decision to meet with URNG chiefs was more a strategy to buffer international criticism. The government figured it could wear down the guerrillas by dragging out the negotiations at a time when the URNG was low on arms and logistical support. It also felt the peace process would strip the guerrillas of their romantic appeal by exposing them and their program to international scrutiny.

This tactical maneuver backfired somewhat as guerrilla proposals to end forced recruitment, abolish the civil patrols, and set up a joint investigatory commission for human rights violations won international support. At the same time the peace talks augmented the political power of the URNG by demonstrating that its demands paralleled those of the popular movement and other progressive forces. Mere participation in a recognized international forum also boosted the prestige of the guerrilla coalition.

Waging a war of attrition against the guerrillas, the army and the Serrano government grew increasingly confident of military victory. By 1992 international reluctance to support guerrilla struggles combined with the URNG's lack of significant political and military power reinforced the government's unwillingness to negotiate a serious accord. Although the URNG had successfully launched an unprecedented military campaign on the South Coast, as well as isolated urban strikes against military vehicles and electric towers, the guerrilla coalition failed in its drive to disrupt economic production. As of mid-1992, the peace talks and associated initiatives had not resulted in sparking the kind of two-front (orchestrating the armed and popular movement) campaign for a negotiated settlement that had been so successful in El Salvador. Despite acquiring credibility in its search for peace, the URNG nonetheless lacked the influence needed to force the government to negotiate seriously.

Ironically, the fading of the URNG as a revolutionary alternative has not served to fortify the position of the armed forces. Instead, unable to justify itself as society's bastion against communism, the military has grown increasingly vulnerable as an institution. Calls to terminate its impunity, trim its size, and narrow its scope emanated from most quarters by 1992. Irked by such proposals, the military high command has adamantly rejected all suggestions that the army budget and size be reduced, arguing instead that the nation's large population and territory require current troop levels, and that the military already suffers from serious equipment shortages and financial shortfalls. Defense Minister García has also argued that once a peace accord is signed, the army will increase its participation in road construction, antinarcotics operations, environmental protection programs, and educational projects in rural areas.[21]

Given the URNG's lack of bargaining power, demilitarization is unlikely in the near future short of international pressure for suspension of military aid, and linking of all economic aid to military cutbacks and an end to gross human rights violations. Equally critical would be a redefinition of the role of the military in Guatemalan society, restricting its responsibility to guaranteeing the nation's "territorial integrity" and eliminating all references to its role in enforcing "internal peace and security."

Guerrilla Opposition

Guatemala has the longest-running guerrilla opposition in Latin America. The origins of guerrilla warfare can be traced to a failed coup in 1960 by a group of reformist officers angry with government corruption and the use of Guatemalan territory to train Cuban exiles for the Bay of Pigs invasion. The uprising's leaders, Lieutenants Marco Antonio Yon Sosa and Luis Turcios Lima, founded the Revolutionary Movement of November 13 (M-13) in early 1962 to avenge their failure.

The two rebel officers, however, had different ideas about revolution. Turcios Lima was more of a nationalist and anti-imperialist than a socialist. In contrast, Yon Sosa criticized Turcios Lima for collaborating with elements of the bourgeoisie, and advocated a peasant-based socialist revolution using China as a model.[22] Shortly after the appearance of M-13, another guerrilla force was formed by the Guatemalan Workers Party (communist-based) with the intention of overthrowing the Ydígoras military regime. In late 1962 the forces united to establish the Rebel Armed Forces (FAR) but went through periodic splits and refusion. A U.S.-backed counterinsurgency campaign in 1966-67 decimated the rural guerrilla forces, although some urban terrorist operations continued.[23] Considering the indian population impossible to organize, the guerrillas of the 1960s took their message of revolution mainly to poor *ladino* peasants in the Izabal and Zacapa departments in eastern Guatemala, where many small landowners had been pushed off their farms by large cattle ranchers eager for new pastures to raise beef for export to the expanding U.S. market.[24]

After a period of reflection and analysis by the remnants of guerrilla forces of the 1960s, two new guerrilla organizations—Guerrilla Army of the Poor (EGP) and the Revolutionary Organization of People in Arms (ORPA)—emerged in the 1970s and were later joined by a resurrected FAR (which broke with the PGT in 1968 over differences about the possibility of a capitalist reform movement setting the stage for a peaceful transition to socialism.). Unlike the 1960s, when the emphasis was on forming "*focos*" or centers of guerrilla operation that would ignite widespread revolutionary war, the new guerrilla fronts place more emphasis on popular education and the political formation of peasant communities. For the first time the guerrillas concentrated their political education and military strikes in largely indian areas.

This new strategy proved successful in mobilizing widespread support for revolutionary objectives. But the newly formed guerrilla armies were neither sufficiently organized nor prepared for the terror that descended upon them and upon the communities where they were working (mainly in the villages of the northwestern highlands, the FTN, and the Petén). Although they met their popular-education objectives, the revolutionary forces had not advanced to the stage where they were able to incorporate large numbers of peasants into guerrilla units. Nor were they strong enough to defend the indian communities from the army's wholesale butchering.

The counterinsurgency war, which reached its height from 1981 through 1983, crushed the defenseless resistance movement and seriously weakened the guerrilla forces themselves. The brunt of the 1981-83 offensive was aimed at destroying or dispersing the guerrillas' unarmed rural followers. This campaign came on the heels of several years of intensive repression against popular organizations, development groups, and community organizations, in both rural and urban areas.

Although the guerrilla armies survived, they could no longer count on ample bases of popular support. The army had clearly made its point: any aid for the "terrorists" would be dealt with in the cruelest fashion—often the elimination of entire villages. Although fear was certainly the main factor in breaking the strong links between the guerrillas and indian communities, disillusionment, fed by army propaganda, also contributed to diminishing revolutionary sentiment. Many rural people felt that the guerrillas had promised more than they could deliver and had failed to protect them when violence struck. The army's developmentalist and democratization strategies also isolated the guerrilla armies. Instead of news of massacres and burning villages, military-sponsored food distribution programs and the electoral process came to dominate international headlines.

Who They Are and What They Want

Since 1982 four guerrilla forces have been united in the Guatemalan National Revolutionary Unity (URNG), which functions as both the diplomatic and military command of the armed revolutionary movement. Although Marxism-Leninism has been the dominant ideological tendency within the URNG, the coalition also embraces strong liberation-theology and social-democratic tendencies. Combatants are largely indian and many have joined the armed struggle from a Christian perspective.

The four guerrilla armies that compose the URNG often operate under common field commands and in some cases have mounted joint operations. They are, however, distinguished by different geographical areas of concentration and varying political philosophies. The EGP, which established itself in the highlands in 1972, operates mainly in northern Quiché and Huehuetenango but also in Chimaltenango. Its commander is Rolando Morán. FAR, the oldest guerrilla army, concentrates in the Petén (along the Mexican border and southeast of Tikal) and in the Northern Transverse Strip (in northern Alta Verapaz). The chief of FAR, probably the most hard-line and militaristic of the four groups, is Pablo Monsanto. ORPA began operations in 1972, and, after years of education and organizing, launched its first military operation in 1979. Its base is found in Sololá, San Marcos, and Quetzaltenango, with a minor presence in Chimaltenango, Escuintla, and Totonicapán. Its head is Rodrigo Asturias (also known as Gaspar Ilom), son of the famous Guatemalan novelist Miguel Angel Asturias who wrote *Men of Corn* and *El Señor Presidente*. The fourth component of the URNG is the PGT Central Committee, led by Carlos González. The PGT joined the guerrilla coalition in early 1989, but maintains little more than a token military presence in the alliance.

The five main points of URNG's 1982 revolutionary platform were the following:

– 1. Elimination of repression, and guarantees of life and peace.

– 2. Distribution of property of the very wealthy, agrarian reform, price controls, and the allowance of reasonable profits.

– 3. Guaranteed equality between indians and non-indians.

– 4. Equal representation by patriotic, popular, and democratic sectors in the new government, equal rights for women, protection for children, and guarantees of freedom of expression and religion.

– 5. National self-determination and a policy of nonalignment and international cooperation.[25]

The Military and Political Fronts

The military high command in the late 1980s toasted victory in the counterinsurgency war. All that remained of the guerrilla armies were small isolated bands that constituted no real military threat.

Defense Minister Gramajo went so far as to say that conflictive zones no longer existed.

The announcement of the demise of the guerrillas proved premature, however. Throughout many areas of the northern highlands and the FTN, army patrols acknowledged that the guerrillas were still active in the late 1980s. Although the army was militarily much stronger, it had failed to instill "security" in the conflictive zones. Road-building plans were stymied by guerrilla sabotage, and rebel units still seized villages for propaganda sessions. Frequent use of civil patrols for scouting missions and large-scale military offensives also testified to the continued guerrilla threat. The reality of enduring guerrilla war was highlighted by the 1988 protests of the army's own Officers of the Mountain, who charged that the desk generals were living the good life while those on the front lines were underequipped and unable to count on the full support of the government.

Military and political initiatives by the URNG revealed the continued viability of the guerrilla movement in the late 1980s. The URNG did not pretend to wield a military force capable of directly confronting the Guatemalan army with major offensive operations. Instead of frontal assaults, it waged a war of attrition relying mainly on ambushes, sabotage, and attacks on isolated military outposts. In 1988 it launched its first joint offensives orchestrating all the guerrilla armies, and the number of its operations doubled in 1989. By 1990 the URNG had forces active in 12 departments and the country's two largest cities.[26] In an apparent effort to develop more popular support, the URNG also began to mount more nonmilitary operations wherein guerrilla troops would occupy villages and explain their political position to gathered villagers.

Stalled army offensives in the highlands and lightning guerrilla attacks in Guatemala City and Quetzaltenango in the late 1980s testified to the URNG's enduring presence. By escalating its levels of sabotage and attacks on military targets in the late 1980s, the URNG did indeed win added recognition as a military force. Yet its operations still ranked more as harassment than actual military conflict.

By 1992 the URNG was demonstrating a surprising logistical capacity to switch its main theaters of activity, initiating military operations led by ORPA forces in the economically vital Escuintla area of the South Coast, and renewing activity in the Guatemala City area. It could claim a military presence in 13 of the 23 departments, though most of its operations were what the army deprecatingly dubbed "assault and asphalt" strikes—lightning attacks on small police or military outposts, infrastructure sabotage, and attempts to block the flow of commerce on the South Coast highway. The URNG held no territory and lacked the capability to mount sustained offensive operations against the armed forces. Most of their military initiatives seemed more designed to disrupt the economy or to announce their existence than to gain ground against the army. A burst of activity in late 1991 was apparently launched with the intent of boosting their standing as a military force at the negotiating table. Assaults against economic targets were designed to precipitate support within the private sector for a negotiated solution. Nonetheless, the URNG's ability not only to survive but also to expand its field of operations was remarkable, especially at a time when international financial, logistical, and ideological support for armed leftist movements had all but disappeared.

Describing the URNG's military strategy, ORPA commander Rodrigo Asturias in mid-1991 explained that its objective "has not been to control territory. It is more a project of expansion instead of remaining in a single area. The concept of hitting more sensitive points has given a new character to the struggle and has generated new political and military conditions—the main one being that the rebel presence is closer to the principal power centers of the economy."[27]

Without the troops or weaponry to mount a serious military challenge, the guerrillas seemed at times little more than isolated bands of saboteurs, occasionally blowing up electrical towers and oil pipelines and launching hit-and-run raids. Exhausted by decades of political violence and besieged by a widening wave of common crime, many Guatemalans began to dismiss the political and military significance of the guerrillas. The URNG contested this evaluation, asserting that the army has never been able to deliver a strategic blow and that the guerrilla forces have constantly expanded their theater of operations. It argued that economic targets were chosen not because they were easier but as part of a strategic campaign to pressure the private sector. Furthermore, the guerrillas claim to have developed a significant "capacity to wear down the army," which has suffered some 20,000 war casualties since 1980.[28] Estimates commonly place the guerrilla force at about 1,000 with perhaps another 1,000-3,000 constituting a support reserve known as the irregular forces.

The URNG describes itself as a "political/military force," reasoning that its military power obligates the government to recognize it also as a political force. However, the URNG's lack of political influence was by the second year of the Serrano administration proving yet a more serious deficiency than its military weaknesses. In contrast with the FMLN in El Salvador, the URNG does not have a strong and unified popular-movement ally poised to exert pressure on the government for a negotiated settlement. And unlike El Salvador, with its broad continuum of revolutionary organizing, Guatemala has no rebel group capable of coordinating armed struggle with popular demands. Squabbles within the guerrilla coalition over leadership roles and strategies for working with the popular movement have also hindered the development of a strong common front between the popular bloc and rebel forces.

Further weakening the URNG's popular influence has been its lack of a viable and well-defined political platform. The sketchy nature of its political agenda has rendered the URNG an unknown quantity in many respects. In attracting supporters, it has relied more on its allure as the only force capable of retaliating against the military than on the coherence of its political and economic demands. This historic failure to offer either a clear analysis of Guatemala's structural problems or a viable agenda for change has hindered the development of a strong groundswell of support among the popular sectors and those Guatemalans of progressive political tendencies. The lack of a well-defined alternative platform has been accentuated by the absence worldwide of credible revolutionary leadership and agendas for progressive change.

Since the mid-1980s the URNG has escalated its criticism of the shortcomings of representative democracy in Guatemala, while placing less emphasis on the urgency of reforms to redistribute income and land. In an interview published in mid-1991 FAR commander Pablo Monsanto acknowledged that the international political and economic climate no longer favored the broader revolutionary goals of the guerrilla forces. As a result, he explained, the URNG's revised emphasis was "limited to gaining political participation and to achieving objectives within the democratic framework. This isn't to say that we have renounced the revolution. But we think that the construction of democracy is an important step on the road to revolution."[29] To this end, the URNG began in the mid-1980s proposing a "historic pact" to terminate the war and open up the political system to leftists and popular coalitions.

The URNG finally achieved its goal of entering into direct negotiations with the government and military in 1991. However, its prospects for either achieving a favorable political settlement to war or increasing its military stature seemed grim by mid-1992. In 1992 the URNG confronted a coordinated counterinsurgency effort by the military that aimed to cripple its military capacity through relentless attacks on rebel infrastructure. At the same time the government and the military mounted a coordinated propaganda blitz that painted the guerrillas as a rapidly decaying band of terrorists devoid of popular support. The counterinsurgency campaign also included the reorganizing of civil patrol units along the South Coast and government sponsorship of peace marches in rural conflictive zones. This double-edged campaign put the URNG on the defensive both politically and militarily while further weakening its position at the bargaining table.

The Peace Process

The Cerezo government initially played a key role in arranging regional talks among the five Central American presidents (Panama and Belize did not participate). Cerezo's ambitions to win international acclaim as a regional peacemaker were thwarted, however, by the more aggressive efforts of President Oscar Arias of Costa Rica. Revelations of Guatemala's support for the Nicaraguan contras and the half-hearted manner in which the Guatemala government implemented the peace accords contrasted sharply with Cerezo's professions of regional neutrality and commitment to peaceful solutions.

The provisions of the Esquipulas II peace accords, ratified by Guatemala in August 1987, were only superficially implemented within the country. In keeping with the accords, the Cerezo government did declare a political amnesty, but its main beneficiaries were military officers who participated in a May 1988 coup attempt against the government. Refugees returning from Mexico or displaced persons rounded up by the army were also granted amnesty during the Cerezo presidency, but only after the military coerced them into signing declarations stating their repudiation of the guerrillas. As specified in the Esquipulas II peace accords, a national dialogue was initiated under the auspices of the newly established National Reconciliation Commission (CNR), which received strong support from the Catholic Church. Representatives of the country's major political parties, churches, and popular organizations were represented in a National Dialogue sponsored by the CNR, but the relevance and impact of the National Dialogue was undermined from the start by its failure to incorporate representatives of the URNG guerrilla coalition and groups of Guatemalan exiles, who also petitioned for the right to participate. The failure of the military and the business coalition CACIF to join the dialogue also foiled the CNR's efforts to promote peace and justice.[30] For all its limitations, the popular movement, represented by the Labor and Popular Action Union (UASP), regarded the National Dialogue as an opportunity to voice demands in a public forum sanctioned by the government. Dialogue participants and observers took advantage of the forum to establish links with each other and to forge a common strategy. The popular movement, however, approached the National Dialogue mindful that past attempts to reach national accords over such issues as wages and human rights had been repeatedly sabotaged by subsequent government agreements with the private sector and the army.

International pressure prompted the Cerezo government to agree to discussions with the URNG guerrilla coalition in October 1987, but this dialogue quickly lapsed due to rightwing reaction in Guatemala. The URNG continued to express interest in reopening talks but was repeatedly rebuffed. It was not until early 1990 that a series of talks between the URNG and the country's political parties, private groups, and popular organizations was initiated. In March 1990 delegations from the URNG and the CNR met in Oslo where it was decided that, through a series of sessions sponsored by the CNR, the URNG would meet with the country's key economic, social, and political groups. The intent of these talks was to lay the foundation for direct negotiations between the rebels, the government, and the military.

Jorge Serrano participated in the CNR meeting with the URNG in March 1990, and he later represented the MAS party at a May 1990 meeting between the URNG and the political parties. During the presidential campaign Serrano announced that he would support direct talks between the government and the URNG. Fulfilling that promise, President Serrano in April 1991 presented his "Initiative for a Complete National Peace," in which he agreed to direct talks between the government and the guerrilla leadership. For the first time, the Guatemalan government agreed to initiate negotiations without requiring that the guerrillas first lay down their arms.

The start of the negotiations in Mexico was marred by an upsurge in human rights violations. This outburst of political violence and the issuing of death threats seemed designed to remind the popular bloc that repression of all popular organizing and left-of-center political mobilization would continue. The extremist army faction Officers of the Mountain issued a statement in mid-1991 dictating that peace will be achieved only "when the last guerrilla is dead"—a sentiment widely shared within the military and private sector.[31] By late October 1991 the fledging negotiations had snagged over human rights issues, while the government began to assume a more triumphant attitude in the face of a weakening guerrilla movement.

From the first meeting in April 1991 many were skeptical about the seriousness of the government and military in negotiating an end to the conflict. Unlike in El Salvador, the UN representative at the talks was only an observer, not a full-fledged mediator. Dismissing this lack of international mediation, Serrano explained: "We are nationalistic. When a foreigner appears on the scene, our hair stands on end."[82] Nationalism was certainly part of the explanation, but more critical was the government's unwillingness to recognize the URNG as "belligerents" and therefore as equal partners at the negotiating table. Similarly, the government refused to consider a temporary cease fire, believing it would imply that the URNG was a legitimate military organization. Rather than a serious commitment to negotiate an end to the war, the peace talks were, according to Vice-President Gustavo Espina "an opportunity that the government and the army are providing the rebels to be reincorporated into the national productive arena because they have already been beat militarily." By mid-1992 the talks seemed to be merely a tactical arena for the government as it awaited the long-predicted demise of the guerrilla forces.

International pressure in 1987 laid the foundation for the peace talks, and this same external pressure prevented either the government or the URNG from unilaterally abandoning the talks. The Serrano administration recognizes that an end to the internal conflict would open doors to foreign aid and financing while boosting Guatemala's trade and investment position. The guerrillas, too, are being prodded internationally to bring the 30-year conflict to a close. In 1991 the Mexican government apprised the URNG that it no longer considered the rebels to be a legitimate military force and that they should settle the war as soon as possible, warning that it would discourage the guerrillas from maintaining offices and supply lines in Mexico. Similarly, Cuba reportedly assured Serrano that it would no longer aid the URNG.

While the guerrillas and the government were being pressured into resolving their conflict quickly, little progress was being made on the major issues. The main obstacle was the URNG's demand for the establishment of a Truth and Justice Commission, composed of three representatives appointed by the UN secretary-general, to investigate human rights abuses. The guerrillas also demanded that measures to ensure respect for human rights—including an end to military impunity, abolishment of civil patrols, government assistance for victims of human rights abuses, an end to forced conscription, and a cleansing and professionalization of the security forces—be implemented immediately rather than upon the signing of a full peace agreement. Realistically assessing its lack of leverage at the bargaining table, the URNG did not initially insist upon major structural changes, such as demilitarization, agrarian reform, or other proposals that would require major revisions of the constitution. It was, instead, apparently opting to use what little leverage it did have to win maneuvering space for the nation's popular movement and progressive political forces.

According to FAR commander Monsanto, the URNG was seeking "political participation within a truly democratic framework—with [political] spaces that could bring revolutionaries not to power but to having fundamental elements of power."[33] To carve a niche in the political process the URNG negotiated for a dismantling of the clandestine repressive apparatus of the state and a new respect for human rights. The rebels have long declared that Guatemala is not a democratic state but rather a militarized one. Democracy, expounded EGP commander Rolando Morán, "must not be understood only as a mechanism for elections."[34]

Demand for a Broader Democracy

Although Guatemala is sorely lacking a left-of-center political party, the prospects for the creation of such an organization are extremely limited. The murder in April 1991 (presumably by security forces) of Dinora Perez, co-founder of a social-democratic political group called United Guatemala, was apparently a warning against any attempts to form a popular political coalition that could serve as a base for the guerrillas' assimilation into electoral politics.

At this point, its seems likely that if the URNG did attempt to operate openly in the political process its leaders and cadres would be quickly eliminated by the security forces and associated death squads. In the mid-1960s, something similar occurred when the guerrilla army threw its support behind the candidacy of Mario Méndez Montenegro. Soon after assuming the presidency, Méndez Montenegro appointed General Carlos Arana as minister of defense. Arana then unleashed an unprecedented campaign of terror against the guerrillas and suspected supporters.

In addition to the absence of an active UN mediator, another structural problem with the peace talks was the lack of direct input from popular and indian organizations. Despite its origins in the National Dialogue, the 1991-92 peace process marginalized the popular movement, thereby bypassing many of the day-to-day social and economic concerns of the nation's workers and peasants. Reacting to the government's refusal to discuss issues not directly related to the conflict, Nineth García of the human rights group GAM retorted that peace means more than a "silencing of bullets." GAM and other human rights organizations also echoed the URNG's position that the war was not the principal cause of human rights violations—a sentiment roundly rejected by government and military negotiators. In mid-1992 six representatives of the country's nongovernmental organizations were permitted to attend the peace talks in the name of the newly created Civil Sector Coordinating Commission (CIC).

In some cases, its own negotiating tactics have been turned against the URNG, as with its demands for the application of the Geneva Convention on war. The army rejects the demand because it regards the URNG as not significant enough to be considered a "belligerent force" with international status. In 1991 the URNG began demanding "prisoner of war" status for captured guerrillas, appealing to the International Red Cross to ensure their safety. But the issue has boomeranged back on the guerrillas as the Guatemalan Human Rights Ombudsman and, to some extent, such groups as Americas Watch and the Washington Office on Latin America began to investigate guerrilla abuses, including extrajudicial killings of civil patrol members, forced recruitment, endangering civilian populations in military attacks, and leaving land mines in the path of noncombatants.[35] The systematic breach of international humanitarian law by the armed forces has been documented, but new attention to the humanitarian rules of war may eventually diminish the standing of the URNG in a nation weary of all forms of violence. Playing on widespread frustration with high crime rates, the army presented a list of violations of humanitarian law by the URNG, urging the citizenry to forge "a common front against the terrorism, vandalism, and arrogance of an illegal organization."[36]

By mid-1992 the peace talks, halted since October 1991 over differences regarding human rights, seemed hopelessly stalled. Both the government and the army seemed to prefer tolerating the URNG as a guerrilla force rather than meeting its demands. Instead of recognizing the advantages of a UN mediator, the Serrano administration forced the removal of UN observer Francesc Vendrell in May 1992, complaining that he was partial to the URNG and apparently hoping that he would be replaced with a more docile observer. Unveiled in May, a new URNG peace proposal titled "For Peace with Justice and Democracy" was immediately rejected by the military and business groups. Its call for broad economic, military, and political reforms, including 11 constitutional amendments, did nothing to advance the peace negotiations, although the "comprehensive proposal" did for the first time publicly present a complete picture of guerrilla demands. Among other points, the URNG advocated: invitation of other social groups to the talks; the restructuring, democratization, and downsizing of the military; land redistribution and an overhaul of all agrarian legislation; recognition of indian rights to land and cultural survival; and broad reforms in the educational, health, and food-production systems. Although too radical to precipitate a negotiated end to the war, the rebel proposals did constitute a reasonable and coherent program for the progressive modernization of Guatemalan society, politics, and economy.

In the early 1980s the leftist refrain, "Nicaragua yesterday, El Salvador today, and Guatemala tomorrow," reflected the belief that revolution was sweeping Central America, and that the successful conclusion of the guerrilla war in Guatemala was almost inevitable. At the start of the 1990s it seemed that a negotiated settlement of the 30-year conflict was also inevitable, following, as if by contagion, the examples of Nicaragua and El Salvador.[37] But the intractable character of the Guatemalan military and business elite, the lack of a strong civil society striving for a negotiated settlement, and the long legacy of political violence continued to obstruct a peaceful termination of the conflict.

With or without a peace accord, it appears that the guerrilla conflict in Guatemala will end in the near future. The URNG has neither the ideology, popular backing, nor international support to sustain it. Lacking sufficient negotiating power to attain structural changes, the URNG was maneuvering what little political and military leverage it had to engineer a resolution of many of Guatemala's longstanding human rights issues and to create more space for popular organizing. The ultimate tragedy of the civil war will be realized if human rights issues are left unresolved as the government, counting on the support of the military and private sector, never enters into serious negotiations in the confidence that the guerrillas are a rapidly fading political and military force.[38]

PART 3

Economy

© David Maung

Overview of the Economy

Guatemala has the largest economy in Central America. Its 1991 gross domestic product (GDP) stood at $9.3 billion—40 percent above that of El Salvador's and about 4 times that of Nicaragua's. But Guatemala's economic size pales to that of Mexico's—whose economy is 21 times larger.

The country's population (9.6 million)—the highest in Central America—and its rich agricultural base contribute to Guatemala's relatively broad economy. However, Guatemala's considerable GDP has not translated into better-than-average social indicators. Mainly because of Guatemala's vastly inequitable patterns of land ownership and income distribution, its population remains among the poorest in Latin America (see State of Poverty).[1]

During the 1960s and 1970s the Guatemalan economy enjoyed annual growth rates of 5 percent or more. But a slump in the world market in the late 1970s combined with escalating internal political turmoil resulted in a sharp economic downturn that burdened the country with negative growth rates through 1986. Renewed foreign aid and the government's economic stabilization plan resulted in moderately positive economic growth through 1991 (Figure 3a). But this renewed economic expansion was only slightly above the rate of population increase and did not result in a return to the per capita GDP level enjoyed prior to the economic decline. In the 1981-91 period the accumulated average per capita GDP growth was a negative 1.7 percent (Figure 3b).

The agricultural sector constitutes about one-quarter of the GDP, employs half the work force, and accounts for more than three-quarters of export income (see The Agricultural Economy). In the Western Hemisphere only in Haiti and Bolivia are such a high percentage of the population employed in the agricultural sector. In contrast, the manufacturing sector represents 15 percent of the GDP and employs about the same percentage of workers (Figure 3c and 3d). Since 1950

81

seek to maintain their privileged access to U.S. markets (through the Caribbean Basin Initiative and other such favored trade agreements). If current proposals are implemented, Guatemala will institute a maximum tariff of 20 percent in the next few years. Domestically produced light consumer goods, such as food, beverages, and shoes, continue to benefit from the highest tariffs—an indication of the uncompetitive nature of domestic industry and the difficulty it faces in competing regionally and internationally.

A trade deficit is not necessarily an indication of economic weakness; it could indicate a revitalized economy importing consumer goods for an expanded domestic market and capital goods for mushrooming investment. Unfortunately, this is not the case in Guatemala, which is suffering from the dual problem of low consumption and low investment rates. In 1991 capital goods represented just 19 percent of total imports. Most imports—about 61 percent—are in the form of intermediate goods, an indication that rather than undertaking new investments businessmen are primarily maintaining old plants with supplies and parts. The balance of Guatemala's imports

Figure 3c
Guatemala's GDP by Economic Sector

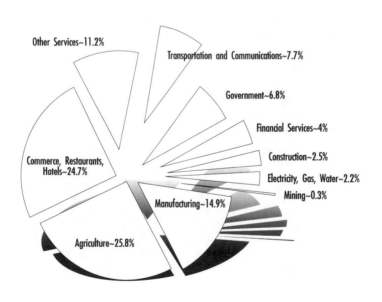

SOURCE: Bank of Guatemala.

are consumer goods, mostly light manufactures consumed by the nation's upper classes.[4] Although imports outweigh exports, consumption levels in Guatemala remain low mainly because inflation has far outstripped wage increases

Guatemala's trade problems are not all the result of a sluggish domestic economy. They date back to the late 1970s, when international terms of trade markedly worsened, meaning that the value of Guatemala's exports declined with respect to the cost of its imports. Although briefly improving in the mid-1980s, mainly due to higher coffee prices, Guatemala's terms of trade deteriorated again and by 1990 were at their lowest level since the late 1970s. Aggravating the country's trade balance in the early 1990s was a sharp drop in coffee prices, reaching a 20-year low by 1992.

A surge in nontraditional exports has compensated for a slackening in traditional exports since the mid-1980s. In 1991, for example, traditional exports (coffee, sugar, cotton, bananas, meat, and cardamom) remained at 1990 levels, but nontraditionals (all others) swelled by more than $100 million. For the first time income from the

Figure 3d
Employment in Guatemala by Economic Sector

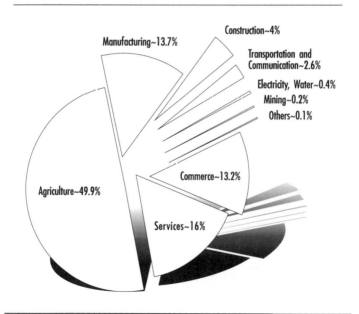

SOURCE: Fundesa, *Guatemala News Watch*, March 1992.

Figure 3e

Change in Guatemala's Exports and Imports, 1981-91

In millions of U.S. $.

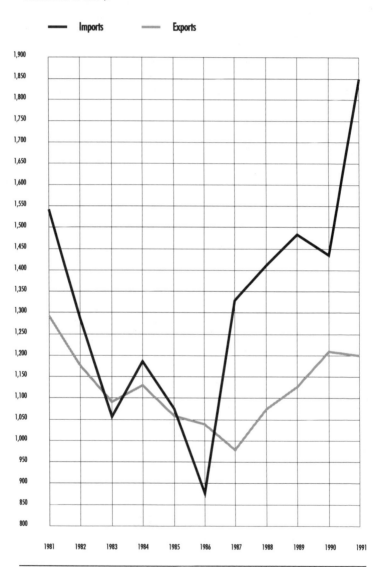

SOURCES: Economic and Social Progress in Latin America 1991 Report; Bank of Guatemala (March 1992).

extraregional export of nontraditionals surpassed that of coffee (Figure 3g).

Financial Woes

Economic stabilization programs launched during the Cerezo administration and embraced by the Serrano government have brought mixed results in terms of balancing the budget, reducing inflation, maintaining debt-service payments, and improving the country's balance-of-payments position. Historically, budget deficits were never very large in Guatemala (held to 2-3 percent of the GDP in the 1970s). Beginning in 1980, however, the government's budget deficit rose sharply, reaching more than 7 percent in 1980, and not until 1985 dipping below 2 percent. During the last two years of the Cerezo administration, the deficit rose again to near 3 percent. Budget cutting and a moratorium on new investment by the Serrano government

Figure 3f
Direction of Trade, 1990

Foreign Suppliers

United States	36%
Mexico	8%
Germany	6.5%
Japan	6%
El Salvador	5%
Venezuela	5%
Costa Rica	5%
Others	28.5%

Foreign Markets

United States	32%
El Salvador	12%
Germany	7%
Costa Rica	7%
Italy	4%
Honduras	3%
Japan	2.5%
Others	32.5%

SOURCE: Bank of Guatemala, Department of Economic and Social Investigation (1992).

contracted the deficit nearly to zero in 1991. The 60 percent inflation rate that assaulted Guatemala during the last year of the Cerezo administration—the result of currency devaluation, deficit spending, and speculation—was also tamed by Serrano.

But the most remarkable achievement of the new administration was the dramatic ballooning of foreign exchange reserves. This new liquidity was largely the result of the issuing of a series of domestic bonds at high interest rates, halting capital flight, and apparently encouraging capital repatriation mainly from the United States where interest rates had plunged. The flood of dollars into the country's banking system was, at least in part, also the result of Guatemala's new role as a regional money-laundering center for narcotraffickers.

The Serrano government's willingness to pass a fiscal-reform package, to raise government revenues, to avoid deficit spending, and to accede to the demands of foreign lenders for the full implementation of structural reform (complete with trade liberalization, privatization, and domestic price liberalization) began to open doors to multilateral funding. By the beginning of the Serrano presidency,

Figure 3g
Guatemala's Principal Exports, 1991

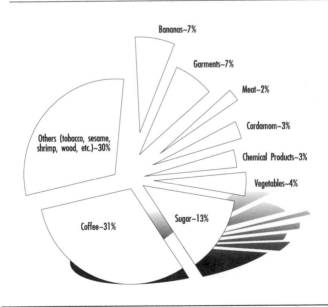

SOURCE: Bank of Guatemala, Department of Economic and Social Investigation (1992).

Guatemala had been blacklisted by the International Monetary Fund (IMF) and the World Bank for failure to honor previous structural-adjustment agreements and for reneging on its debt-service schedule (Figure 3h). Deep in arrears in its external debt payments, the country, now flush with unprecedented foreign exchange reserves, began to catch up with its debt service in 1991. Serrano also began debt-renegotiation discussions with the United States, Mexico, and Venezuela. Guatemala's external public debt by type of creditor is roughly divided as follows: private financial institutions (8 percent), international bonds (9.5 percent), multilateral banks (43 percent), bilateral loans (37 percent), export credits (2.5 percent). Banks from the United States hold about 56 percent of the debt outstanding to private financial institutions, and the U.S. government is the leading creditor country holding 32 percent of the bilateral loan debt, followed by Spain. The United States is also owed about 40 percent of the outstanding export credits. The Inter-American Development Bank (IDB) retains 62 percent of Guatemala's outstanding multilateral debt.

For all the fiscal fundamentalism of the Serrano administration, the country's financial stability is far from ensured. Its unprecedented foreign exchange reserves in 1992 were not the result of a surge in private investment or trade surpluses. Instead the flush state of the Central Bank was largely attributable to low international interest rates compared with the high rates that the government was willing to offer. Any rebound in foreign rates might precipitate an outflow of foreign exchange. Because of the exorbitantly high interest rates that the Serrano administration offered on new bond issues, Guatemala had to pay dearly for the bloating of its cash reserves. In fact, the debt service on the domestic debt now rivals external debt service. Furthermore, government payments on

Figure 3h
External and Domestic Debt

External debt (1991)	$2.5 billion
External debt per capita	$263
Public external debt as % of total external debt	96%
Debt service as % of exports	44%
External debt as % of govt. expenditures (1992)	12%
Domestic debt as % of govt. expenditures (1992)	15%

SOURCE: Bank of Guatemala.

bond issues accrued mostly to the financial elite, thereby intensifying concentration of wealth in Guatemala.

The Serrano administration received good marks from the U.S. embassy, the World Bank, and the IMF for its fiscal reform in 1992. Guatemala's pre-reform tax system—collecting only 7 percent of the GDP—had ranked as one of the least demanding in the world. Yet at best Serrano's reforms will increase the tax bite to only 10 percent, still far short of the amount needed to expand social services and to bolster public-sector investment. Furthermore, the fiscal reform did nothing to make the tax system less regressive.[5] In fact, the biggest source of new revenue will come from an expanded sales tax (known as the IVA) that falls disproportionately on the poor and working class. It was even estimated that IVA receipts, which will now include taxes on food, might double as a result of the fiscal reform. Some tax loopholes may have been eliminated, but the income tax rate on the highest bracket of personal and corporate wealth was actually lowered, equating tax rates paid by the middle class with those of the economic elite. Direct taxes on wealth and income constitute about a quarter of total tax revenue in Guatemala, and with property and export taxes having been progressively reduced, the tax burden borne by the poor and middle classes has become relatively heavier. Tax evasion—representing at least $125 million annually—remains a major impediment to healthier fiscal revenues.

Attempts to establish a consensus among the government, private sector, unions, and popular organizations about economic policies have repeatedly failed. During the Cerezo administration, the popular bloc found that agreements reached with the government were later ignored. In an effort to ensure social stability, President Serrano renewed attempts begun by Cerezo to shape a *concertación* accord. But his call for a social pact was roundly rejected by the popular bloc as an attempt to coopt the labor movement into accepting the dictates of conservative structural adjustment and, as such, reflecting the economic platform of the business elite.[6] This was certainly the case, although it did appear that both the government and important elements of the private sector were willing to make a few concessions in the interests of maintaining social stability. Theoretically, at least, the modernizing private sector recognizes that a certain degree of social consensus is needed to keep neoliberal reforms moving forward. But when substantive compromises affect business leaders in the pocketbook or challenge their hegemony over economic and social policy they are automatically rejected. Another irritant mitigating against the *concertación* or social-pact method of governing is the dual approach of the private sector in mounting a campaign of attrition against labor unions while espousing social harmony.

The credibility of the government's call for a social pact is also questionable given that Serrano's economic cabinet is drawn exclusively from such business associations as CACIF and the Free Market Chamber (CLE), the very same groups representing the private sector at social-pact negotiations. The ministers of agriculture, public works, economy, energy, development, and the Central Bank are all former directors of prominent private-sector associations (see The Business Lobby).

Economic Prospects

The economic prospects for the 1990s are less than hopeful despite the moderate recovery of growth and stability achieved in the late 1980s. Among the major characteristics and weaknesses of the economy as it approaches the mid-1990s are the following:

– *Inflation*: The economic vise of rising consumer prices—without corresponding wage increases—has put the squeeze on the Guatemalan work force. Whereas the average inflation rate was 1 percent in the 1960s and 9 percent in the 1970s, it rose to 15 percent in the 1980s with a 22 percent average in the 1986-90 period, mainly because of the devaluation of the national currency, the *quetzal*. The government's failure to support cost-of-living wage increases not only means that workers will become poorer but also that the domestic market will continue to contract in the face of falling demand.

– *Government Debt*: Guatemala's per capita external debt is relatively low when compared with such countries as Costa Rica and Panama. Yet debt service nonetheless remains a drain on limited public revenues, causing the government to short-change social services so as to meet debt payments. Of growing concern is the rising domestic debt which obligates the government to pay out annually in debt service to local creditors more than it does to foreign ones. Interest payments as a percentage of total government expenditures jumped nearly five-fold between 1980 and 1991. In 1992 the government dedicated 15 percent of its budget expenditures for domestic debt payments, 12 percent for external debt payments—together more than the government intended to spend on education (12 percent), public health (8 percent), urban and rural development (1 percent), agriculture (3 percent), and culture (1 percent) combined.

– *Trade*: Although Guatemala has been successful in nurturing its nontraditional-export sector, serious trade deficits remain. A boom in garment exports has done little to improve the country's trade balance since virtually all the inputs for this industry are imported. The low proportion of capital imports (a reflection of new investment) darkens the long-term economic picture.

— *Remittances*: At least $250 million enters Guatemala each year in remittances from Guatemalans living abroad, chiefly in the United States. Equivalent to a fifth of the country's exports, remittances help sustain the poor while keeping Guatemala's current-account balance from sinking deeper into negative figures.

— *Economic Growth*: Despite maintaining positive economic growth since 1987, Guatemala's per capita income is still considerably below levels experienced in the 1970s. Even when economic expansion does outpace population growth there is no guarantee that the benefits are broadly shared. In fact, income distribution is worsening in Guatemala (see State of Poverty).

— *Investment*: Gross domestic investment has failed to recoup earlier levels. Annual investment growth rates, averaging near 7 percent in the 1960s and more than 5 percent in the 1970s, plummeted to a negative 1.3 percent in the 1981-90 period. Furthermore, most recent economic activity has occurred in construction and services as well as financial speculation, rather than manufacturing and other productive investment. As a percentage of total domestic expenditures, public-sector investment shrunk from 22 percent in 1981 to 9 percent in 1990, with capital investment cut by three-quarters in the same period. As a percentage of the GDP, total investment stood at 13 percent in 1990, down from 17 percent in 1981. Current investment levels— by both the private and public sectors—fall far short of the amount needed to spark a new wave of economic development.[7] One problem is that the Guatemalan private sector has historically been averse to sinking its money into long-term investment. Another obstacle is that investors view producing for the external market as too competitive and too risky, while low domestic consumption levels due to deepening poverty render any expansion in locally oriented production unfeasible. Yet without vigorous investment, sustained economic stability will not be possible.

— *Budget Deficit*: Austerity measures have brought the budget deficit under control but at the cost of slashing already scant social services and bringing public-sector investment to a standstill. These cuts not only lower Guatemala's abysmal education, health, and housing standards but also undermine its ability to compete regionally and internationally because of deteriorating infrastructure and the lack of an educated and healthy work force.

— *Free Trade*: Entrance into the General Agreement on Tariffs and Trade (GATT) and the signing of a "framework agreement" with Washington in 1991 mark Guatemala's tilt toward full trade liberalization. Regional trade accords with Mexico and other Central American countries have set the stage for free trade in the region. Liberalized trade focuses prime attention on export production. Little concern is expressed about the virtual exclusion of the majority of Guatemalans from the domestic market because of their almost insignificant purchasing power.

— *Social Investment*: Promised social investment, or increased spending on social services and economic development programs for the most deprived regions, has been repeatedly postponed. Although the central government is obliged to assign 8 percent of its budget expenditures to municipalities, these funds are often late or not forthcoming. Plans to establish a social investment fund rely for the most part not on internally generated revenues but on foreign donations. The neoliberal model needs social stability for its implementation, yet it fails to provide either for the structural reforms needed to encourage participation of the majority in the economy or for the funds necessary to guarantee that basic needs (adequate food, education, health care, housing, etc.) are met. A new threat to plans for a social investment fund is that allocated resources may be directed to combatting the rising crime wave and to pacifying—rather than truly assisting—the population in former conflict zones.

— *Structural Adjustment*: In a certain sense the structural-adjustment measures implemented since 1986 have resulted in a measure of economic stabilization as evidenced by positive economic growth rates and the narrowing of budget deficits. Trade and domestic prices have been steadily liberalized, and the currency has been devalued to reflect its worth more truly. But the emphasis on conservative fiscal management has failed to spark new private investment and has resulted in declining public-sector investment. Exports have eased upward but not sufficiently to cover imports, and by 1992 there were signs that earlier growth in nontraditional exports was tapering off. Traditional exports are also unlikely to improve substantially. Economic-reform measures have as yet failed to address structural impediments to the expansion of the domestic market (such as grossly inadequate wages, lack of access to land, concentration of credit within the business elite, and a highly regressive tax system). Instead of encouraging a productive regeneration of the economy, financial structural adjustment has led to the rise of speculative investment in real estate and construction and to the spectacular growth of the banking industry.

— *Role of the State*: Under the pressure of neoliberal reforms, the state is becoming ever less a mediator between social classes. Instead, government has increasingly come to be an instrument of the business elite, particularly of export and financial interests. The patent danger of such an arrangement is that it heightens the potential for social and political instability—a danger implicitly recognized in the military's own "security and development" and the subsequent "national stability" models of governance. Yet another danger is that in their campaign to promote the private sector as the only motor of development, those calling for the privatization of state enterprises are undermining the potential for future economic growth by allowing the further deterioration of the nation's social and economic infrastructure (see Privatization Plans).

State of Poverty

Poverty statistics are dramatic in Guatemala (Figure 3i), but they sometimes fail to convey the human face of deprivation. More revealing than numbers and percentages are scenes from daily life—images of how the vast majority of Guatemalan people live: the indian woman who walks barefoot to the town market from her mountain village, carrying her sandals until she reaches town so as not to wear them out; the hundreds of thousands of Guatemalans who can no longer afford to eat beans with their tortillas; the peasant women who labor more than five hours (including gathering loads of firewood to cook the maize) every day to make their own tortillas in order to save the one or two *quetzales* it would cost to buy them at the local *tortilleria*; the misery of urban squatters, living in makeshift shelters without water, sanitary facilities, or electricity.

Poverty is officially separated into two categories: 1) those without the ability to meet basic material (housing, transportation, medicine, etc.) and food requirements are defined as living below the poverty line, and 2) those who cannot even meet their basic food needs, let alone other basic needs, are classified as experiencing extreme poverty.

Poverty statistics vary according to agency, but all surveys show that poverty has mushroomed since 1980 and that approximately four out of every five Guatemalans live below the poverty line. Even when the economy is expanding, as it has been since 1986, the rate of economic growth has been unsubstantial, often lagging behind the rate of population growth. Yet even positive per capita economic growth would be no guarantee that poverty would ease in a nation where resources and income are so unevenly distributed.

According to the National Statistics Institute (INE), 59 percent of all Guatemalans and 71 percent of rural residents endured extreme poverty in 1989.[8] The United Nations Children's Fund (UNICEF) considers 86 percent of Guatemalans to be impoverished.[9]

Figure 3i

Poverty Indicators

Population living below poverty line (1990)	80-87%
Population living in extreme poverty	36% (urban); 71% (rural)

Work and Wages

Average monthly wages (1991)	
Agriculture	$36
Industry	$95
Commerce	$105
Active work force without any schooling	42%
Unemployment/underemployment (1989)	43%
Children between 10 and 14 years of age who work (formally or informally)	18%
Minimum wage compliance:	60% (urban); 15% (rural)

Housing

Guatemala City residents living in shantytowns	30%
Housing deficit	840,000 homes
Homes constructed of discarded materials	26%
Homes without potable water	62%
Homes without sanitation or drainage system	59%

Informal Sector

Portion of GDP represented by informal sector	20%
Annual rate of women entering informal sector	13.5%
Annual rate of men entering informal sector	9.2%

Income Distribution

Income shared by bottom 10% of population in 1980	2.4%
Income shared by bottom 10% of population in 1987	0.9%
Income shared by top 10% of population in 1980	40.8%
Income shared by top 10% of population in 1987	44%

Average Family Size according to Condition of Poverty

Extreme poverty	6.2 members
Below poverty line but not extreme	5.2 members
Above poverty line	4 members

SOURCES: INE-FUNAP, *Perfil de la pobreza en Guatemala* (Guatemala City: 1991); CEPAL, *Bases para la transformación productiva y generación de ingresos de la población pobre de los paises del istmo centroamericano* (Mexico City: January 1992); UNICEF, *Situación de pobreza: Guatemala* (Guatemala City: May 1991); World Bank, *Guatemala: Country Economic Memorandum* (April 1991).

The Guatemalan government's planning agency, SEGEPLAN, estimated in 1991 that 89 percent of Guatemalans live in poverty, 67 percent in extreme poverty. According to the World Bank, the percentage of the population living in poverty rose from 63 percent in the early 1980s to 83 percent by 1987, aggravated by a doubling in extreme poverty from 32 percent to 64 percent.[10] In actual numbers, then, between 7.7 million and 8.5 million Guatemalans cannot afford to satisfy their basic necessities of life.

The large majority of Guatemalans were worse off at the end of the 1980s than at the beginning of the decade—a decade during which Guatemala "democratized" by instituting elected civilian rule. The cynical sentiment of one Guatemalan that "democratization means you don't eat" is shared by many of her compatriots who watched the value of their wages erode, unemployment spread, and social service spending contract during the last half of the 1980s.

Real wages have been falling since the early 1970s, but the rate of decline accelerated in the late 1980s. During the 1980s real wages plunged 35 percent, with the reduction in real minimum wages approaching 50 percent.[11] Minimum wages have risen since 1980 but their growth has been overtaken by the galloping pace of inflation. The average monthly salary in Guatemala is less than $40, with the highest wages paid by the commercial sector and the lowest by the agricultural sector. The legal minimum wage was increased to $84 a month in November 1991, and the legal minimum in the agricultural sector, which accounts for nearly a quarter of the GDP and half of national employment, is about $2.25 a day. The Ministry of Labor estimates that compliance with minimum wage standards by employers is 60 percent in urban areas and only 15 percent in the countryside. Average agricultural wages were cut in half during the 1980s, amounting to about one-third of average wages in the manufacturing and commercial sector by decade's end.[12] In the capital city, a family requires two workers earning the minimum wage just to cover basic food needs. According to INE, the average monthly family salary in Guatemala City in 1990 was $52, yet a family needed at least $205 per month simply to meet its basic needs. Between 1983 and early 1992 the consumer price index in Guatemala charted the cost of basic goods rising more than 400 percent.[13]

As real wages depreciated, so did employment opportunities. During the 1980s employment expanded by 2.1 percent annually, considerably below the 2.9 percent population growth rate. There are no good measures of unemployment, but even the government's conservative calculations showed unemployment more than doubling from 3 percent in 1980 to 8 percent by 1990, and underemployment swelling from 30 percent to 35 percent. In 1992 the U.S. embassy estimated that combined unemployment/underemployment was at least 50 percent.

Guatemala's income distribution—already one of the worst in the hemisphere—polarized even further during the 1980s. The bottom 10 percent of the population suffered a reduction in its share of total national income from 2.4 percent to 0.9 percent between 1980 and 1987, while the top 30 percent of the population enjoyed relative gains. The wealthiest one-tenth of Guatemala's families strengthened its 40.8 percent of total national wealth in 1980 to 44 percent by 1987. These figures indicate that while the wealthiest sectors succeeded in consolidating their grip on national income, the poorest Guatemalans were unable to protect themselves against the ravages of inflation, unemployment, and currency devaluation.[14]

One way that many poor Guatemalans have been able to stave off complete destitution has been through their participation in the informal economy of street vending and household businesses. In 1977 the informal sector represented just 8 percent of the GDP, but by 1990 accounted for 20 percent of total national income.[15] About a quarter of all new employment in Guatemala is generated by the informal sector, where compensation is generally below the minimum wage.

Low government social spending is another factor explaining the desperate socioeconomic conditions in which most Guatemalans live. Whereas Costa Rica dedicated about 15 percent of its national income to social spending in 1990, Guatemala spent about 3 percent—down from 7 percent in 1980.

Another way to understand the country's impoverishment is to compare Guatemala with Haiti—the country with the lowest life quality index in the Western Hemisphere. Haiti's per capita GDP is about one-fifth of Guatemala's. Yet in some categories its quality of life indicators are superior to or equal to those of Guatemala. Haiti spends more of its GDP on education than Guatemala does, and has a much higher percentage of its children in primary schools. In Haiti 30 percent of the children are seriously malnourished, about half the proportion of children underfed in the Guatemalan highlands. Only 20 percent of births in Guatemala are attended by medical staff, on a par with the pitiful figure in Haiti of 19 percent.[16]

The degree of impoverishment in Guatemala is directly related to family size, with larger families suffering more severe destitution.[17] Low levels of education, lack of access to birth control information, and resistance to family planning by male partners are among the leading reasons for high fecundity rates in Guatemala. Large families, especially in rural areas, are commonly regarded as a type of social security. However, as infant mortality rates drop, landlessness intensifies, and rural labor opportunities dwindle, this folk wisdom no longer holds true.

Housing prices are beyond the range of many families. One-room apartments in Guatemala City in 1992 were renting for $50 per month, and many landlords prohibited children and charged extra for each electrical appliance that their tenants used. As the cost of housing and land increase, homelessness is becoming a major social problem. According to the government's planning institute, there is a housing shortage of 840,000 units, which will rise to 1.2 million units by the year 2000.[18] Each year there is a demand for 35,000 new homes, but virtually no low-income housing is being built. As a result, more Guatemalans are invading state and private land to erect shantytowns, usually in precarious locations such as under high-tension lines, along the edge of ravines, or next to dumps and sewage canals.

Until the 1980s the phenomenon of "street children" was rare in a society where families and neighbors took in unwanted or orphaned children. War, deepening poverty, and the breakdown of traditional value structures have created a new social underclass of 5,000-10,000 children in Guatemala City who survive on the street through begging, scavenging, stealing, and prostitution. In response to the rising urban crime wave, the police have struck out at these street children with a campaign of torture and killings. Children's Rights International has charged that the Guatemalan police prey on these children, dealing out "cruel and life-threatening extrajudicial punishments." To protect themselves against charges by human rights organizations and child-advocacy groups, police either intimidate witnesses through torture or inflict fatal beatings.[19]

The Agricultural Economy

Perhaps more clearly than any other Central American country, Guatemala has two agricultural economies. The dominant economy is one of commercial estates located chiefly along the fertile South Coast and secondarily to the north in the department of Izabal. An extreme concentration of land and an export orientation characterize this dominant agricultural economy. Paralleling the agroexport economy is a system of peasant agriculture, characterized by small plots of land devoted to subsistence agriculture. These two economies—while markedly different—are interdependent. The below-subsistence nature of *minifundios* (small parcels) serves to keep wage rates low in Guatemala by enabling a large sector of the peasant population to survive and feed themselves during the off-seasons, facilitating temporary work during harvest seasons for the substandard wages ($1-2 daily) paid by the agroexport estates.[20]

Although still pervasive, this dual structure that has for so long defined rural society and economy is gradually disintegrating. With the agricultural frontier shrinking, the number of landless peasants is increasing while the average size of the *minifundios* is decreasing. Peasant agriculture is no longer able to supply the growing population with sufficient basic grains, and the escalating importation of beans, rice, and corn further undercuts Guatemalan basic grains producers. The rising cost of inputs (fertilizer, etc.) has also meant that many peasants can no longer feed themselves, even for just part of the year, off their small plots. Traditional export agriculture is also suffering as fickle international markets and generally low world-market prices have caused export production of some traditional crops to stagnate and others to decline markedly.

Another factor affecting the historical dual structure of agriculture has been the expansion of nontraditional agricultural production. Both in the highlands and in the fertile lowlands many farmers and new investors have switched to the cultivation of fruits and vegetables for the foreign, mainly U.S., market. Nontraditional-export production has benefited a class of medium-level producers, many of whom have bought out their poorer neighbors thereby changing the class structure, particularly in the central highlands.

Land Reform Stalled for Four Decades

No other issue in Guatemala is so volatile as the use and ownership of land. It is one of the issues that sparked a CIA-sponsored coup in 1954 and later gave rise to death squads and civil war. As Guatemala enters the 1990s the inequities resulting from skewed patterns of land ownership and use continue to divide its society and stifle its economic development.

In 1952 the Arbenz government instituted an agrarian reform as part of its plan to rid the country of its feudal elements and open the doors to a more modern capitalist economy. For the landed oligarchs, the Catholic Church, and United Fruit Company, agrarian reform meant godless communism—in other words, the loss of land and privilege. That attempt at economic modernization was aborted by the 1954 coup, and the country has suffered the political and economic consequences ever since.

Despite harsh repression, the issue of land reform will not go away. Fewer than 2 percent of landowners own 65 percent of the farmland—the most highly skewed land-tenure pattern in Latin America. The latest agricultural census in 1979 confirmed that land-tenure patterns had grown progressively more skewed since previous censuses in 1950 and 1964. Guatemala's unequal distribution of land is compounded by the fact that most postage-stamp plots of land straddle mountain slopes while the richest land is held by the largest producers. According to the U.S. Agency for International Development (AID), about a third of the population lives on farms too small or too poor to support a family.[21]

The government has long recognized that landlessness gives rise to serious social and economic problems. Yet rather than expropriating private estates or encouraging their sale by heavily taxing uncultivated farmland, the government—through the National Agrarian Transformation Institute (INTA)—has distributed state lands to state-organized peasant cooperatives. Between 1955 and 1982 a total of 664,525 hectares of state land was distributed to 50,267 families. In comparison, during 1953-54 more than 78,000 families received 602,000 hectares of land. Most of the land distributed by INTA was done through colonization projects that aimed to open up the country's agricultural frontier, first along the South Coast and later in the Northern Transverse Strip and in the Petén. Surprisingly, at a time of mounting landlessness and inadequate grain production, the amount of uncultivated land along the South Coast has been increasing since the late 1970s.

In 1986 Father Andrés Girón and his Pro-Land Peasant Association dared to put agrarian reform once again on the national agenda. A year before, presidential candidate Vinicio Cerezo had promised the Union of Agricultural Producers (Unagro) that his government would not institute an agrarian reform. In fact, he promised he would not even mention land reform because "to use the term in this country causes emotional reactions." Shortly after Cerezo's inauguration, Girón led 16,000 *campesinos*, mainly from the South Coast, to the National Palace to demand that the government distribute land to the landless.

Even though Girón's movement was not demanding that the government expropriate land, but rather that it redistribute estates purchased from private owners, the Pro-Land organization stirred vitriolic opposition from Unagro and large landowners. The Pro-Land leaders argued, in the Social Christian tradition, that their movement represented an alternative to communism and arbitrary land expropriations. But the hard-liners of Unagro felt that any government involvement in land redistribution, even in controlled land sales, would open the way to wholesale agrarian reform.

The government did eventually respond favorably to the Pro-Land movement. Several estates that had been mortgaged to state banks were sold to the Girón organization, but this token measure fell far short of the great need for land and could scarcely be termed an agrarian reform. Instead it represented an extension of a land-sales program financed by AID and implemented by a local nongovernmental organization called the Penny Foundation with the approval of Unagro. As an added onus, the Girón movement had to pay the government for land sold to them at higher-than-market-value prices.

Agrarian reform again came to the fore when the Catholic bishops in 1988 circulated a pastoral letter known as "The Cry for Land." Although the bishops offered no concrete remedies, they did conclude that "it is necessary and urgent to change our country's sinful and obsolete social structures." Acting quickly to distance itself from the Catholic Church, the Cerezo government pledged: "There will be no agrarian reform." For its part, Unagro reproved the bishops asserting that it "rejects any project or idea that looks or smells like expropriatory agrarian reform."

Although President Serrano carefully avoided all talk of agrarian reform, expanding landlessness in the countryside and homelessness in Guatemala City returned the issue of inequitable land distribution to the center of public attention. No longer even hoping that the government would legislate some type of agrarian reform, groups of landless peasants began occupying uncultivated estates while poor city residents mounted invasions of government land in early 1992. Father Girón, who had been selected as a congressional deputy on the Christian Democratic slate in 1990, acted as an intermediary for the Guatemala City squatters. Most of the land invasions both in the countryside and in the city were crushed by the police, but the pressure for land distribution continued apace. Adding to this pressure was the planned return of more than 40,000 refugees to Guatemala from Mexico, all demanding to return to their former lands or to receive new cultivable acreage.

Yet simply distributing land equally to all the country's small farmers and landless peasants will not solve either the county's agricultural production problems or to its socioeconomic crisis. As concentrated as land tenure patterns are, there is not enough land to create commercially viable farms for the entire Guatemalan peasantry. Nonetheless, an agrarian reform program could contribute to the easing of rural tensions while spurring productivity and resuscitating the domestic market (by boosting rural purchasing power) if such a program redistributed the largest of the *latifundios*, encouraged the farming of all uncultivated land, and offered technical advice, credit, and marketing services to small farmers. The main objective of the 1952 reform had been just such a modernization of Guatemalan agriculture.

For all the talk of economic modernization by the government, the private sector, and foreign donors, however, there has still been no serious discussion about adopting the structural-adjustment measures needed to modernize agricultural production and land tenure. Although the landed oligarchy has watched its influence diminish as new industrial and financial interests have gained power, large estate owners still possess sufficient clout to veto major structural reforms in the agricultural sector.

Traditional Exports

Export crops represent about 28 percent of total agricultural production in Guatemala, led by such traditional exports as coffee, bananas, sugar, and cotton.[22] Coffee, which accounts for about 30 percent of the country's income, is grown virtually everywhere in Guatemala, except for the departments of Petén and Totonicapán. Although some 44,000 farms produce coffee, the production is concentrated on the 395 largest estates that average 582 acres in size. These large estates, representing only one percent of the farms producing coffee, account for 45 percent of total production. In contrast, more than 30,000 farms with an average size of less than 4 acres represent 69 percent of the units but account for only 14 percent of total production.[23]

Since the 1880s coffee has provided the financial base of the Guatemalan oligarchy. Many of the country's wealthiest families—including Aragón Quiñones, Plocharsky, Brol, and Falla—own vast coffee estates. Since the largest growers have easy access to credit, technical assistance, and marketing as well as their own processing facilities, they capture the lion's share of the profit margin on coffee sales. Small producers receive less than 25 percent of coffee profits, while medium and large producers accrue about 75 percent.[24] Large producers also have the financial flexibility to stockpile coffee until international prices improve.

Unlike in many other coffee-producing nations, export trade is not nationalized in Guatemala. As a consequence, a great deal of the income from the coffee business flows into the coffers of the export houses. These private companies not only arrange the sale of Guatemalan coffee on the international market but also finance coffee production itself.[25] The United States absorbs slightly over half of Guatemala's coffee exports, with Germany being the next largest importer. About 9 percent of the U.S. market is supplied by Guatemalan exporters. The Guatemalan coffee industry, the largest producer of mild beans in Central America, has benefited from the booming gourmet market. Gourmet coffees—marketed under such regional brands as Atitlán, Antigua, and Huehue—now constitute about 60 percent of total coffee exports.

The termination of international quotas and the resulting drop in coffee prices in 1989 cast a dark shadow over the coffee industry. Guatemala's large coffee producers and traders initially celebrated the collapse of the International Coffee Agreement because Guatemala was no longer restricted to export quotas and could sell to nonagreement countries. Soon, however, the coffee industry was demanding that the government devalue the currency, eliminate export taxes, and otherwise subsidize coffee producers to make up for the precipitous drop in international prices. Support for resurrection of an international quota system has grown due to stiffened competition and the threat by European countries to impose higher import tariffs.

The some 300,000 coffee workers are always the most adversely affected by downturns in the international market, suffering depressed wages and deteriorating working conditions. Yet when the fortune of the industry improves, these workers are not similarly benefited with higher wages. Currency devaluation, for example, results in windfall profits for coffee exporters since it lowers local costs while in effect bloating their profits, which are measured in dollars. Reduced export taxes for the coffee industry also benefit the exporters but this extra income is not reflected in higher wages. For coffee workers to earn enough to afford one pound of gourmet Guatemalan coffee, they would have to pick 500 pounds of coffee beans—about five days work.[26] By 1992, coffee prices had plunged to half their 1985 level, resulting in producer support for the renewal of an international coffee agreement in the interests of stabilizing prices.

Bananas bring in about 8 percent of the country's foreign-currency income. As a function of rising international prices, banana income rose steadily in the late 1980s. All banana production is located in the departments of Izabal and Zacapa—the low-lying eastern area lapped by the Caribbean. Del Monte (a subsidiary of RJ Reynolds) dominates the banana export business, controlling 80 percent of production through its local branch BANDEGUA. Six independent producers (organized as the Independent Banana Company or COBIGUA) account for the other 20 percent. Seventy percent of Guatemalan bananas enter the U.S. market.[27]

Most of the country's sugar comes from Escuintla on the South Coast, where extensive sugar estates and giant mills dominate the land. The local sugar industry was sustained during years of low prices in the mid-1980s by a strong domestic demand and fixed prices on the local market, as well as by preferential prices obtained by sales to the United States. Pressure from the sugar oligarchs resulted in a doubling in guaranteed sugar prices. One of those benefiting from artificially high domestic prices was the Botrán family, which in addition to owning a sugar mill produces the country's leading brand of rum. The United States, under its sugar quota system, buys about 40 percent of Guatemala's sugar exports at nearly twice the world market price. Declining U.S. quotas and international prices periodically affect Guatemalan sugar producers, but low wages and cheap land keep them producing with a healthy profit margin.

Cotton production suffered a major decline in the 1980s, sinking to a 25-year low in 1987. Although cotton production has since recovered somewhat, the industry is but a thin shadow of its former self—with acreage sown in cotton having receded 60 percent between 1980 and 1990. Like sugar, cotton production is concentrated on the South Coast. The cotton industry is extremely concentrated in Guatemala—just 15 families control half the production. The average size of a Guatemalan cotton estate was 638 hectares in 1979, compared to 25 to 40 hectares for the rest of Central America.[28]

As with elsewhere in the region, the expansion of the beef industry over the past 25 years has been devastating both for indian communities and for the environment. Whereas the agroexport boom in cotton and sugar did not extend beyond the South Coast, the rise of the beef industry has affected some of the most isolated and previously unspoiled areas of the country. Using peasant colonists to clear the land, the beef industry has leveled great expanses of tropical forests in the last four decades. It was just this type of expansion that led to the Panzós massacre of some one hundred Kekchí indians in 1978, after cattle growers complained to the military that the indians were protesting their land-grabbing. All beef exports—which constitute over one-fifth of local production—are shipped to the United States.[29]

In the mid-1970s, Guatemala entered the cardamom market and by 1986 was supplying over 60 percent of world demand. In the development pole of Playa Grande, AID and CARE used food-for-work and agricultural-development programs to integrate peasants into this cardamom boom. Cardamom had become one of the country's leading sources of foreign exchange, and accounted for nearly half of nontraditional agroexports.[30] By 1988 the world's small market for cardamom (mainly Arab countries) had become saturated. Other countries—Costa Rica, Ecuador, Honduras, and India—had joined Guatemala in the cardamom exporting business, and prices had plummeted. So weak was the market that nearly half of the country's cardamom exporters did no business in 1988, and peasant farmers who had been growing cardamom in the Northern Transverse Strip were left without any source of income and with a harvest they could not eat. In 1990-92 the value of cardamom exports—now considered a traditional agroexport—had slumped to half of what the country earned in the early 1980s.

Nontraditional Exports

The promotion of nontraditional agroexports is nothing new in Guatemala. In the 1950s and 1960s international lending institutions promoted the cotton, beef, and sugar industries as a way to diversify the economy's dependence on coffee and bananas. In the 1970s, AID prompted a new type of agricultural diversification, this time encouraging vegetables, flowers, and spices. These nontraditionals, which increased gradually during the 1980s, currently account for about 22 percent of total exports—up from 14 percent in 1980. The best performers among the nontraditional agroexports in the 1980s were sesame, shrimp, fish, lobster, fresh and processed fruits, wood and wood manufactures, and vegetables. Other emerging exotics like miniature broccoli, snow peas, and assorted vegetables are raised for the gourmet market in Japan and the United States.

Nontraditionals face many of the same problems confronted by more established agroexports like coffee and cotton including oscillating prices and shrinking markets. The fluctuations of the world market are compounded for nontraditional agroexport producers by the sparsity of customers for which they produce. There is also more risk involved since nontraditional exports usually spoil faster and crops commonly require more frequent applications of fertilizer and pesticides, compounding a farmer's risk.

There is little doubt that the agricultural sector needs to pursue diversification, but it is a development path fraught with difficulties. While the diversification into fruit and vegetable production was encouraged by the Caribbean Basin Initiative (CBI), Guatemalan producers have discovered that the U.S. market is a fickle creature. Competition from nontraditional agroexport sectors in other Caribbean Basin countries, mainly the Dominican Republic and Costa Rica, also narrows the market space for Guatemalan products. Protectionism by U.S. producers and rising consumer concerns about pesticide-saturated produce cast a further shadow over the future of diversification attempts.

Small growers who gamble on nontraditional crops are very vulnerable. A 1989 AID study found that most small farmers cultivating nontraditionals relied on chemical company representatives for advice about pesticides and application frequency and that only one in 40 farmers surveyed had ever been visited by a government extension agent.[31] Furthermore, some exporters have stopped purchasing from small farmers because they feel that buying from larger growers "enables them to better control both quality and cosmetic appearance, and that it is more profitable and efficient to concentrate on a few growers with large amounts of land than on many smaller growers."[32]

Although nontraditional agroexports often spell high profit margins, they also involve high costs of production and high risks. A producer of snow peas risks about $4,000 a hectare in costs versus only $250 to $375 a hectare (ranging from manual to mechanized production) for corn or $750 per hectare for mechanized production of coffee.[33] The market for nontraditionals is also extremely volatile. When the U.S. market for such items as snow peas or broccoli becomes saturated or when pesticide residues are judged to be too high by U.S. customs officials, Guatemalan producers find themselves stuck with produce they can not sell on the local market. As a result, it is not unusual to see mounds of vegetables dumped by the side of the Pan American Highway. Whereas AID poses nontraditional agroexport production as an alternative for Guatemalan farmers, it is generally a venture only affordable to commercial-level farmers, not the hundreds of thousands of peasant farmers that cultivate the country's poorest land. Copycat production of nontraditional exports by farmers throughout the region also casts doubt on the future profitability of nontraditionals.

Basic Grains Production

Since 1980 basic grains production (corn, beans, and rice)—expanding at an annual average rate of 2.4 percent—has failed to keep pace with the 2.9 percent population growth. Local farmers have little incentive to grow basic grains despite this shortfall in production in part because food imports from the United States undercut the local market and keep prices low. As a result of lower per capita production, the country has had to import an ever-increasing proportion of its basic grains. Mainly because of falling international prices and the dramatic rise in imports, price indices for basic grains have generally deteriorated since 1980, especially for beans and wheat but also for sorghum and maize (corn), thus fueling the vicious cycle discouraging Guatemalan farmers from producing for the local market.

Since 1984 Guatemala has received a burgeoning amount of U.S. food aid. According to the U.S. Department of Agriculture, "Nearly all of Guatemala's agricultural commodity imports come from the United States, and since 1985, virtually all U.S.-origin imports have been donated or financed under concessional and commercial assistance programs."[34] By the late 1980s, 20 percent of the population was receiving nutritional assistance from U.S. and other foreign food aid programs.[35] From constituting less than 1 percent of national grain supply in 1980, food aid sprouted to approximately 14 percent by decade's end. Only about 20 percent of foreign food aid goes directly to poor recipients, leaving as much as 80 percent to compete directly with domestic food production and commercial imports.[36]

Guatemalan wheat production has been seriously affected both by food aid and by a more liberalized market. Local wheat production was slashed by two-thirds between 1988 and 1991, and the industry may soon fade away in the face of foreign competition.[37] Neither can Guatemalan producers meet the domestic demand for dairy products. The country has the lowest rate of milk production in Latin America—providing an average daily per capita allotment of only two tablespoons.

The Guatemalan government does have a policy of food security with the stated objective of promoting local food production, but it has not been enforced. In fact, the government has welcomed additional food aid to ease budget deficits and to pacify targeted social sectors (urban slums and displaced families in conflictive areas). Both the army and the government share the concern that food shortages and high food prices will aggravate social tensions. But rather than initiate the kind of sectoral adjustment needed to prioritize food security, food aid and cheap food imports have provided a short-term avoidance mechanism.

Trade liberalization could deepen the country's agricultural crisis and addictive dependence on imports. With the demise of protectionist tariff and nontariff barriers, Guatemalan basic grain farmers will increasingly have to compete in the international market against foreign producers that benefit from greater mechanization, better infrastructure, and more extensive government services. In Guatemala, government agricultural expenditures as a percentage of GDP were sliced in half during the 1980s, meaning that grain farmers now get little or no government credit or technical assistance.

Industry, Tourism, and Narcotics

The industrial sector boomed in the 1960s and 1970s as a result of the creation of the Central American Common Market (CACM) in 1961, which opened up a regional market for goods manufactured in Guatemala. Many transnational corporations, chiefly from the United States, set up factories inside Guatemala to produce food products, pharmaceuticals, tires, chemicals, and other products for Central American customers. Kellogg, for example, established a plant in Guatemala City to produce Corn Flakes and other processed foods for all of Central America. As the Central American market began to constrict in the late 1970s, so did the Guatemalan industrial sector. The outbreak of war in the region shut down the CACM, greatly slowing regional trade and throwing Guatemalan industrialists into a state of shock.

The deepening regional crisis paralleled a sectoral crisis in Guatemalan manufacturing. Having developed within a protected domestic and regional market with high import tariffs on competing goods, Guatemalan industry had grown inefficient and lax. Not forced to contend with international producers, local manufacturers operated with obsolete plants and technology. As the regional market shrank due to economic crisis and war, Guatemalan industry also increasingly operated far below productive capacity.

From 1960 to 1980 Guatemala's manufacturing sector expanded at an average annual rate of 7 percent—hiking the sector's share of the GDP from 12 percent to 16 percent. Industrialization came to an abrupt halt during the first half of the 1980s, with manufacturing exports plummeting by 45 percent and real growth declining by 2 percent annually during the 1980-85 period. The combination of government efforts to promote manufactured exports, new U.S. trade and investment initiatives, and the easing of political violence, resulted in slight sectoral growth in the 1985-90 period. This growth was attributable to the boom in nontraditional exports, mainly garments, with the traditional manufacturing sector remaining stagnant. By 1990 manufacturing represented 15 percent of the GDP, down slightly from 1980 despite the boom in nontraditionals. Riding the coattails of assembled goods, manufacturing's share of extraregional exports rose from 11 percent in 1980 to 16 percent by 1991.

The traditional manufacturing sector, concentrated in food processing, consumer products, printing, and chemicals, comprises about 2,000 firms, with an average employment of 20 workers. Less than one hundred companies employ 100 or more workers. Food, tobacco, and beverages account for about 45 percent of manufacturing output. The next largest category is chemicals, which includes pharmaceutical production and accounts for 27 percent of total manufactures.

Mining is of minor economic significance, constituting 0.3 percent of the GDP and employing 0.2 percent of the labor force. Many minerals are found in Guatemala—including nickel, lead, copper, iron, gold, silver, antimony—but few are commercially mined.[38] In the late 1970s the Canadian company Eximbal opened a major nickel-mining operation but closed down in 1981 after prices slumped.

Since the late 1980s the crisis of the Guatemalan model of industrialization has been highlighted by the encroaching liberalization of international trade. Realizing that they were unable to compete with often cheaper and better-quality foreign goods, numerous industrialists shut down their plants or sold them to small investors or even cooperatives of workers. Such has been the case in the domestic textile and chemical industries, which now consist of a jumble of small shops operating with outdated equipment. Other industrialists revamped their factories, equipping them with newer technology in hopes of better competing in regional and international markets. Some textile manufacturers simply shifted from domestic production to export-oriented assembly operations.

In reference to Central America, Guatemalan industry, historically one of the most developed in the region, has the potential of capturing a better-than-average share of the market, particularly when compared to the industrial sectors of Honduras and Nicaragua. With the end of the civil war in El Salvador, however, Guatemalan industrialists face new competition from a revived Salvadoran industrial sector, potentially the most dynamic and aggressive in the region. Probably an even greater threat lies to the north—from both Mexican and U.S. industries—should free trade advocates prevail.

Mexico, which already enjoys a hefty trade surplus with Guatemala, is interested in establishing a free trade regimen with Central America—with Guatemala as a key ingredient due to its large population and strategic location at the doorway to the region.[39] Although Guatemalan exporters are eager for Mexico to dismantle its tariff and nontariff trade barriers, Mexico may stand to gain more in a free trade relationship because of the greater efficiency, diversity, and economies of scale of its industrial sector. As trade obstacles tumble, Mexican investors are casting a hungry eye toward Guatemala. The Mexican bread company Pan Bimbo has already seriously eroded the business of Guatemalan-owned bakeries, and other food processing industries may find themselves challenged by Mexican traders and investors as well. Mexican moguls are also said to be interested in acquiring stock in state-owned enterprises in Guatemala, especially the telephone and electricity companies, when they are privatized.

Nontraditional *Maquiladora* Manufacturing

The one dynamic industrial subsector is export-oriented garment assembly, which benefits from the "drawback" provisions of the U.S. tariff code and the duty-free exemptions offered by the Caribbean Basin Initiative. Only in the mid-1980s did the drawback or *maquila* manufacturing industry emerge in Guatemala. From a humble beginning in 1986 of only 20 *maquiladoras* employing some 4,000 workers, Guatemalan *maquilas* mushroomed in five years' time to at least 225 assembly factories employing 50,000 or more workers. Ninety percent of these factories are garment plants where workers sew together, iron, and package garment pieces shipped from the United States. The remaining 10 percent are dedicated mainly to the assembly of electronic and mechanical parts.[40]

Tax exemptions and investment subsidies initiated by the Cerezo administration together with promotional efforts by the U.S. Agency for International Development (AID) sparked *maquila* industry growth in the late 1980s. Most *maquiladoras* are small plants owned by Guatemalans who subcontract with U.S. clothing manufacturers and retailers. Some 20 U.S. firms have their own assembly factories, although the largest foreign investors are South Koreans, who operate more than 50 factories including a couple with more than 700 employees.[41] More than 90 percent of the garments produced in Guatemalan *maquilas* enter the U.S. market, with the rest shipped mainly to Germany and Canada.

Groups like the Guatemalan Nontraditional Exporters Association (Gexport) boast that *maquilas* are leading the way to economic modernization and growth. Gexport members compare Guatemala's *maquila* industry to the export-oriented sectors in Taiwan, Hong Kong, and Singapore. They brag that this new industry not only generates employment but also encourages technology transfer and a greater efficiency and competitiveness on the part of Guatemala industrialists. The *maquiladoras* do indeed provide tens of thousands of jobs, mostly to young women (see Labor and Unions). More doubtful, however, are claims that they provide a new base for economic development. Besides labor, paid $2-4 a day per worker, the only local inputs are water, electricity, and the factory itself. Generally, all the garment parts and machinery are imported, creating an enclave sector with few links to the national economy. Garments have become a leading Guatemalan export, but the economic benefits, either in terms of foreign exchange or GDP growth, are meager since the manufactured goods are nothing more than assembled imports with little value-added and are exempt from most taxes and tariffs.

The *maquila* industry is concentrated in Guatemala City, home to nearly 80 percent of the country's *maquiladoras*, with another 15 percent in the department of Guatemala and the rest in the departments of Chimaltenango and Quetzaltenango. In addition to the *maquiladoras* themselves, usually occupying windowless warehouse-like buildings, there is a thriving cottage industry sector of garment businesses, in which assembly and sewing operations are contracted out to families or small subcontractors. Because whole families are involved in these enterprises, sometimes called "*maquilas de hormigas*" or ant *maquilas*, contractors find that labor costs are as much as 25 percent less than in Guatemala City factories. Villages such as San Francisco el Alto in Totonicapán that formerly concentrated on traditional weaving have lately become centers for *maquila* subcontracting.

Gexport and the Guatemala Development Foundation (Fundesa) have been wooing foreign-owned *maquilas* to rural Guatemala to take advantage of the low wages and sewing skills of highlands indians. In its English-language publication, *Guatemala Viva*, Fundesa notes: "In the past years, these communities have had to abandon their productive activities due to political violence, thus increasing the supply of skilled labor." In 1992 such companies as Generation One, Van Heusen, Liz Claiborne, and Gitano were considering government plans to establish a *maquiladora* zone in former conflict areas, dubbed "Zones of Peace" by the Serrano government. One plan calls for creating of a duty-free manufacturing park in the Ixcán near the Mexican border and expanding the military airstrip to facilitate cargo planes, with the government pledging to rebuild (free of charge) installations damaged in war-related incidents. Beamed Gitano's general manager for Central America: "We definitely support the president's effort to trade sewing machines for guns, if that's what you want to call it."[42] According to government officials, the Liz Claiborne company was negotiating a contract to manufacture handwoven sweaters that would employ as many as 20,000 people.[43]

In the 1970s, Guatemala hoped to expand industry through mining and oil ventures, but these diversification dreams have since been dispelled. Large nickel mining operations near Lake Izabal were shut down in 1981. Guatemala does produce oil, but after peaking in 1983, foreign sales dropped 70 percent by the end of the decade. In a setback to the country's plan to reduce its dependence on the agricultural sector, Amoco Corporation announced in early 1989 that it was discontinuing its oil exploration project in the Franja Transversal—complaining that it suffered a constant siege by guerrillas. Like Amoco, several other foreign companies have suspended exploration operations. Meanwhile production by Basic Resources, another private oil corporation, has fallen short of the high expectations of the company and the government.

Problems with Electricity

Since the advent of the Cerezo administration the issue of electricity rates and the efficiency of state-owned electric companies have been a focus of popular protests against structural adjustment and privatization. In 1987 labor confederations and popular organizations united to protest proposed electricity rate hikes by the government, and in the early days of the Serrano administration, plans to raise the price of electricity also sparked cries of protest from the nation's popular sectors. While the popular bloc has led the fight against higher rates, the country's business associations have been urging the privatization of the National Electrification Institute (INDE).[44] A series of blackouts in 1990—the immediate result of low water levels for hydroelectric generation—bolstered the position of those calling for privatization. The inability of INDE to meet the country's electricity needs inspired the daily *Siglo Veintiuno* to quip that it was a good thing that the government did not also have an Institute of Oxygen.

The union movement, led by the electrical workers' union (STINDE), has, in turn, been desperately trying to block privatization of state enterprises. Those calling for the privatization of INDE contend, however, that the electricity company's 7,000-person work force is far more than necessary to run the enterprise efficiently. Yet since personnel costs constitute only 6 percent of the cost of electric service, trimming the payroll will not be sufficient to solve INDE's serious financial difficulties.

Although it is true that proposed rate hikes will exceed what most families can afford, it is also true that since the mid-1980s the government has been subsidizing electricity production and that INDE is deep in debt. Rather than raising electricity rates to offset currency devaluation and inflation, the government has kept rate hikes below true production costs. In terms of the U.S. dollar, electricity rates declined from 13 cents per kwh in 1982 to 4.9 cents per kwh in 1990, which according to the World Bank is 54 percent below actual long-run production costs.[45] This cost differential is borne chiefly by INDE, which sells electricity well below cost to the EEGSA distribution company. But cheap electricity is not the only explanation for INDE's financial crisis. The institute suffers from weak management, low investment in infrastructure, and a large external debt resulting primarily from cost overruns and inefficiencies at its Chixoy Hydroelectric Power Plant, which came on line in 1986 after numerous delays.

Per capita electricity consumption (240 kwh per year) and access to electricity (40 percent of the population) are the lowest in Central America. Industry and commerce are the major electricity users—and beneficiaries of low rates—absorbing respectively 32 percent and 29 percent of total production, followed by residential users consuming 31 percent and the government using the remaining 8 percent. Nearly two-thirds of Guatemala's electricity is generated by hydroelectric projects, principally Chixoy, with the remainder supplied by oil-fueled thermal plants.[46]

Privatization Plans

A prominent plank in the neoliberal platform is the privatization of state enterprises. Ideologically, public corporations are regarded as obstacles to private investment and free market economics. Neoliberal proponents of privatization also argue that the sale or dissolution of state entities furthers the democratic process, touting privatization as the "democratization of property." In terms of budget balancing, state enterprises are often criticized because they are inefficient, function at a loss, and lead to government budget deficits. In keeping with the structural adjustment of the Guatemalan economy, in process since the mid-1980s, privatization of state enterprises and institutions has frequently been proposed.

A 1991 study undertaken by the Enterprise Chamber (CAEM) on behalf of the U.S. Agency for International Development concluded that of the 38 state enterprises 32 should be privatized in three stages over a ten-year period. Among those that CAEM recommended for immediate privatization were the telephone company, the electricity-generation firm, the electricity-distribution company, the railroad corporation, the Santo Tomás Port Authority, and the government's San Bartolo Free Trade and Industry Zone. As a second stage, the social security institute, national housing institute, national institute of cooperatives, national finance corporation, agricultural marketing institute, and the national agricultural school are recommended for privatization in the mid-1990s. By the end of the decade such non-business entities as the national university, national wheat association, public administration institute, and the national statistics institute are slated by CAEM for state divestment. Under CAEM's plan, the state—other than government ministries themselves—will only control such minor institutes as the sports confederation, national planning institute, volunteer firefighters' agency, and the Guatemala City water agency. CAEM would also exempt from privatization the Military Social Welfare Institute (IPM), the financial arm of the army.

Rather than proceeding directly to sell state entities to the private sector, a process that the government and business community call "demonopolization" is under way. By cutting government subsidies to state entities and by liberalizing prices, the government is opening up some areas of the economy, such as electricity generation, to the private sector while at the same time weakening the financial position of the state corporations. For the private sector, such a strategy has the advantage of allowing investors to assume gradual control over the most profitable operations of what was previously a state monopoly. For the government, gradual demonopolization of state enterprises like INDE, rather than their outright sale, keeps the issue of privatization from turning into a flashpoint for worker opposition.

Contrary to the image perpetuated by CACIF and other private-sector groups, the nonmilitary branch of the public sector in Guatemala is not a giant octopus with tentacles reaching into every sector of the economy and society. In fact, the Guatemalan government is quite small, accounting for only 10 percent of the GDP. Most state enterprises are strategic institutions concerned with promoting public welfare and economic growth. In Guatemala the public sector does not operate its own restaurants, hotels, or other businesses that have no social function.

Public expenditures on social services in Guatemala are among the lowest in the world. Rather than obstructing economic growth, public sector investment is a critical component of economic development and its decline in recent years has helped create a stagnant economy. One branch of the public sector that does indeed sap revenues without enhancing economic development is the military, but the issue of demilitarization is still too sensitive to be discussed seriously by politicians and business leaders. Nor have foreign lenders included demilitarization as an objective of structural adjustment or as a condition for further financial assistance.

Prospects for Tourism

The tourism industry, like nontraditional export production, is a bright spot in the Guatemalan economy. Guatemala has long been a favorite travel destination for those interested in native culture and Mayan archeology. In the 1960s young, budget-minded travelers discovered the allure, beauty, and cheap living of Panajachel (affectionately called Pana by locals and foreign tourists alike) on the shores of Lake Atitlán. By the 1970s tourists began streaming into Guatemala. Initially, the escalating repression of the Lucas García regime did not stem the tourist boom. In 1979 Guatemala attracted a record high 502,000 visitors, who brought $201 million into the country. By 1980, however, the encroaching militarization of the highlands started scaring off would-be visitors. In 1981 the U.S. State Department's "travel advisory" warning citizens of the dangers of visiting Guatemala virtually shut down the tourism industry.

It was not until 1984, when the counterinsurgency war let up and the State Department's travel advisory became considerably less ominous, that the industry gradually began to revive. The drop in the value of the *quetzal* in 1985-86 rated Guatemala an even more attractive vacation spot. With the number of tourists rebounding by 20 percent annually, the industry quickly rose to a position as one of the country's chief sources of foreign exchange. In 1991 more than 509,000 tourists visited Guatemala, generating $210 million in foreign exchange and providing work directly and indirectly for nearly 50,000 Guatemalans. Tikal, Antigua, Lake Atitlán, and Chichicastenango are the main attractions for visitors from the United States, Canada, El Salvador, and Europe.[47] Despite the strong showing of the tourism industry, travel services registered negative in the current account (balance of trade plus services and unrequited transfers) in the 1980s, mainly due to frequent trips to Miami and other U.S. locations by members of the country's upper class. Beginning in 1990, however, Guatemala once again began enjoying small net foreign-exchange gains from travel services.

Since 1989 the tourism industry has ranked third after coffee and nontraditional exports as a source of foreign exchange. The country's improved international image—the result of the slowdown in counterinsurgency operations and the transition to civilian rule—accounted for the new influx of tourists. The industry also benefited from increased international publicity about Guatemala's tropical rainforests and Mayan ruins. Foreign investors, like Club Med (which is considering establishing an "archeological villa" near Tikal), have expressed a keen interest in profiting from this upswing in tourism. Inguat, the government's tourism institute, projects that one million or more foreigners will be visiting Guatemala annually by the year 2000. But that projection may be overly optimistic, especially considering rising foreign concern about expanding crime and lawlessness in Guatemala. Embassies from several European countries as well as the United States have issued increasingly severe travel advisories warning prospective visitors of the crime wave that has gripped Guatemala since the late 1980s (see Lawlessness and Human Rights).

The Business of Drugs

It used to be that the drug business was just a relatively minor sideline of the Guatemalan underworld. The police managed the domestic marijuana market on the San Carlos University campus, while customs officials along the Mexican border looked the other way (for a fee) as the opium poppy produced in Guatemala was smuggled into Mexico for processing into heroin. Drugs were small time—particularly when compared with the ever-booming black market in cars and electrical appliances. However, in the late 1980s narcotrafficking suddenly became big business, artificially boosting the economy while adding another layer of corruption to an already lawless society.

A crackdown spearheaded by the U.S. Drug Enforcement Administration (DEA) made life more difficult for marijuana producers in neighboring Belize, and some of this illegal agribusiness shifted to Guatemala, especially into Petén department. Similarly, a vigorous war against drugs in Mexico enhanced the relative importance of poppy production in Guatemala and also resulted in the emergence of an elementary processing business. Farmers in the remote valleys and canyons of San Marcos and Huehuetenango (along the Mexican border) who cultivated the beautiful orange-red poppy did so because this illegal flower was at least 20 times more profitable than other crops. When the DEA moved into Guatemala in the late 1980s, it focused almost exclusively on eradicating poppy and marijuana production through aerial spraying.[48] While these eradication efforts continue, the main objective of antinarcotics operations since 1990 has been suppression of cocaine smuggling.

Most of the cocaine moving northward from Colombia and other South American countries used to be smuggled through the Caribbean or along Central America's Atlantic Coast. But the launching of a major antidrug campaign by Washington in the 1980s—complete with new radar monitoring facilities in Honduras, Puerto Rico, Cuba (at Guantanamo base), and Florida collectively called the Caribbean Basin Radar Network—has rendered this traditional smuggling route more risky. As a central point between Colombia and the United States, Guatemala became a favored transshipment point for cocaine smugglers by 1990.[49] Unmonitored by radar (except for a station at Aurora International Airport in Guatemala City) and possessing hundreds of hidden airstrips, Guatemala was selected as an ideal place to unload cocaine for temporary storage and subsequent shipment north by land, air, or sea. In 1990 a record 15.5 metric tons of cocaine were confiscated by authorities—a fivefold leap over the amount confiscated the year before. In early 1992 narcotics officials estimated that 1-3 metric tons of cocaine were being smuggled into Guatemala every week by South American drug cartels. An average of five cargo drops a day were being made to clandestine airstrips, located mostly on extensive estates along Guatemala's Pacific Coast. A grower allowing smugglers to land on his property receives $50,000 per landing and $500 per kilogram if the cocaine is then temporarily stored before being shipped north.[50] Involvement in narcotrafficking extends to all sectors of society, with the police, politicians, and military each taking their cut.

By 1992 the evidence that Guatemala had become a major cocaine transshipment point was indisputable. There were also indications that the country was no longer just a bridge for international cocaine trafficking but was developing into a regional money-laundering center as well. Luxury construction was booming, the country seemed awash in dollars, new banks were opening every month, and real estate prices were skyrocketing—all telltale signs that narcodollars were being laundered. In 1991 new construction expanded by an unprecedented 60 percent. Not since the reconstruction following the 1976 earthquake had there been so much building. But the difference was that almost all the new construction activity was for the elite market. High-rise condominiums, shopping centers, and plush apartment complexes were popping up on the outskirts of the city at a time when the low-income housing crisis was exploding in frequent land invasions by homeless squatters. Struck by all this new construction, Guatemalans nodded knowingly and murmured, "Narcodollars."

The attempt by narcotraffickers to "wash" their dirty money by investing it in the local economy was also thought to explain soaring real estate prices. By the second year of the Serrano administration it was becoming apparent that drug traffickers were buying up stores, restaurants, discotheques, and other commercial ventures with their new wealth. It was, however, the sudden reversal in Guatemala's foreign exchange reserves that led most observers to conclude with certainty that Guatemala had become a money-laundering center. A dramatic rise in local interest rates in 1991—and a parallel decline in U.S. rates—brought a sudden halt to capital flight and apparently encouraged a considerable repatriation of dollars. But so massive was the influx of dollars and so persistent, continuing even when interests rates began falling in 1992, that many close observers deduced that narcodollars were also contributing to Guatemala's largest dollar accumulation in more than a decade.

PART 4

Social Forces

© Derrill Bazzy

Popular Organizing

The 1954 coup that struck down the reformist Arbenz government and the subsequent repression of the organized popular movement cast Guatemala into a political winter. Not until the early 1970s did the popular movement begin to recuperate. At first, the surge in popular organizing came in response to dramatic price hikes brought on by the sudden rise in the cost of oil in 1973. Later, the 1976 earthquake and the limited political opening during the Laugerud regime (especially in its last two years, 1976-78) sparked much broader levels of popular organizing, in which economic and political demands were increasingly linked. The wave of popular organizing during the 1970s differed markedly from that which occurred in the 1944-54 period in that this more recent effort was largely of grassroots origins—neither tied to government initiatives nor dependent on the guidance of leftist intellectuals.[1]

The teachers' strike of 1973, popular protests against higher bus fares in the winter of 1973-74, and the 1976 formation of the National Committee for Labor Unity (CNUS)—the first united labor front since the Arbenz years—signaled the renewal in urban organizing. In the wake of the earthquake, which left 25,000 dead and 1.25 million homeless, new types of popular organizations sprang up such as an association of shantytown dwellers called MONAP and a Consumers Defense Committee.[2] Also following the earthquake was a burst of rural organizing as devastated communities, often supported by foreign aid, formed self-help groups and agricultural cooperatives to improve their social and economic conditions.[3] The courageous march of the Huehuetenango miners in 1977 and the founding of the Campesino Unity Committee (CUC) in 1978 were other signs of the resurrection of popular organizing in rural Guatemala. Throughout the country, but especially in the western highlands, there emerged a new social consciousness and confidence inspired by activist interpretations of the gospel propagated largely by foreign missionaries and Catholic Action organizers.

This crescendo of popular organizing reached its zenith in 1978, after which heightened repression made demonstrations and social activism ever more dangerous. Following the labor marches and strikes of 1978 dozens of labor leaders were killed and some 800 strike supporters were arrested. Similarly, a demonstration for land by Kekchí indians in the town of Panzós in Alta Verapaz was met by military gunfire leaving more than one hundred dead and three hundred wounded. Organizing by indians—both in the highlands and among South Coast farmworkers—was considered particularly threatening by the army and large landowners. Compounding this threat were new attempts to unify the indian and *ladino* sectors of the popular movement—a phenomenon not seen since the 1944-54 period.[4]

The Lucas García regime directed its repression against all sectors and individuals that raised reformist agendas. Not only were workers and peasants victims of this crackdown but also politicians, intellectuals, and students. In early 1979 the country's two most prominent and respected social-democratic politicians, Alberto Fuentes Mohr and Manuel Colom Argueta, were assassinated, and more than one hundred Christian Democratic politicians were killed in the 1980-81 period. Students and professors, regarded as the ideologues of the popular movement, were targeted for elimination, with some 400 being murdered or disappeared in the 1979-80 wave of violence. Banding together to protest the mounting violence against the popular movement, urban and rural groups in early 1979 formed a popular coalition called the Democratic Front Against Repression (FDCR), coalescing virtually every active progressive and democratic organization.

The official violence continued unabated, forcing most social justice activists into exile or clandestinity. The January 31, 1980, burning of the Spanish embassy—occupied by 39 protesters, including 27 CUC members and supporters—revealed just what measures the military government was willing to take to repress popular organizing. Later in the year, 41 labor activists belonging to the National Confederation of Workers (CNT) were disappeared. Despite this mounting repression, some popular organizations continued to protest openly. In 1981 several came together to form the January 31 Popular Front (FP-31), which offered itself as a "unitary structure to deepen support and coordination between mass organizations." This popular alliance was short-lived due to the continuing wave of terror spread by the Lucas García regime. One of the last manifestations of the popular movement that emerged in the late 1970s was the February 1980 strike by CUC in the cotton and sugar plantations of the South Coast. The successful strike, which organized more than 75,000 farmworkers, greatly alarmed the agroexport oligarchy. The solidarity of CUC-affiliated farmworkers temporarily blocked the harvest while demonstrating the broad organization and militancy of the peasant population.

The wholesale violence against the popular movement—combined with the deepening counterinsurgency campaign to destroy the guerrillas and their base of civil support—silenced all forms of public protest by 1981. It was not until 1983—and especially after 1985—that the civil society began to show new signs of life. With the popular movement decapitated, the highland population terrorized and corralled into militarized zones, and the guerrillas in retreat, the military regime slowly began relaxing its repression. This created space for a reconstitution of the civil society and civilian political activity. One of the first groups to form was the Confederation of Guatemalan Trade Union Unity (CUSG), founded in 1983 with the blessing of the Ríos Montt regime.

Gradually, as the military proceeded with its institutional reform project, other popular groups began to establish themselves, notably the Mutual Support Group (GAM), founded in 1984. The creation of the left-leaning Union of Guatemalan Workers (UNSITRAGUA) in 1985 was another bold attempt to test the extent of the country's new political opening. By the second half of the decade during the civilian government headed by Vinicio Cerezo, popular organizing picked up momentum. Although never approaching the degree of strength or cohesion of the late 1970s, the popular movement of the late 1980s and early 1990s had acquired new dimensions. No longer the sole domain of peasant and worker organizations, the struggle for justice and peace was now being championed by new groups of human rights activists, the landless, the displaced, indian farmworkers, religious workers, and women. Forming an important new component of the popular movement were the Communities of Population in Resistance (CPR), comprising entire communities of displaced families and returned refugees (see Refugees and the Internally Displaced). Beginning in 1990 the communities in resistance (along with Guatemalan refugees living in Mexico) escalated their demands to be integrated into civil society. With the advent of the reintegration of refugees and displaced persons, concern arose within the military and the Serrano administration that the returning populations might spark new popular organizing in rural areas. One of the most notable developments within the popular movement in the 1985-92 period was the emergence of a strong indigenous-led sector including such groups as CONAVIGUA, the CPRs, CERJ, CUC, and other peasant organizations. Equally striking was the fading of the labor unions, the traditional vanguard of the popular movement, as the leading voice of the popular sectors.

The Clamor for Land

Conflicts over inequitable land distribution resulted in Guatemala's first mass organizing of the 1980s. The spark igniting this peasant organizing was a maverick Catholic priest, Andrés Girón, a rotund padre with a flair for publicity. In 1986 Girón tapped the deepfelt need of South Coast peasants for agrarian reform. From his parish in Nueva Concepción, Padre Girón organized the Pro-Land Peasant Association to demand land from the new Christian Democratic government. This movement, with wide support among the country's more than 500,000 landless peasants, dared to call for agrarian reform and brought its demands directly to the National Palace via several mass demonstrations. Internal splits and ideological differences, however, debilitated the group led by Girón and other similar pro-land organizations.[5]

Although Girón's movement and other pro-land groups gradually waned, they did create the space for the reemergence of other peasant groups, notably CUC. Unlike the Pro-Land movement, CUC was not demanding that the government sell land to landless campesinos. It focused, instead, on the plight of the farmworker. Before being driven underground in 1981, CUC organized a highly effective strike against the sugar mills of the South Coast. In early 1989, as it surfaced from hiding, CUC organized numerous strikes against the large estates and mills of the southern coastal plains.

Inequitable land distribution and the plight of the country's seasonal farmworkers persisted as acute social issues in the early 1990s, but viable solutions remained elusive. The Cerezo government did distribute some land to organized pro-land groups but as in previous land distribution and land colonization projects the peasants were left without credit or technical assistance and were heavily burdened by land payments. Similarly, the Serrano administration signaled that there would be no real agrarian reform. Recognizing that landlessness remained a volatile issue, in 1992 Serrano called for the creation of a government foundation, Fonatierra, to facilitate the sale of private lands to small farmers—hardly a solution for those without any financial resources or ability to pay back bank loans.

The fight for land, the one issue that more than any other highlights the highly uneven distribution and use of resources in Guatemala, continued into the early 1990s. But rather than facing one united rural movement calling for agrarian reform, the government and landed elite now confronted multiple threats by community groups to invade uncultivated land. Demands by farmworkers for higher wages persist, although the task of organizing rural labor has become more difficult as competition escalates among the landless and unemployed for low-paid seasonal jobs on the country's agroexport estates. Continuing military repression and the vehement opposition of the agroexport oligarchy have also stymied rural organizing.

UASP: A New Popular Coalition

In late 1987 unionists, human rights activists, and students came together to form the Labor and Popular Action Unity (UASP) coalition to present a united front in the face of economic crisis, repression, and government unresponsiveness. Besides the specific demands of the constituent groups, an overriding objective was to retain and even widen the political space that had opened up in the country beginning in 1985.

Leading UASP was the UNSITRAGUA labor confederation, drawing on the collective strength of the entire popular movement. Members of this new popular coalition included three human rights groups (GAM, CONAVIGUA, and the Runujel Junam Council of Ethnic Communities, known as CERJ), two student organizations (AEU and the secondary students' organization, CEEM), numerous unions (UNSITRAGUA, FESEBS, STINDE, STEG, FENASTEG, and Luz y Fuerza), a progressive religious association called the Monsignor Romero Group, CUC, South Coast Workers Front, and the National Council of the Displaced (CONDEG).

In 1988 UASP presented to the National Dialogue (see The Peace Process) a list of demands that constituted a platform for moderate social change in Guatemala. This call for change incorporated the full spectrum of demands of the popular movement, ranging from respect for human rights to a moratorium on external debt payments and an end to sexual harassment and discrimination. But rather than a cohesive alliance, UASP represented the convergence of disparate popular demands.

Beyond its role in merging important elements of the popular sector into a single coalition and opening a political space for popular organizing, UASP can point to few concrete achievements. Its major success—the March 1988 negotiation with the government for wage hikes and a price freeze on basic goods—was later ignored by the Cerezo administration, which found itself increasingly under attack by hard-line elements of the military and the private sector. Though unsuccessful, one of the most impressive displays of popular organizing was the 1989 teachers' strike, which despite strong teacher support ended after almost three months without achieving any of its fundamental objectives. The utter failure of a general strike called by UNSITRAGUA in August 1988 and the inability of CUC to maintain mass support for its farmworker strikes in January 1988 and 1989 highlight the relative weakness of the organized popular sectors and reflect the difficulties they face in mobilizing around economic demands.

The State of Popular Organizing

Although the popular movement made an impact in the late 1980s, particularly in light of the repression it faced, it did not approach the degree of popular organizing experienced in the 1970s. Nevertheless, UASP did create a base of unity from which a resurgent popular movement voiced its demands. It set the tone of resistance by demanding that the government honor its commitments to respect human rights and meet the basic needs of the country's poor majority.

The transition to civilian rule provided the popular sectors with a political opening to express their concern about such matters as low wages, forced service in civil patrols, landlessness, and human rights violations. But though marches and demonstrations were once again permitted, the still-palpable atmosphere of repression braked any rapid expansion of popular organizing. No longer were there massive killings and disappearances of activists, but speaking out against the government, business, or the army remained hazardous. Following the army revolts of May 1988 and May 1989, the political opening for popular organizing narrowed further. Those who dared to join the struggle for social change received death threats or sometimes were killed or disappeared. Students, peasant activists, unionists, journalists, and community organizers became victims of a new scourge of selectively administered, anti-popular-sector terrorism that continued into the Serrano administration.

At the end of the 1980s the level of organizing and political consciousness among the popular sectors was low. Deepening poverty and economic uncertainty brought on by conservative structural policies left poor Guatemalans ever more reluctant to risk what limited security they had in social activism. For many Guatemalans the daily fight for survival took priority over popular struggles that usually proved unsuccessful.

The popular movement's courageous determination to voice its demands to the country's oligarchs, generals, and politicians has helped retain a limited niche for democratic reform and popular organizing. But there have been few concrete advances, on either the human rights or economic fronts. When the unions and popular coalitions sat down to negotiate accords with the government and private sector, the resulting accords were routinely violated. When they went out on strike or dared to confront the perpetrators of human rights abuses directly, they endured the wrath of the vigilante and security forces.

On the positive side, the popular bloc in Guatemala gained new dimensions in the 1985-92 period with the more prominent presence of women, indians, and religious groups, such as the ecumenical Campaign for Life and Peace. No longer did the popular movement restrict itself to class-based issues or certain ideological lines. Also notable, especially in the early 1990s, was the rising community response to local repression, corruption, and deteriorating living conditions. Most impressive was the unified response by the community of Santiago Atitlán to an army massacre, resulting in the military abandoning its post in that indian town.

Noteworthy too was the explosion in 1991-92 of numerous community protests against town mayors for failing to address local problems. In many cases the local mutinies were led by political parties or competing local bosses. But at its heart this rebellion against the installed political leadership represented a popular rejection of traditional politics and an added aggressiveness in demanding that basic needs, such as potable water, be met by governing authorities.[6] Reflecting a widespread dissatisfaction with lawlessness, popular organizations also began to challenge the impunity of government officials and the security forces.

At a July 1991 conference six popular organizations (CONAVIGUA, GAM, CERJ, Communities of Population in Resistance or CPR, CONDEG, and the Permanent Commission of Guatemalan Refugees) called for the legal prosecution of ex-generals Benedicto Lucas García and Efraín Ríos Montt, the uncovering of clandestine graves, and the establishment of a commission to investigate the fate of the disappeared. The presence of popular organizations demanding an end to impunity and respect for human rights lent weight to similar demands increasingly raised by foreign lenders. The reconstitution of local self-help groups in many towns and a new wave of land occupations by squatters in the 1989-92 period were other signs indicating a more assertive popular sector in Guatemala.

Perhaps the most remarkable development in popular organizing has been the burgeoning strength, creativity, and unity of what has become an indigenous- and rural-led popular movement. Organizing around an array of social, economic, and cultural demands, this movement has succeeded in focusing international attention on human rights violations and military impunity. In a nation where the popular movement has long been dominated by a *ladino* and urban leadership, the rise of indian leadership and organizations signals an important change in the composition and direction of popular organizing. The joint demonstration by GAM and CONAVIGUA on Father's Day 1992 in which 2,000 indian children marched to the National Palace with placards demanding that the government give them back their missing fathers was further evidence of the leading role of indigenous people in the human rights movement. The massive presence of peasants in the International Labor Day protest—reported to be the largest since 1980—a month earlier also signalled the presence of an increasingly active and organized rural population.

On the whole, however, the popular bloc has remained weak, fractionalized, and lacking a coherent program of political and economic reform. Perhaps its greatest problem is the weakened state of its leadership. Decades of systematic repression isolated the popular bloc from its history and the experience of previous struggles. But repression alone does not account for the leadership problems facing the popular movement. Cultural, ethnic, and linguistic divisions in Guatemalan society obstruct popular unity. The paternalistic, dogmatic, hierarchical, sexist, and often racist working styles of entrenched leaders inhibit popular organizations, keeping them insular and ineffective. Rather than launching training programs to develop new cadres and leaders, honchos have often monopolized decision-making power within the organizations. Lack of representative democratic structures—or any formal structure at all—within these organizations also weaken their claim to be voices of a new democratic movement.

Requiring unity in the face of repression and crisis, leaders of the popular movement tolerate little dissent. Those who raise issues or who question leadership styles and policies are often marginalized. Similarly attempts to introduce gender-specific or culture-specific demands have sometimes been denounced as sectarian or destabilizing. Although the various guerrilla groups stress the importance of unity in the popular movement, they have been known to favor certain groups over others as the selected vanguard. Another factor contributing to internal problems within popular organizations has been corruption and powermongering resulting from the flow of funds into these organizations from foreign churches and foundations.

Both a strength and a weakness of the popular movement has been the way that different groups or issues temporally assume a leading role and then fade in importance and impact. When GAM or UNSITRAGUA lost momentum, other groups such as CONAVIGUA or the religious Campaign for Life and Peace gained prominence. But neither UASP nor any other coalition has been able to forge all these diverse movements into a coordinated force for social change.

Also limiting the influence of the popular movement has been its alienation from the political process in Guatemala. Political parties have cultivated few links with popular organizations, and when they do reach out to individual groups or leaders it is usually to manipulate them for short-term electoral objectives. The popular organizations, in turn, dismiss the political parties as corrupt and self-interested elite clubs that offer little hope for real social and economic advances for the poor majority. The demands of the popular bloc have yet to find a place in the electoral arena despite the dramatic decline in the country's socioeconomic conditions.

The 1981-83 counterinsurgency campaign broke most popular links with the guerrilla movement—keeping the popular movement and the guerrillas operating in relative isolation from each other. Both movements have suffered from the absence of a strong infrastructure of support and the lack of a well-defined platform of political and economic change. As a result, their efforts only rarely complement one another, leaving both movements relatively weak. Although the popular organizations certainly supported negotiations to end the war, they had neither the strength nor the political vision to assert themselves as a principal force in forging peace and developing a new social order. For their part, the guerrilla leadership, though successful in getting the negotiations to focus attention on such problems as human rights violations, proved incapable of articulating a modern platform for social and economic change.

The popular movement has also suffered from the lack of a coherent analysis of the rapidly changing economic and political forces internationally and regionally. As a result, popular organizations continue to rely on such historical demands as the maintenance of price controls, a wholesale rejection of privatization, and lower public utility rates. The labor sector, in particular, has proved uncreative in formulating its demands in the context of realistic possibilities. The weaknesses of progressive social organizations are not singular to Guatemala but are akin to those confronting the political left around the world.

Overall, repression remains the chief cause for the weak state of the popular movement, eliminating its most experienced leaders and severing it from its base of support. Guatemalans have internalized the long campaign of terror and they fear the consequences of any form of organizing. Nevertheless, economic desperation, the indignity of living without rights, and the courage of selfless activists have kept the movement alive.

As socioeconomic conditions deteriorate, the state of severe deprivation in which at least three of every four Guatemalans live will likely ignite renewed popular protests. Landlessness, the unresponsiveness of public officials, price hikes for public utilities and transportation, a lack of adequate water, public-sector layoffs, and the dearth of urban housing will likely be the principal sources of future conflicts with the government. The danger, however, is that this social justice mobilization will take the form of spontaneous and unrelated outbursts of popular frustration—rather than constituting part of a cohesive social movement for substantive political and economic changes. Without a unifying strategy or vision, such popular protests may result in individual and temporary gains but may also have the unintended effect of propelling the country further into a state of social anarchy and hopelessness.

Nongovernmental Organizations Strengthen Civil Society

In promoting social demands, popular organizations create a more participatory civil society—an arena for community development and social realization outside the structures defined by business, government, and the military. Also key in the effort to develop a more active and influential civil society are nongovernmental organizations (NGOs), private institutions founded for specific social or economic objectives. In a society where government social initiatives have been so limited, local and foreign NGOs serve as a privately sponsored social infrastructure. Given the absence of government institutions and the major social problems facing Guatemala, NGOs could potentially occupy an important place in civil society through their role as agents of economic development and democratization.

Most NGO activity in Guatemala is characterized by its paternalistic, welfare nature, in contrast to a style that could be more supportive of community organizing and popular education. The most beneficial NGO activity is sponsored by European and Canadian agencies and, to a lesser extent, by progressive Protestant churches and Catholic orders in the United States.[7] The two principal NGO umbrella groups are the AID-funded Association of Development and Services Entities of Guatemala (ASINDES) and the more progressive Council of Development Institutions (COINDE), which is more closely associated with popular organizing.

Neoliberal economic strategies emphasizing the free market along with private initiatives that gained prominence in the late 1980s have combined to create new space for NGO operations. For the most part, however, the business sector rather than the popular sector has taken the lead in exploring new possibilities for NGOs in areas such as education and microenterprises. In such areas as refugee resettlement, health care, economic subsistence strategies, and community development, more progressive NGOs could contribute to the broadening of Guatemalan civil society by offering innovative and viable programs.

Labor and Unions

Enlarged photographs of eight murdered unionists adorn the walls of the labor union representing workers at the Coca-Cola bottling plant in Guatemala City.[8] Those martyrs are among hundreds who have fallen victim to death squads and military repression since 1954. Union activists, however, need no reminder that union organizing is a life-threatening activity. Although wholesale murders of union organizers waned during the later part of the 1980s, union activists were still frequent targets for death threats and killings during the Cerezo government and the early part of the Serrano administration.[9] (For a chronology of the labor and union movement in Guatemala, see Figure 4a.)

Few Guatemalan workers are organized into unions. There are no hard figures on union membership, but most estimates put the figure at 5 percent or less of the work force. Repression is the main obstacle to labor organizing, but it is not the only one. An antiquated Labor Code, the large pool of cheap labor, union-breaking tactics by employers, and the growth of *solidarista* associations are among the impediments faced by unions. The lack of unity between urban workers and peasants together with the lack of popular support for union struggles (factory and public-sector employees often being regarded as a kind of labor elite) also undermine labor organizing in Guatemala.

Following the darkest years of repression and counterinsurgency operations (1978-1983), the union movement tentatively began to reestablish itself in 1984, as illustrated by the occupation of the Coca-Cola factory.[10] Unions took advantage of the new, although still limited, political opening represented by the Cerezo administration (1986-91) to present wage demands and to link themselves with the wider popular movement.[11] Factories that tried to break unions or to shut down in the face of unionization were occupied by workers, pub-

Labor Chronology

1870s: Reforms of Liberal era privatize communal lands, while *mandamiento* labor system presses indian labor into work gangs for agroexport plantations and the state.

1894: Debt-bondage replaces *mandamiento* system to guarantee supply of farm labor for coffee oligarchs.

1920s: First trade unions formed among shoemakers, bakers, railroad, banana, and port workers.

1926: Labor Law recognizes right to strike but establishes obligatory system of arbitration.

1931: Regime of Jorge Ubico (1931-44) clamps down on unions, strangling many in infancy.

1934: Vagrancy law obligates indians to work as wage laborers 150 days each year, replacing debt-bondage system.

1945: New constitution enacted by reformist Arévalo government greatly expands worker rights, establishing eight-hour day, minimum wage, social security system, and right to bargain collectively and strike. For the first time, workers' right to freely sell their labor is recognized, propelling Guatemala toward capitalist modernization.

1947: Comprehensive Labor Code promulgated. First union to register under new code is SETUFO, representing workers of United Fruit Company.

1952: Agrarian reform law sparks burst of peasant organizing.

1954: Right-wing coup ousts President Arbenz. 534 registered unions and dozens of rural associations repressed by Castillo Armas administration. Armas outlaws labor and peasant organizations formed during 1944-54 period, allowing new associations to form only if they can guarantee they are free of communist influence. Hundreds of union and peasant leaders jailed or killed.

1956: New constitution prohibits union participation in politics and in public sector, creating new obstacles for union organizing and effectively barring strikes.

1970-76: Industrial growth, spurred by Central American Common Market and reduced repression, gives rise to new unions and rural associations. Kjell Laugerud regime (1974-78) backs formation of rural associations and unions that support government, but new openness begins to break down during last year of his administration as popular organizing mushrooms.

1976: Formation of National Committee of Trade Union Unity (CNUS), indicating expanded popular organizing.

1977: Protest march by Huehuetenango mine workers.

1978: Lucas García regime (1978-82) dramatically increases level of repression against unions and rural organizations. Prominent labor attorney Mario López Larrave assassinated. Formation of Campesino Unity Committee (CUC). In 1977-78 period, 68 rural cooperative leaders killed in Ixcán.

1979-80: Repression of Coca-Cola union leaves four union leaders being shot and wounded, four disappeared, and seven killed.

1980: 41 National Confederation of Workers (CNT) organizers disappeared by security forces in two incidents in Guatemala City and Escuintla. Along with other protesters, leaders of CUC die in Spanish embassy fire. Labor movement driven underground.

1983: State of emergency bans all union activity. A condition of U.S. aid and CBI eligibility, Ríos Montt regime authorizes formation of new labor federation named CUSG and headed by his personal attorney, Juan Francisco Alfaro.

1984: Less repressive climate exemplified by noninterference of security forces in year-long occupation of Coca-Cola plant by unionized workers.

1985: Formation of UNSITRAGUA by an alliance of unions formerly active in 1970s (some affiliated with leftist CNUS) and others active in support of Coca-Cola workers' struggle.

1986-87: Formation of CGTG, affiliated with CLAT and associated with Christian Democratic Party. Cerezo government fulfills promise to permit labor organizing and strikes by public-sector employees with Decree 71-86, sparking a wave of public-sector strikes and new union formation. Ruling party proves unable to control these unions as it had hoped. Formation of UASP popular coalition whose main members are UNSITRAGUA, STINDE, STEG, FESEBS, FENASTEG, CUC, and GAM.

1988: After Cerezo government (as part of its social consensus or *concertación*) signs a wage and price accord with labor confederations, it later ignores terms of agreement and repression escalates against union activists.

1991-92: Determining that Serrano administration's invitation to participate in a new "social pact" between government, private sector, and labor is a disingenuous attempt to manipulate popular sectors, UNSITRAGUA, FENASTEG, and FESEBS boycott meetings, although CUSG, CGTG, and CTC initially participate in social pact talks. Death threats and killings continue against union and peasant organizers. Labor unions continue to lose members to *solidarista* associations. Private and public sectors employ legal and illegal tactics to minimize role of unions in Guatemalan society.

SOURCES: Mario López Larrave, *Breve historia del movimiento sindical Guatemalteco* (Guatemala City: Editorial Universitaria, 1979); James A. Goldston, *Shattered Hope: Guatemalan Workers and the Promise of Democracy* (Boulder, CO: Westview Press, 1989); Miguel Angel Albizures, *Tiempo de Sudor y Lucha* (Mexico City: Praxis, 1987); Maria Guadalupe Navas Alvarez, *El movimiento sindical como manifestacion de la lucha de clases* (Mexico City: Editorial Universitaria, 1979)

lic-sector employees went out on strike, and new links were established with international labor and solidarity groups.

The main growth in unionization occurred among government employees, whose right to organize was recognized for the first time in 1986. Continued repression and union-breaking tactics have checked the movement's advance in the private sector. In the face of strikes and occupations by unions, numerous factories have simply closed, frequently reopening with newly hired employees who are included in management-sponsored *solidarista* associations. Private companies, especially after the May 1988 coup attempt, have been able to rely on ready police support. In contrast, unions find that neither the police nor the Ministry of Labor will act forcefully either to protect workers' rights or to enforce court decisions favorable to the workers.

By appointing Mario Solórzano of the social-democratic PSD as his minister of labor, Serrano hoped to create a wider social base for his government while avoiding destabilizing labor conflicts. Although the Ministry of Labor under Serrano did give workers a more sympathetic hearing than in previous administrations, the Ministry proved less an advocate of labor interests than some had hoped. At least part of the Ministry's problem is that it has been grossly underfunded (about 0.2 percent of the government's budget) and has little or no enforcement power.[12] Its few inspectors are routinely denied access to factories to investigate worker complaints, and the fines the Ministry is authorized to levy are only nominal. Like other government bureaucrats, the labor inspectors are low-paid and easily corrupted. In addition to an ineffective labor ministry, unions are hampered by a labor code that bars strikes in certain public sectors and during agricultural harvests. The outdated code hamstrings unions through complicated and lengthy judicial procedures that favor business owners. Numerous proposals to revise and upgrade the labor code were under consideration by the National Congress in 1992, but a substantially improved code was not a priority for either the Serrano administration or the main political parties.

At the beginning of the 1990s the labor movement encompassed one minor and three major confederations, various independent unions, and a few peasant associations. The main confederations and unions are as follows:

The **Confederation of Guatemalan Trade Union Unity (CUSG)** originated on May Day 1983 with the official blessing of the Ríos Montt government. A principal reason for its founding was to demonstrate that Guatemala qualified in terms of labor rights for the benefits of the Caribbean Basin Initiative. The union's main figures are Juan Francisco Alfaro Mijanos and his brother Antonio. Francisco

Alfaro, a lawyer, was a member of the Council of State during the Ríos Montt regime, and in the 1990 elections won a place in Congress as a representative of the UCN party.

Internationally, CUSG is associated with the International Confederation of Free Trade Unions (ICFTU) and regionally it relates to the Interamerican Regional Organization of Workers (ORIT). Its main affiliation, however, is with the American Institute for Free Labor Development (AIFLD), the principal source of its funding. AIFLD, in turn, receives its funding from the U.S. Agency for International Development (AID) and the United States Information Agency (USIA). CUSG shares the center-right, social-democratic politics of AIFLD, an associate of the AFL-CIO labor confederation in the United States.

CUSG, the best-financed confederation in Guatemala, offers instruction in "free trade union" principles at local and U.S. workshops to any Guatemalan unionist willing to attend. Its base has mostly been found among rural associations formed to receive inexpensive agricultural inputs and to benefit from community development projects sponsored by AIFLD and AID, although it has made some inroads in the *maquila* sector.[13] Despite its antileftist orientation, CUSG temporarily joined the UASP popular coalition in early 1988, dropping out in mid-1990 and angering other labor confederations by throwing its support behind the center-right UCN party. Internal divisions and the friction between Alfaro's political ambitions and the demands of labor have weakened CUSG's effectiveness.

The **Union of Guatemalan Workers (UNSITRAGUA)** was founded in February 1985 and is identified with the most progressive sectors of the labor and popular movements. Many of the nearly 25 unions that form UNSITRAGUA were previously affiliated with the National Committee of Trade Union Unity (CNUS), which disintegrated under the repression of the Lucas García regime. UNSITRAGUA is not affiliated with any international or regional confederations. It is concentrated primarily in the industrial sector and secondarily in banking and services, with little outreach into the public sector. Yet the influence of UNSITRAGUA extends beyond the confederated unions. As the most progressive confederation, it has opened up political space for all unions. In its battles to defend the rights and demands of associated unions in the private sector, UNSITRAGUA suffered numerous defeats, leaving it weak and with little mobilizing ability among private-sector trade unions. Beginning in 1988 UNSITRAGUA provided critical institutional support for the struggles of CUC farmworkers.

Unable to force management to the bargaining table through strikes, unions associated with UNSITRAGUA have resorted to plant occupations. Such an occupation by Coca-Cola workers in 1984 was brought to a successful conclusion thanks to broad international support for the determined union members. Subsequent occupations have not met with the same success. The seven-month strike at the Acumuladores Víctor factory ended in a union defeat in late 1987 when the company fired union members, reorganized under a new name, and hired nonunion employees. After an 14-month occupation of the Lunafil textile factory in 1988 an accord was reached, but the union was decimated and is only now recovering. In June 1990 the government ended the four-month occupation of the Cavisa glass factory by sending in riot police to remove the protesting workers. The workers were fired and their union was broken.[14] Like the other confederations, UNSITRAGUA's presence has been largely limited to denouncing government actions and policies. Debates both about whether the confederation should participate in social pacts with the government and private sector and about how closely it should ally itself with the antimilitary positions of other UASP members have caused splits within the UNSITRAGUA leadership.

The **General Confederation of Guatemalan Workers** (CGTG), a Christian Democratic labor confederation, was formally established in April 1986 although it had been in the works since 1982. Based largely on public-sector unions, CGTG has been closely tied to the Christian Democratic party. Its financial support comes from the Latin American Confederation of Workers (CLAT) and the Konrad Adenauer Foundation of Germany. The leading figure within CGTG was Julio Celso de León, a longtime Social Christian labor leader, who was replaced in late 1988 by José Pinzón, a CLAT organizer from Costa Rica. Celso de León, who became an associate of the ASIES think tank, has since joined the PSD political party along with ASIES associate Héctor Rosada. Aside from its base among state institutions, CGTG contains some private-sector unions, including those that represent the workers of *La Prensa Libre* and Kern's food-processing company. Intense competition exists between CGTG and CUSG, neither of which will enter a labor coalition to which the other belongs.

Formerly one of the main union groupings within CUSG, the **Central Federation of Guatemalan Workers (FECETRAG)** and its leader, Ismael Barrios, broke with CUSG to form a separate confederation in late 1988. A longtime Social Christian leader, Barrios developed political and personal differences with the Alfaro brothers. FECETRAG has been outspoken in its condemnation of UASP and UNSITRAGUA, which it claims have been infiltrated by insurgents and foreigners.[15]

Formed in 1969, the **Bank and Insurance Workers Federation (FESEBS)** includes 19 unions, several of which joined the federation after 1986, when state financial workers began to organize. FESEBS claims to represent 80 percent of the banking sector, although it includes only one insurance union. The **National Electric Workers Union (STINDE)** is probably the largest and best-organized union in Guatemala. Created in 1985 as the union of the National Electrification Institute (INDE), STINDE has been the repeated target of repression and now faces the likelihood that INDE will be privatized.

Public-sector employees are, in general, better organized than their counterparts in the private sector. During the Christian Democratic government, civil servants were at the forefront of the labor movement. Like STINDE, others joined the UASP coalition, including the **National Teachers Union (STEG)** and the **National Federation of State Workers Unions (FENASTEG)**. Public-sector unions have been widely criticized for focusing too narrowly on their own economic goals rather than using their comparatively privileged position to demand economic changes that would benefit the entire working class and other poor sectors. Many Guatemalans consider public-sector employees to be part of the middle class, and resent them for the corruption that pervades the civil service.

Organizing in the *Maquiladoras*

The booming *maquila* sector, comprising nearly 250 factories and employing as many as 45,000 workers is virtually unorganized.[16] The work force is largely female (75-85 percent) and young, with most workers between 16 and 24 years of age.[17] Attempts to form unions in this sector have been routinely repressed by owners with the support of the government, which has proved reluctant to recognize *maquila* unions and to enforce labor laws.[18]

To prevent union organizing, many factory owners subdivide their operations or incorporate under new names. Others try to preempt unions by imposing *solidarista* associations. When threatened by worker organizing, some *maquila* owners simply fire their employees, replacing them with others eager for the $1.80- to $3.00-per-day jobs. The U.S. owner of the INEXPORT factory (which has assembled garments for Sears, K-Mart, and Montgomery Ward) fired its 180 unionized workers shortly after a collective-bargaining pact was signed in 1988. Similarly, in 1991 union organizers at the Phillips-Van Heusen (PVH) factory were pressured to quit, sparking an international campaign to support worker demands for better pay and working conditions.[19]

Typically, *maquila* workers are young women who work six-day weeks with obligatory but uncompensated overtime. Twelve-hour days are not uncommon, with workers at the Korean-owned Royal-Tex plant charging that in 1990 they were locked inside the factory all night to ensure that a contracted shipment of garments was finished on time. In windowless and unventilated *maquila* factories clogged with cloth dust, workers crouch over sewing machines, sitting on backless stools. Most complain of chronic shoulder and elbow pain and of burning eyes.[20]

Farmworker Struggles

CUC, revived in 1988, remains the largest peasant organization and claims to represent more than a million and a half rural workers.[21] CUC did succeed in pressuring the Cerezo government to raise the rural minimum wage to ten *quetzales* (Q10) a day, but by the end of the first year of the Serrano administration most farmworkers still received between Q4 and Q8 a day.[22] In addition to CUC, other peasant organizations also emerged in the 1980s. Some groups, emboldened by the Pro-Land movement led by Father Andrés Girón, formed to demand land from the Christian Democratic government. For its part, CUSG also sponsors various rural associations, though these are mostly self-help community organizations rather than actual unions. Other peasant organizations include the Highland Campesino Committee (CCDA), Campesino Union of the South (UCS), and the Rural Workers Central (CTC).

Solidarismo: Labor/Owner Cooperation

The 1980s witnessed an upsurge of worker groups called *solidarista* associations. *Solidarismo* is a philosophy of labor/ownership formulated in Costa Rica in 1947, where it has received important support from the Catholic Church, big business, and more recently the U.S. Agency for International Development (AID). Its origins in Costa Rica can be traced to the emphasis placed by the Catholic Church on class cooperation rather than class conflict, or the "harmony between capital and owners."

In practice, *solidarismo* takes the form of financial associations in which workers and businesses form credit cooperatives, food services for workers, and investment projects. Most of the capital used for these projects comes from employee savings and the investment by the company owner of the severance pay due each worker. It is supported by businesses as an alternative to class confrontation, unionism, and collective bargaining. Instead, workers and their employer form a *solidarista* association with the declared objective of pooling resources for their mutual benefit. For the most part, *solidarista* associations do little more than sponsor credit unions and other employee services. At their more advanced stage they may form associated businesses to do contract work for the parent company. Associations frequently start spin-off businesses, such as a bottle-washing venture (created by the PepsiCo association) whose main customer is PepsiCo. Only infrequently are wage levels and working conditions discussed by these *solidarista* groups.

Solidarismo first appeared in Guatemala in 1963. At the behest of business owners, Alvaro Portela, a *solidarista* organizer, helped form the first *solidarista* association in the department of Quiché. The movement did not, however, experience rapid growth until 1983 with the founding of the Guatemalan Solidarista Union (GSU).[23] From only three fledgling associations in 1983, the GSU mushroomed to 223 groups in 1989, and by 1992 boasted of 336 associations with some 100,000 members.[24]

An ever-growing and enthusiastic portion of the Guatemalan private sector regards *solidarismo* as a modern response to the threat of unionization. Rather than simply repressing union activists, businesses can now promote the alternative of *solidarista* associations, as has happened at the Lunafil, Petrosteel, and Duralita factories, on the banana plantations, and at several *maquila* plants, including the U.S.-owned INEXPORT.[25]

Promoted by both U.S. and local corporations and financially backed by AID, *solidarismo* is expanding throughout Central America from its base in Costa Rica.[26] In Guatemala *solidarismo* has been touted not only by businesspeople to counteract unions but also by the army and landowners to combat rural unrest. The Arenas brothers, directors of the national *solidarista* council, installed an association on their coffee estate, La Perla, in northern Quiché. The La Perla Solidarista Association claims it has armed its members to defend the estate against leftist insurgents and that workers themselves have forgone wage hikes so that the association could purchase more weapons. In 1987 the association helped build a 12-kilometer road in this conflictive area, for which the army gave it a plaque noting its appreciation. A *solidarista* association has also been installed in the Las Minas antimony mine in Huehuetenango, a longtime hotbed of labor unrest.

One trait distinguishing *solidarismo* in Guatemala is its attempt to establish employee stock-ownership plans (ESOP). Such plans were introduced by Joseph Recinos, who (in addition to directing a consulting firm that advocates privatization of state corporations) was a counselor to the U.S. Presidential Task Force on Project Economic Justice in Central America headed by Ambassador J. William Middendorf, a member of the rightwing Santa Fe Committee.[27] The ESOP concept proposed by Recinos represents the most advanced stage of *solidarismo* to date and is in place in only a few businesses in Central America.

Although *solidarismo* is in essence an anti-union and antiworker philosophy, *solidarista* associations have provided some benefits to workers and in some cases have improved worker morale by enhancing labor-management cooperation. Instead of simply attacking *solidarismo* as a union-breaking movement, many labor activists in Guatemala recognize that if unions are to compete effectively with *solidarista* associations they will have to provide their members with concrete social and economic benefits. Workers are actively participating in *solidarismo* not necessarily because they agree with its philosophy of labor-management relations, but because the alternative of unionism usually evokes repression and provides few material benefits.

The Business Lobby

The backbone of Guatemala's business elite or oligarchy has historically been the agroexport producers, dominated by the coffee growers. This narrow group, together with associated mercantile interests and foreign investors, traditionally set the economic and political agenda. The feudal-type economy that resulted was challenged for the first time in 1944 when a democratic alliance overthrew General Jorge Ubico. Although the traditional oligarchy, together with the most reactionary political elements in the country, eventually succeeded in crushing the ensuing experiment in capitalist modernization, many of the social and economic reforms of the decade of democracy persisted—such as the creation of a broader economic infrastructure and the encouragement given to new business associations.

Over the last four decades the traditional agroexport oligarchy—inveterately conservative—has remained powerful, although new commercial, financial, and industrial interests have been integrated into oligarchic circles. Although Guatemala now enjoys a broader economic base, the private sector maintains its narrow-minded and self-interested character as well as an unrelenting opposition to economic and social reforms that might threaten its immediate interests.[28]

The Guatemalan business elite is a netherworld where the intrigue of politics and economics intertwine and where differences are often solved by force rather than by negotiation. Historically, the business class has not wedded itself to any one political party; instead, it has regarded itself as a political power in its own right, negotiating directly with the government and military rather than lobbying for its interests indirectly.

Although it sometimes may appear so, the Guatemalan private sector is by no means monolithic. Divisions exist between the historic agroexport families and the new money of families such as Paiz and Castillo. Big businessmen and small entrepreneurs have little in common; and the various business chambers are often split between hard-liners and modernizers, trade liberalizers and protectionists, and merchants and industrialists. An influential sector of modernizers, urging a concerted government-business commitment to nontraditional agricultural and industrial export production, emerged among the private-sector elite in the 1980s. These modernizers, generally operating through new business associations funded by the U.S. Agency for International Development (AID), have also promoted a new rhetoric that equates economic and political freedoms.

Encouraged by a flurry of AID private-sector-strengthening projects, the business elite has become more sophisticated in its self-promotion. This new finesse has often taken the form of cloaking reactionary demands in the rhetoric of democratization. To defend its immediate interests, the private sector has also attempted to popularize neoliberalism, using slogans like "What is good for Business is good for the Country" and "I too am a businessman." In its opposition to tax hikes in 1987, the National Coordinator of Agricultural, Commercial, Industrial, and Financial Associations (CACIF) paid for an advertisement that screamed, "Big Government, Poor People." For its part, the Chamber of Industry reminded Guatemalans: "Private property does not only refer to big capital. Your plot, your house, your car, everything you own are also private property."[29]

In the past, during the long decades of overt military rule, the oligarchy never presented itself as a champion of democracy. But adapting to the new spirit of "democratization," the economic elites have seized the rhetoric of democracy as their own, professing a one-to-one correspondence between democracy and economic freedom. When opposing a government or army initiative, business organizations invariably haul out the constitution, charging that the sacred constitutional and democratic rights of all Guatemalans are being trampled upon. In the name of democracy, the modern business elites attack taxes and increased minimum wages as infringements on their economic freedom.

Private Sector: Front and Center

The business elite, long operating in the shadows of government, assumed an overt role in governing Guatemala with the election of Jorge Serrano. Although Serrano's initial cabinet did include a social democrat and two members of a policy institute associated with the Christian Democratic Party of Guatemala (DCG), it was dominated by representatives of business and private-sector organizations. The Ministry of Agriculture is led by a former director of the country's premier business association (CACIF) and of the leading agricultural pressure group in the late 1980s (Unagro).[30] Similarly, the new heads of the Central Bank, economy ministry, development ministry, and presidential-affairs office were drawn from the business elite.

Never before has the private sector assumed such a direct role in government, as the business-government tensions that characterized the Cerezo years vanish. The business elite, particularly its modernizing vanguard, is not yet content with the status of the private sector in Guatemalan society and politics. Reinvigorated by the ideology of neoliberalism, the private sector is seeking to impose its own political and economic agenda on society as a whole. Since the early 1980s the private sector has been undergoing a process of reorganization and redefinition. As a result of this process, numerous new business associations, policy centers, and development foundations have been formed. The business elite has also permeated areas, such as education, previously considered the exclusive realm of the government or nongovernmental organizations (NGOs). More importantly, the new activism of commercial figures as well as groups in the media and in politics has left traditional political and military elites feeling threatened.[31]

A bit reluctantly at first, the dominant elements of the private sector have come to embrace the principles of neoliberalism, including trade liberalization, privatization of state enterprises, and the promotion of private investment. With the guerrilla threat much diminished and the political left not offering an ideological alternative, business elites have promoted the ideology of free enterprise and the financial bottom line as a political, social, and economic platform. They argue that only by unleashing the productive energy of free enterprise can Guatemala grow economically, thereby benefitting all Guatemalans.

Emerging from the modernizing private sector—consisting largely of nontraditional exporters, technocrats, young entrepreneurs, and their ideological supporters—is a new right wing that is reducing the influence of the old, extremist, and violent right wing.[32] Although all sectors of the business elite recognize the need for security forces that can keep peasant and worker organizations tame and powerless, there are elements within the new right wing that perceive less need for a bloated and repressive military. Instead, the military is increasingly seen as a destabilizing element in that it violates the "rule of law" needed for efficient business and it squanders scarce resources for essentially unproductive purposes while scaring off international investors with its violent image.

This is not to say that challenges to military impunity and support for demilitarization are projects that a cohesive new right wing publicly and unhesitatingly promotes. Rather, in its embrace of neoliberal logic the private sector finds that an uncontrolled military is increasingly counterproductive to creating a state and society ruled by trade and profit imperatives. This effort by the modernizing private sector to distance itself from the military and the extreme right wing is paralleled by a similar estrangement between Washington and extremist anticommunist forces in Guatemala. The abrupt change in U.S. posture on human rights issues was not a function of a nascent sensitivity but rather the result of heightened attention to international economic issues. Rampant political violence and a wildcard military simply are not conducive to free trade and economic stability. Although similarity exists between the policy agendas of Washington and Guatemala's modernizing private sector, there is not total coherence. Within the Guatemalan private sector, as throughout Guatemalan society, there is a strong nationalist streak that resents foreign domination. And while the private sector is quick to criticize the military for any "nation-building" pretensions, it still depends on the armed forces to maintain the social "stability" of a repressed and underpaid work force. It is likely, however, that the private sector would support, at least tacitly, measures to reduce the army and to strengthen a civilian police force that could carry out its repressive functions.

Tensions between the private sector and the military are nothing new. The expansion of the army into state enterprises coupled with personal aggrandizement and land acquisition by individual officers (particularly in the Northern Transverse Strip) set the private sector and the military at loggerheads in the 1970s. Frustrated with the hidebound private sector, military regimes, beginning with that of General Carlos Arana (1970-74), viewed themselves as nation-builders. As such, they backed new road and port infrastructure projects, created new state corporations, and even toyed with state-directed developmentalism through colonization projects and cooperative creation—all the while personally enriching themselves. As if by military dictate, Arana declared that he intended to "modernize capitalism, no matter what the cost."

Although virulent anticommunists, military chieftains have also harbored a reformist philosophy that recognizes the need to widen the economic base of capitalist development. This reformist tendency—and no small measure of political opportunism—helps explain the Christian Democratic Party's support for the Ríos Montt candidacy in 1974. Reformism within the military also gave rise to such agencies as the National Reconstruction Committee, which has overseen development assistance projects in the highlands since its creation in 1976. One after another, Guatemala's military regimes also attempted to modify the tax structure in order to provide more government revenue and to maintain a social services infrastructure while paying the military budget. But all proposals for higher taxes were rejected by the private sector, which was usually able to rally wider public opposition to tax increases.

During the 1980-83 period the military dropped all pretense of state developmentalism or of maintaining a lawful government. Instead, Guatemala became a counterinsurgency state, where the priority was crushing the guerrillas and suppressing all popular dissent. As the country recovered from the upheaval of the early 1980s, and particularly during the Cerezo presidency, ideological differences began to emerge between the private sector and the military high command. Recognizing that political instability and popular rebellion were, in part, functions of poverty, the marginalization of rural and indian society, and the absence of legitimate government, the military adopted a strategy of "democratization" leading to the establishment of civilian rule. This democratization was part of its larger National Security and Development Plan, renamed National Stability during the tenure of Defense Minister Gramajo (see Saving the Nation).

For its part, the business elite, while supporting a return to civilian rule, was concerned that it was being sidelined by a Christian Democratic-military alliance. It repeatedly opposed tax reform and rejected outright the notion that increased revenues were needed to pay a "social debt" to the poor majority. All talk of national stability, social debt, development councils, or higher taxes on income and property was dismissed as "uneconomic thinking." Instead, the private sector counterposed a neoliberal philosophy, taking its lead from several U.S.-funded business associations. In opting for the international neoliberal bandwagon, the business elite discovered a philosophy that not only idolized trade and investment but also provided an ideological framework for the group's social and political doctrine.

Organized Business

The concrete manifestation of private-sector power and influence is embodied in Guatemala's business chambers and associations. These are the representatives and the bureaucracy of the country's elite. Most are organized by type of business, such as industry, commerce, or finance, and have many affiliated members. The largest agroexport producers have organizations of their own, such as the National Association of Coffee Producers (Anacafe). There are also several development foundations, think tanks, and ideological organizations sponsored by the business elite.

In addition to functioning as a lobby for private-sector interests, business groups also play a direct role in policy making through their representation on most government commissions. These include the tourism institute, national wage commission, national export council, national mortgage bank, social security institute, national sugar committee, national environmental committee, coffee policy council, and numerous other commissions.[33]

The commercial sector was the first to organize itself, with the formation of the Guatemalan Chamber of Commerce (CCG) in 1894, but not until the post-World War II era did business associations begin to flourish.[34] Currently there exist over one hundred such groups, most of which are either directly or indirectly represented by the National Coordinator of Agricultural, Commercial, Industrial, and Financial Associations (CACIF).

CACIF, founded in 1961, purports to represent the entire private sector, but it generally acts only on behalf of the country's larger business interests. There were few challenges to CACIF's supremacy until the early 1980s, at which time the dominance of the traditional agroexport and industrial oligarchs began to be questioned by modernizing elements. In the 1983-87 period CACIF almost disintegrated, with different chambers bickering over what should be the unified business response to tax increases proposed by the Ríos Montt and Mejía Víctores regimes. Rather than letting CACIF respond to government proposals as the voice of the entire private sector, leading business chambers began publishing their own *campo pagado* or political advertisements in the daily papers.

Two new business groups, both representative of the modernizing capitalists and neoliberal thought, emerged in the early 1980s. The Enterprise Chamber (CAEM), founded in 1982, includes the same sectoral chambers as CACIF—agriculture, tourism, commerce, finance, and industry—as well as four development foundations that also were established in the early 1980s: the Foundation for Integral Development (Fundap), Guatemala Development Foundation (Fundesa), Technology Foundation (Funtec), and Foundation for Financial Assistance to Development Institutions (Fafides). While CAEM serves as a promotional organization for the private sector, another new business organization called the Free Market Chamber (CLE), founded in 1983, functions as an unabashed proponent of neoliberal thought and policy. Both CAEM and CLE have counted on U.S. financial backing in their drive to create a more effective bureaucratic infrastructure for the private sector.

The fractionalization resulting from the rise of new business groups and the neoliberal challenge was largely smoothed over midway into the Cerezo presidency. It was by then largely an accepted fact that the old models of industrialization and dependence on a few traditional agroexports were obsolescent. As a result, differences between the commercial sector and industrialists over such matters as trade liberalization began to ease. The private sector also became increasingly unified in its opposition to the Cerezo administration, particularly to an attempt to push through tax reforms and a social investment fund. Another unifying factor was the private sector's strong moral support for the counterrevolution against the Sandinista government in Nicaragua.

Crucial in the configuration of business organizations are the various agricultural interest groups. The General Association of Farmers (AGA) includes the country's largest estate owners and has long been one of the most reactionary forces within the private sector. The Agricultural Chamber is a newer and less adamant group of large producers resulting from a 1973 split in AGA. Unlike AGA, the Agricultural Chamber functions as a true business chamber with sectoral members such as the National Cotton Council and the Rubber Producers Association. The two chambers created a coalition called the Union of Agricultural Producers (Unagro) in 1986 to present a unified stance against proposed farmworker wage increases and land redistribution measures. Differences between AGA and the Agricultural Chamber later resulted in Unagro's dissolution. Other major agricultural groups include Anacafe, the coffee-growers club, and Azagua, the powerful association of sugar producers.

In addition to CLE, there are several other private-sector organizations engaged in educational and ideological functions. The oldest of these, Association of the Friends of the Country (Amigos del País), traces its origins back to 1795 but was greatly reinvigorated in 1967. With funds from AID, Friends of the Country has launched a private-sector educational program and is also publishing a history of Guatemala, both of which project the organization's conservative outlook. The Manager's Association of Guatemala (AGG), founded in 1959, offers training programs for businessmen and sponsors forums and speeches on a national level. The influential National Economic Research Center (CIEN), an economic think tank closely associated with CLE, presents detailed studies of major economic and social problems. More ideological than investigative, the Economic and Social Studies Center (CEES) is one of the country's most conservative policy centers. It is associated with Francisco Marroquín University, the private university founded in 1971 that has trained a new crop of young managers and entrepreneurs in neoliberal economic principles and neoconservative political thought. Both CEES and Francisco Marroquín University benefit from U.S. government funding.

An increasingly important business group is the U.S.-funded Guatemalan Nontraditional Exporters Association (Gexport), founded in 1982. Gexport represents more than 750 exporters and is organized by commissions concerned with the promotion of different nontraditional products. Although the Guatemalan private sector has its own identity and dynamism, many large corporations are actually affiliates of transnational corporations and many exporters are closely linked through credit and trading relations to foreign investors. This intermingling of local and foreign-based private sectors merges under the American Chamber of Commerce, established in 1967 in Guatemala City.[35]

Only recently has the business elite concerned itself with small and micro enterprises. Recognizing that the informal sector was expanding and worried that foreign development programs and government were gaining influence over these businesses, CAEM together with Funtec created the System of Microenterprises soon after the Cerezo government initiated the Federation of Small and Medium Businesses (FEPYME).

Most of Guatemala's private sector is represented in an obscure umbrella committee called the Greater Association of Presidents (APA), which (under the auspices of CACIF) brings together the directors not only of CACIF's own member organizations but also of the ideological and promotional groups and foundations as well as CAEM.[36] The APA provides an image of unity to the private sector, and in most instances the business elite is indeed unified. But tensions and divisions continue to break out particularly between the new right or modernizing business community and the more traditional sector.

Limits of Neoliberalism

Although a neoliberal economic philosophy accents the rhetoric of today's business lobby, the private sector is, as a whole, more pragmatic than ideological. Except for a small faction of intellectuals, neoliberalism is more an instrument of attack than a set of operating principles. Business adopts the rhetoric of neoliberalism only when its suits its interests—as in its opposition to government price controls. Rather than calling for the complete liberalization of the economy and the elimination of all government intervention, the business class demands that the state function as its servant. As CACIF is well aware, many elements within the private sector depend on government intervention and investment. Sugar producers, for example, profit from high domestic price levels set by the government. Domestic industry still relies on government protections, and the construction industry is propped up by public-sector investment. Even the export sector, while espousing neoliberalism, often pressures the government to expand those public-sector services (infrastructure, irrigation projects, marketing and credit assistance) that augment export production.

When its immediate interests are threatened, the private sector in Guatemala is not accustomed to compromise. It accepted Cerezo's policy of *concertación* only when the government adopted private-sector recommendations—while rejecting all measures designed to meet the demands of the poor majority. Although trying to maintain some semblance of policy independence, the Cerezo administration consistently bowed to the demands of CACIF. But it has never bowed low enough for CACIF's liking. Curiously, when the Serrano administration announced its intention to seek a social pact among business, labor, and government, the private sector—led by its modernizing wing—seemed more receptive to an agreement with labor and the popular movement that would enhance social stability than it had been when such steps were suggested by Cerezo. Having set the economic direction of the new administration, the business elite at least initially appeared willing to negotiate on such matters as minimum wage increases and electricity rate hikes.

Both the government and CACIF agree that private-sector investment needs to be the motor of national economic growth. But that investment has not been forthcoming, despite an abundance of ready capital in the nation's private banks and a cascade of government incentives including the elimination of export taxes and liberalization of prices. Traditionally, the private sector in Guatemala declines to invest its own money in productive ventures, preferring instead to rely on government and foreign credit.

What little investment the private sector has demonstrated has been in areas where its way has been paved with subsidies and incentives provided by the government and AID. Only in construction—the traditional piggybank of the rich—has the private sector shown any real inclination to invest. Instead of sinking capital into the future of Guatemala, the private sector, thus far, has tended to blame the government for its failure to provide a secure investment climate. With starvation wages, a terrorized labor sector, and an array of new incentives to promote private-sector investment, one might ask what more CACIF could need to be satisfied.

Bolstered by the tenets of neoliberal philosophy and the private-sector development theories proffered by AID, modern oligarchs say, instead, that the type of reformism needed in Guatemala is of an economic, not social, character—namely reforms designed to strengthen their immediate financial prospects within the traditional context of an export economy. In their demand for economic reforms (reduced export taxes, investment incentives, privatization, liberalized prices, etc.), there is a coincidence of interests among most private-sector factions. Differences among the business community emerge around such issues as devaluation (advocated by coffee producers but opposed by those businesses relying more on imports), free trade (favored by the commercial sector but feared by industrialists who produce mainly for the domestic market), and wage hikes (vehemently opposed by most businessmen but seen as necessary by more forward-looking modernizers).

By no means are these modernizers all squeaky-clean entrepreneurs following the principles of free trade and demanding an end to government corruption. In the Guatemalan tradition of seeking easy, short-term profits, many have little respect for the niceties of the law when money is at stake. In 1992, not satisfied with the return on broccoli exports, one exporting firm was discovered shipping cocaine along with the frozen vegetables to the United States. Money laundering and foreign-exchange speculation are other "modern" business activities in Guatemala.

There does exist a small, silent minority of businessmen professing interests tied to an expansion of the domestic market. These entrepreneurs, who feel stifled both by the lack of a large domestic base of consumers and by the monopoly control of the private-sector elite, would support the kind of economic and social reforms needed to modernize the Guatemalan economy. But to articulate such social-democratic sentiments is regarded as treasonous among the private sector and, in some cases, has spelled death sentences for these would-be reformers.

Business and Politics Mix

It was not until the late 1980s that the elite business community began to take a direct interest in politics. Previously, the private sector had been content with wielding its influence from the sidelines in deals worked out with the politicians and the military. The most reactionary elements, usually old agroexport families, frequently lent their financial support to rightwing extremists within the military or political arena.

Caught up in the neoliberal wave, where economics and politics merge, the private sector has in recent years adopted a different view regarding its place on the political stage. Determined to prevent the reelection of a Christian Democratic government, an oligarchic clique under the auspices of CACIF formed the secretive Pyramid Club, designed to back the presidential candidate most likely to bow to a private-sector agenda and with the best chances of winning. This elite group selected Jorge Carpio of the National Union Center (UCN). In an attempt to keep a pulse on the electorate and on changes in the political climate, private-sector interests associated with CLE and the daily *Siglo Veintiuno* also sponsored a series of opinion polls. Not until late in the campaign was it discovered that public opinion was swinging sharply in favor of dark horse Jorge Serrano. In a post-election evaluation of its electoral strategy, Pyramid Club associates reportedly decided that although they had misjudged the political scene, their strategy of selecting and supporting a candidate was sound. All that was lacking for future elections was better preparation in terms of a media strategy and opinion surveys. In the meantime, anticipating the 1995 elections, the task before the business elite is to ensure that there is no resurgence of the Christian Democratic Party and that no viable center-left popular coalition develops.

PART 5

Social Sectors and Institutions

© Derrill Bazzy

Women and Feminism

The women's movement in Guatemala is the least developed in Central America, both in terms of organizing at the popular level and among educated women.[1] The profoundly conservative and patriarchal nature of Guatemalan society, along with its stark class, ethnic, and cultural divisions, have slowed the development of feminism and women's organizations. Male leaders accuse women who place a priority on gender-specific issues of creating unnecessary divisions within the popular movement. The history of repression against all forms of popular organizing is another important retarding factor. In a society of such economic deprivation and political violence, gender-specific concerns have long been ignored.

During the 1944-54 period of economic and political reforms, Guatemalan women first began organizing. In 1945, women obtained the right to vote. The Guatemalan Women's Alliance, an organization of teachers and other working women, was also formed during those years. But the military coup of 1954 brought a violent conclusion to this decade of democracy, halting as well the advance of women's organizing. In the late 1960s, another women's group formed and was named after Dolores Bedoya, a heroine of the country's independence movement. This new group, however, was an association of professionals and upper-class women with few connections to the popular sectors. Among the earliest women's groups comprising poor and middle-class women were the Housewives Clubs (Clubes de Amas de Casa), which encouraged women to improve household conditions and family health through educational programs and events.

In 1975, at the beginning of a new stage of popular organizing, the Women's Solidarity in Action committee flowered briefly. Another fleeting attempt, the National Women's Union (UNAMG), disbanded shortly after its founding in 1980 due to the intensifying violence of the Lucas García regime. Those women's organizations that did exist were mostly associations of upper-class women who met for charitable or professional purposes rather than to organize for social change.

The advent of the Cerezo government opened up political space for serious popular organizing, and women took advantage of this opportunity to form human rights organizations and groups concerned specifically with the situation of women. In addition, the new administration's placement of women in high government positions played a role in increasing feminist consciousness in Guatemala. The Mutual Support Group (GAM), a human rights organization directed principally by women, has succeeded in focusing international concern on continued human rights violations and on the plight of widows.

In 1988 GAM was joined by another women's human rights organization called the National Coordinator of Guatemalan Widows (CONAVIGUA), whose directors and members are mostly indian widows of the murdered and disappeared. According to indian leader Rigoberta Menchú, CONAVIGUA is "the first organization in all the 500 years of Guatemala that was born of indigenous women. It is an organization so powerful that the indigenous women can channel the convictions of thousands of other Guatemalan women."

Another step forward for the women's movement in the 1980s was the creation in 1986 of the GRUFEPROMEFAM, a women's organization linked to the UNSITRAGUA union confederation. From its inception as an auxiliary organization to raise political consciousness among the wives of union activists, GRUFEPROMEFAM quickly expanded to include union women and later women from all popular sectors. Its agenda is closely linked to the popular movement, but includes a distinct focus on gender issues, one being to formulate a history of women's organizing in Guatemala. The success of the First Conference of Guatemalan Women Workers, which GRUFEPROME-FAM sponsored in 1989, encouraged the organization to seek new ties with the popular movement and to strengthen its links with the women's movement in other Central American countries.

Between 1988 and 1992 gender-specific issues were brought to the public attention by several new feminist groups, including the Association of Guatemalan Women, Tierra Viva Women's Group, Network Against Violence Against Women, Women's Committee of Guatemalan Food Workers Union (COMFUITAG), and the Guatemalan Women's Group. In 1990 the Support Center for Domestic Workers (CENTRACAP) was founded to offer alternative job training, literacy classes, and shelter for domestic laborers fired without notice. For their efforts the CENTRACAP activists received death threats and were ordered to leave the country.

In the universities and within the popular movement gender-specific concerns, such as discrimination, sexual harassment, and violence against women, have arisen. Although lacking the focus of a centralized feminist movement, numerous small organizations and mutual-support groups have emerged, some of them with the capacity to deliver public statements and make demands. Within many sectors of the popular movement—land squatters, the displaced, human rights, and religious communities—women form the base and in many cases the leadership. Supported mostly by the United Nations, the government's National Office on Women (ONAM), part of the labor ministry, provides information about the state of women in Guatemala and is promoting sorely needed changes in the country's civil and labor codes that discriminate against women.[2]

In recent years women have assumed a more visible role in the political life of Guatemala although they remain poorly represented in national and local governments (Figure 5a). Among those who have carved a new niche for women in Guatemala are Catalina Soberanis, 1991 president of the National Congress; Rigoberta Menchú, representative of the Campesino Unity Committee (CUC) and the RUOG; and Nineth de García, leader of GAM.

Breaking the Silence on Harassment and Battering

The increase of women in the work force and the rise in women's organizations in Guatemala have resulted in an expanding awareness of the problems of sexual harassment and female battering. Battering of women occurs at all social levels—among rich and poor, in the factory and university. There is little statistical information on battering but what is available is shocking. In 1991 a doctor concerned about the problem discovered that three-quarters of women treated for injuries at his hospital had been beaten by their spouses.[3] A survey in Antigua, one of the wealthiest towns, found that 48 percent of women interviewed had on at least one occasion been a victim of male aggression.[4] According to ONAM, four of every ten women murdered are killed by their husbands. There are no government services for battered women. One women's group, however, opened a small shelter for battered women in 1991.

A group formed by women professors has denounced sexual harassment at the national university, while members of the university's blue-collar work force have charged that male superiors and co-workers have physically assaulted them. In the *maquila* industry, women sewing machine operators have denounced beatings and sexual harassment by male factory managers. Particularly in the Korean-run factories, these practices are routine and considered by the Korean bosses as part of their management technique.[5]

Incest and rape have long been a hidden part of family life in Guatemala. As traditional cultural and community life erodes and lawlessness spreads, Guatemalan women are also increasingly subject to violent assaults and rape outside the home. Battering and sexual harassment of women have only recently become publicly discussed issues. To a large extent they are still regarded as family or

Figure 5a

Women in Statistics

Government

National Assembly	6 of 116 seats
Local government	3 of 330 mayors
Women as percentage of registered voters	40%

Economy

% of union members	9%
% of cooperative members	20%
% of active work force	24%
% of informal sector	56%
% of Guatemala City work force	38%
% of working women who head households	21%

Education

Female (15 years or more) illiteracy	64%
% women who finish primary school	42%
% women who finish secondary school	9%
% women who finish university	1%

Health

Life expectancy	67 (women); 62 (men)
Mortality rate	9 of 1000 women annually
Maternal death rate (5th leading cause of death among females age 15-44)	2 per 1000
% of deliveries in medical centers	23%
% of deliveries by trained midwives	43%
% of deliveries by untrained midwives	34%
% of mothers receiving prenatal care	38%

SOURCES: Instituto Nacional de Estadística (1987); Organización de la Mujer (1991); *Política nacional para el desarrollo y promoción de la mujer en Guatemala* (Guatemala City: Oficina Nacional de la Mujer, August 1990); UNICEF, *Análisis de situación del niño y la mujer* (Guatemala City: August 1991).

cultural matters not subject to legal or governmental action. But as women's groups begin to speak out against the culture of violence and intimidation against women, progress is being made in recognizing the prevalence of household violence, rape, and sexual harassment on the job in Guatemala.

As yet unaddressed—either by women's organizations, the government, or human rights activists—is the issue of abortion. Illegal and widely condemned by the Catholic Church, abortion is nonetheless commonly practiced. Owing to the clandestine and unclinical circumstances in which it is usually performed, abortion is a major cause of female mortality, accounting for 10-50 percent of maternal deaths. At Guatemala City's municipal hospital, three of every eight maternity cases suffer from complications due to induced abortion.[6] Still, at only $25 per back-street visit, abortion is a relatively cheap and common form of birth control.

The topic of birth control itself is little discussed on a public level, due mainly to the influence of the Catholic Church and the traditional nature of Guatemalan society. Among couples birth control is largely regarded as a "female problem" and the use of male contraceptives is uncommon. A study by the Family Improvement Association (APROFAM) in the mid-1980s revealed that only 25 percent of women of child-bearing age were practicing birth control (other than those relying on natural birth control as advocated by the Catholic Church). More than 40 percent of those surveyed had been surgically sterilized—most apparently at the time of their last childbirth.[7] Because of the lack of education about other birth control methods and the reluctance of men to use contraceptives, sterilization continues to be a leading, if not the most common, form of birth control practiced in Guatemala.

Within the popular movement and the revolutionary left, birth control programs are regarded with great suspicion. Educational efforts by APROFAM and other family-planning groups have been denounced by leftists as part of a conspiracy by U.S. imperialism in league with the local elite to reduce the threat represented by the poor majority and indian population. Foreign financing, especially from the United States, for APROFAM has been compared to eugenic projects sponsored by the Nazis in the 1930s to eliminate undesirable portions of society and promote the white race. Referring to birth control programs, one prominent organization of Guatemalan leftists asserted that "the intentions and objectives of the dominant groups have been basically the same as the Nazis."[8]

Along with the Catholic Church, the political left has charged that women, especially poor indian women, have been involuntarily sterilized. It is common wisdom within the dogmatic left that U.S.

support for birth control is primarily motivated by a counterinsurgency logic—that it is better to kill children in the uteruses of Guatemalan mothers than to face growing guerrilla challenges. It is argued that the high fecundity of Guatemalan women is more the product of economic necessity—more children mean more sources of income and labor for peasant families—than a result of lack of education and access to birth control methods. Furthermore, the left in Guatemala has historically contended that if land were justly distributed, enough wealth would be generated to ensure the welfare of the entire peasant population.[9]

Women at Work

Conditions facing Guatemalan women are among the worst in the hemisphere. Nowhere else in Latin America are illiteracy rates so high for women. War in the early 1980s and the deepening economic crisis have aggravated the socioeconomic conditions in which women live and work. Although more men died as a result of the army's counterinsurgency campaign, the majority of the country's refugees and internally displaced are women.[10]

To maintain themselves and their families, more women have entered the work force (economically active population). Since 1981 the percentage of women in the work force has nearly doubled; about one of every four workers are now female. Participation of women in the informal sector has exploded—soaring 13 percent a year (9 percent for males). In Guatemala City, 38 percent of the economically active population is female. The formal sector employs 61 percent of these women, 33 percent create jobs in the informal sector, 4 percent work as domestic help, and 2 percent are employed in other activities.[11] Some 275,000 girls and women work as domestic help, most toiling 12-14 hours daily earning less than minimum wage and enjoying no government protections or benefits such as social security.

Earning their own income affords women more freedom, but their own household work must still be done as well. UNICEF has estimated that most housewives in Guatemala work 15-16 hours a day. In rural areas, many women spend as many as five hours daily preparing tortillas. In both urban and rural areas, women find that they now have to find ways to work a double shift—one to earn income and a second unpaid one in their own homes.

The labor bind that women experience is clearly manifested in the agriculture sector. In general, women constitute only a small portion—11 percent—of the agricultural work force, mostly in basic grains and coffee. In the production of such nontraditional crops as snow peas, however, women constitute about a third of employees, averaging 20 percent in other nontraditionals. Commonly women's work is unpaid in family and cooperative enterprises. When women are paid for agricultural work they often receive less than men even when they perform the same or higher skilled work. Women employed in quality control for agribusinesses are often paid less than men who do physical labor, such as carrying bundles of produce.[12] In many indian communities, where land is the most prized possession, women are not property owners and only sons can inherit family land.

Within the home, both *ladino* and indian women suffer from pervasive *macho* behavior by male household members. The conflictive state of gender relations in highland Guatemala is reflected in an old riddle that asks: "How is a husband like an avocado?" The answer: "A good one is hard to find." Good or not, Guatemalan women seek out male partners for their economic survival. The devaluation of childcare and homemaking along with the marginalization of women in the cash economy contribute, according to a social anthropologist studying Guatemalan gender relations, to a belief that men are "valuable scarce resources who can misbehave with impunity, assured that their wives and mistresses need them for economic reasons more than men need women."[13]

Recent integration of indian communities into commercial activities has for the most part degraded the position of women and bolstered male dominance. Men tend to be the major beneficiaries of entrepreneurial activities, new labor markets, and other sources of cash income. Traditional economic survival patterns that relied on female labor in such activities as grain processing and preparing agricultural produce for market have been disrupted as men have come to dominate cooperatives and commercial weaving businesses in the past two decades. Because of their reduced economic profile within the household, women have been increasingly victimized by abandonment, mistreatment, and parallel marriages.[14]

Unequal by Law

The Guatemalan constitution recognizes the equality of women, stating that "man and woman, irrespective of their civil status, have equal rights and responsibilities." Nevertheless, the governing statutes and legal practice blatantly discriminate against women. Under the labor code, women and children are considered separately from men; under the civil code, the male is recognized as the legal representative of a married couple while the woman is relegated to the care of children and other domestic chores. The civil code also grants the husband the right to deny his wife from participating in activities outside the home. In addition, the code gives the husband prime authority in disposing of joint property. Under the penal code an adulterous man can only be penalized if he has a mistress living within the family house. For females, the legal marrying age is 14 years—two less than for males. The statutes also include such reverse discrimination as a wife's right to inherit her dead husband's social security benefits, but not vice versa.[15]

Under consideration by Congress in early 1992 were revisions in the country's statutes that would improve the legal status of Guatemalan women. But even if passed, such provisions would be difficult to enforce given the inefficiency of the country's judicial system, the depth of male domination in Guatemalan society, and the weak state of feminism and women's groups.

Health and Welfare

Guatemala is a patently unhealthy place, ranking as the Central American nation with the highest infant and child mortality rates, the lowest life expectancy, the most malnourished population, and the lowest level of public health expenditures (Figure 5b). In contrast, Costa Ricans, who have benefited from traditionally higher levels of government spending on health and education, enjoy an average life expectancy nearly ten years more than Guatemalans and a child mortality rate one-fifth that of Guatemala.

Mainly due to foreign aid and the work of nongovernmental organizations health statistics markedly improved during the 1960s and 1970s, but war and economic crisis combined with the budget cutting of the Cerezo and Serrano administrations have contributed to worsening health conditions in recent years. Since 1988 moderate and severe malnutrition rates among children under five in many areas have nearly doubled.[16] During a 1991 vaccination campaign in rural areas medical workers found that 76 percent of all children were malnourished and 41 percent were severely malnourished. So severe and widespread are hunger, malnutrition, and illness in Guatemala that they can only be described as a type of social violence. Even at the height of the counterinsurgency campaign in the early 1980s, more Guatemalans were dying of malnutrition and preventable disease than from political strife.

The overall averages, as appalling as they are, mask the alarming disparities between Indian and *ladino* health. Life expectancy for non-indian men is 65 years, and 64 years for non-indian women. But indian males can expect to live only 48 years, and indian women only 47 years. While the national average for underheight children is 37 percent, the average soars to above 60 percent in many indian villages: San Marcos La Laguna (92 percent), San Pedro La Laguna (76 percent), and Santa María de Jesus (68 percent).[17] According to World

Bank estimates, malnutrition has worsened over the past two decades.[18]

The two top causes of death in Guatemala are gastrointestinal and respiratory infections brought on by malnutrition and poor sanitary conditions that stem primarily from a lack of potable water.[19] A leading cause of death for Guatemalan children is measles due to the large number of unvaccinated children in the country. During a 1986

Figure 5b

Health in Statistics

Life expectancy	63.4 years; 69.5 years (Latin America)
Mortality rate per 1000	8.9; 7.4 (Latin America)
Access to potable water	61% (nation); 43% (rural); 92% (urban)
Access to sewage facilities	59% (nation); 52% (rural); 72% (urban)
Homes without interior plumbing	54% (Guatemala City)

Health Care Access

Doctors per 10,000 people	
nation	7.3
Alta and Baja Verapaz	1.1
Guatemala City	28
% of doctors working in Guatemala City area	80%
% of nurses working in Guatemala City area	56%
% of hospital beds in Guatemala City	46%
% population served by health care	54%
% private	14%
% Guatemalan Social Security Institute (IGSS)	15%
% Ministry of Health	25%

Budget

Government health budget as % of GDP	1.9% (1980); 1.0% (1990)
% of government health budget for infrastructure and equipment	46% (1980); 34% (1988)
Government health budget as % of total budget	12.5% (1980); 9.4% (1991)
% of health budget spent in Guatemala City	67%
% of health budget spent maintaining hospitals	80%

Nutrition

% of population with vitamin A deficiency	
children	9%
women	19%

visit to Guatemala, the regional director of UNICEF addressed this tragedy of preventable death, lamenting: "Guatemala has the worst infant mortality rate in Central America. Every day 115 Guatemalan children under five—that's five children every hour—die from such diseases as diphtheria, whooping cough, tetanus, measles, or polio."[20] Fifteen percent of Guatemalan children suffer from eye diseases, and one of every six afflicted children is blind.[21]

% of population with iodine deficiency	
urban women	37%
rural women	23%
all teenagers	13%
Malnutrition in children under 3 years	60%

Infant Health

Principal causes of infant mortality: diarrhea (30%), respiratory infections (23%), and perinatal (childbirth) problems (20%).

Infant mortality per 1000 live births	
national	66
Western highlands	84
Child mortality (under five years) per 1000	102
Number of pediatric hospitals	0
% of child mortality from preventable diseases	80%
% of children under three years with low weight	
national	34%
Western highlands	46%
ladino	29%
indian	41%
% of children under three years with low height	
ladino	48%
indian	72%
% of children under five malnourished as measured by weight/height deficit	
Guatemala	58%
Costa Rica	6.4%
born of indian mothers	72%
born of illiterate mothers	68%
Western highlands	75%

SOURCES: *Situación alimentaria nutricional de Guatemala* (Guatemala City: IN-CAP and OPS, March 1991); *Human Development* (UN Program for Development, 1991); *Análisis de la situación: Guatemala* (UNICEF: May 1991); *World Bank, Social Investment Funds in Guatemala, Honduras, and El Salvador* (1991).

Health care facilities are of notoriously poor quality in Guatemala. Only the wealthy and the military enjoy reasonably good health care. Two government agencies, the Ministry of Public Health and Social Assistance (MSPAS) and the Guatemalan Social Security Institute (IGSS), administer the government's health care budget. Although there is a social security system, it covers only 15 percent of the total population, or one-quarter of the active work force. Even if a person is covered by social security or does have some income to pay for health care, the country's clinics and hospitals are extremely underbudgeted, understaffed, and undersupplied. With the help of foreign aid hundreds of health posts and centers have been constructed in rural areas, but at least 100 of the 735 health posts that exist have never been put into operation for lack of equipment, medical staff, and medicines. Yet another deficiency of the health care system in Guatemala is its concentration on curative rather than preventive health care—as illustrated by the fact that four out of five *quetzales* designated by the government for health care are spent in maintaining hospitals.[22]

During the 1980s the government's health care budget was repeatedly slashed, even though it was already one of the lowest in the hemisphere at the beginning of the decade. At a public hospital in Guatemala City in 1992 there was only one doctor on duty to handle all deliveries, emergencies, and surgery for 200 hospital patients. Government officials themselves acknowledge that only five of the country's hospitals provide adequate services and that at least half the medical equipment in the country's hospitals is in poor or nonworking condition. To feed their patients, hospitals generally rely on foreign food aid and on food brought by families. Besides the lack of food, equipment, staff, and medicines, public hospitals in Guatemala City have also had to restrict service for lack of sufficient water and laundry services. Workers at one Guatemala City hospital erected a banner explaining: "This is not a strike. There is no budget."

Government health officials have largely ignored the public health threat of AIDS, leaving public education about the disease to a couple of underfunded nongovernmental organizations. In the mid-1980s when the first AIDS patient died in Guatemala, the government—in a fit of nationalism—claimed that the disease was limited to foreigners and to those who had contact with them. In subsequent years the government continued to downplay the health problem represented by AIDS, undercounting those infected with the disease and charging that infections were limited to those who had sex abroad and to homosexuals. The national commission established to monitor the disease has consistently underrepresented the portion of heterosexuals and intravenous drug users among those infected with HIV.

Since the mid-1980s there have been more than five hundred AIDS cases reported, although nongovernmental sources estimate that the number of HIV-infected people could be as high as 70,000-100,000.[23] More than half of those infected are heterosexuals, as many as one-fifth are intravenous drug users, and less than 5 percent contracted the virus outside the country. Due to sparse use of contraceptives, AIDS and other sexually transmitted diseases can quickly spread in Guatemala. According to the Guatemalan Red Cross, 70 percent of Guatemalans do not use contraceptives. Opposition by the Catholic Church coupled with the government's own lack of commitment to health education and population control retard expanded AIDS awareness in Guatemala.

Similarly, the government has been slow to acknowledge the threat of cholera, even though Guatemala was the first Central American country to experience an outbreak of the infection in recent times and is the country where the disease is advancing the most rapidly. When a teenage boy died after eating cholera-infected shrimp from the Naranjo River, the government claimed that he had drowned, even though his father was also affected by the same cholera symptoms.[24] The widespread lack of sanitation facilities and potable water leave Guatemala particularly vulnerable to the spread of cholera, which by early 1991 had killed more than three dozen people in the departments of Sololá, San Marcos, and Retalhuleu. The last time cholera struck Guatemala was in the late 1850s, killing more than 12,000 people.

Stepping in to fill the health care gap in Guatemala have been numerous foreign humanitarian and religious organizations. In the absence of a national nutrition strategy and a preventive health program, many private organizations have mounted their own efforts. But because of the uncoordinated and distributive character of these private undertakings they have also largely failed to seriously address the country's deplorable state of health. One exception has been the Maryknoll project in Huehuetenango, which for the last 25 years has been training health care promoters. Like other endeavors that incorporate a certain degree of community empowerment and popular education, the Maryknoll project was hard hit by counterinsurgency terror as over 160 health promoters either fled the country, quit, or were killed between 1981 and 1989. Another group working to improve the health status of rural Guatemalans through popular-education techniques is ASECSA, a community health organization based in Chimaltenango.

Medical workers assume great political risk in Guatemala. Doctors, nurses, medical students, and health care promoters are prime targets for repression. Medical neutrality is not respected by the government, which has failed to ratify the Geneva Conventions on the safety of medical personnel. From 1980 to 1988 there were 125 cases of serious violations of medical neutrality, including the killing and disappearance of medical students, health professionals, and patients (abducted from medical facilities and killed). During this same period some 500 health promoters were killed or disappeared.[25]

Schools and Students

Education is a privilege in Guatemala. With a 48 percent rate of literacy, Guatemala is the least-educated society in Central America (Figure 5c). Among children ages 7 to 14, more than four of every ten do not attend school. Of those who do attend, less than 20 percent finish the sixth grade. Most rural schools do not even extend beyond the third grade, and about 40 percent of Guatemalan primary schools are unitary schools that do not have different classrooms or teachers for different grades. Although there is no tuition charged for elementary education, the high cost of books and materials as well as transportation discourage higher enrollment in rural areas.

The Ministry of Education has set as its goal for the year 2000 an 80 percent literacy rate and an 80 percent enrollment rate for primary schools. Numerous nongovernmental organizations have joined with the government in mounting adult literacy campaigns, but the combination of economic crisis, inadequate government spending, and high fertility rates mitigate against their efforts. Unless dramatic measures are implemented, the literacy rate may sink to 40 percent by the mid-1990s.

Increasingly the depressing state of education is being recognized as a national crisis. Realizing that economic modernization will be impossible without an educated populace, the business community has demanded that the Ministry of Education improve its services. Overcentralization, a top-heavy bureaucracy, and an unmotivated teacher corps are among the Ministry's problems. But neither decentralization nor the efficiency strategies announced by the Serrano administration address the chief obstacle to better education in Guatemala—insufficient budgetary resources. During the 1980s the government did raise teachers' salaries, although far short of what they demanded. However, the investment budget for education was slashed by half, meaning that no new schools were built and school facilities were left to deteriorate. Students themselves, led by

Figure 5c
Education in Statistics

Literacy (over 15 years)	48%
Rural literacy	28%
Indian literacy	23%
Average schooling	2.9 years

Enrollment

% enrolled in preschool	26%
% enrolled in primary school	
nation	58%
Western highlands	38%
% enrolled in secondary schools	16%
% enrolled in postsecondary schools	1%
% of students enrolled in first grade who finish primary school	
urban	27%
rural	15%
% of primary school students who repeat first grade	25%
% of primary school students who quit school during first grade	15%
% of primary school students who finish 6-year cycle in 6 years	34%
% of handicapped (physically or mentally) who receive education	2%

Teachers

Average number of teachers in primary schools (first six years)	
Nation	3.7
Guatemala City	8.4
Western highlands	2.3
Unemployed teachers	30,000
% of schools operated by private sector	25%
% of teachers employed by private sector	62%

Budget

UN-recommended minimum % of GDP to be dedicated by government to education budget	5-7%
% of Guatemalan GDP spent on education	2.4% (1980); 1.7% (1990)
% of Costa Rican GDP spent on education in 1990	10%
% of national budget spent on education	15.8% (1980); 13.5% (1911)
% of national education budget spent in Guatemala City	71%
Decline in funds dedicated for investment in construction and upkeep of schools in 1981-89 period	-52%

SOURCES: *Análisis de situación: Guatemala* (Guatemala City: UNICEF, May 1991); Ministry of Education (1992); National Statistics Institute (1990); SEGE-PLAN (Guatemala City: 1991).

the Coordinator of Middle School Students (CEEM), have increasingly responded to this inattention by occupying schools and joining street demonstrations to demand new school rooms, equipment, and the filling of vacant teaching posts.

National University and its Continuing Crisis

The University of San Carlos (USAC), the national university, has long enjoyed a reputation as one of the best universities in Latin America. Founded in 1676 by Dominican priests, it was the first (and, until the 1800s, the only) university in Central America. The university has served as a vanguard and barometer of the popular movement, and in its activist phases has accordingly been a prime target of government repression. Like many other Latin American universities, it functions as an autonomous institution with its own governing body and budget.

USAC's history of social activism began in 1944 when its students, professors, and workers expressed strong support for the junta that overthrew dictator Jorge Ubico. By the end of the subsequent ten-year window of democracy, however, USAC had evolved into a center of opposition to the Arbenz government with law professors and students publishing strong denunciations of the government's agrarian-reform program, claiming that the expropriations violated the property rights of the affected landowners. Yet after 1954, USAC became a leading source of leftist and antimilitary criticism.

In the 1960s many students graduated directly from youth clubs and political discussion groups into the ranks of the guerrillas. A leftist critique continued to dominate student thinking at USAC during the 1970s, a time when its academic prestige peaked. But repression leveled against USAC professors and students plunged the university into academic decline. The violence reached its zenith between 1980 and 1982 during the Lucas García regime, when hundreds of students and professors were killed. As a result of this siege, the nature and quality of instruction at USAC changed dramatically. Most courses that involved social criticism were dropped from the curriculum, and many of the best professors were either killed or forced into exile. Progressive university rectors and deans gave way to conservative, less academically qualified replacements.

Student Movement Revives

After 1983 the student movement, decimated during the Lucas García years, gradually came back to life. The University Students

Association "Oliverio Casteñeda de León" (AEU), the elected student organization, is attempting to reclaim its former role in the popular movement. Founded in 1920, the AEU now includes the name of an assassinated student leader in its full designation. A wall mural on the USAC campus, commemorating the 1978 murder of Oliverio Casteñeda, admonishes: "You can massacre our leaders, but as long as the people exist, there will be revolution."

Being a student activist is a risky undertaking, as the elaborate security measures adopted by the AEU testify. Security checks and a system of unspecified meeting places are responses to the frightening history of persecution of AEU leaders. The disappearance of members of AEU's executive committee in 1984 forced the organization underground. In 1987 its executive secretary was murdered. Despite the repression, the AEU emerged from the shadows in 1988 and joined the UASP popular coalition and began playing a major role in the National Dialogue. AEU activism encompasses economic-justice issues, human rights concerns, labor solidarity, and student issues. On the USAC campus, the AEU provides critical support for the workers' union, while aggressively demanding better quality education and more socially relevant studies. In 1988 it stood firmly behind a strike by secondary students who had organized to gain better school facilities and an increased education budget.

In March 1989 the entire AEU government council received death threats, with repression against student activists reaching a new peak in August 1989 when 11 students were disappeared. By September 1989 only three of the 16 members of the AEU directorate remained, the others having been killed, disappeared, exiled, or in hiding. The killing of yet another AEU leader in 1991 seemed designed by the army as a reminder to students that their activities were being closely watched. The ongoing repression has been at least partially successful in disrupting AEU activities and keeping the AEU from playing a leading role in the popular movement.

Dating back to 1898, the Huelga de Dolores has been the most prominent manifestation of student dissent in Guatemala. The tradition, originated by medicine and law students at the national university during the Estrada Cabrera dictatorship, includes the election of an "ugly king" (and a queen for the first time in 1992), street theater, and a costume parade through the streets of Guatemala. Providing the Guatemalan version of carnival, students organize parades during Palm Sunday week in Guatemala City, Quetzaltenango, and other cities. These parades, while part student exuberance, have also served as an important outlet for political and social dissidence. This dual focus is reflected in the clandestine paper *No nos tientes* (*Don't Tempt Us*), published each year by the Huelga de Dolores organizing committee, including revolutionary poems and analysis in addition to the sarcastic humor so characteristic of the Huelga de Dolores tradition.[26]

The Huelga de Dolores has repeatedly fallen victim to government repression. In 1903 the police interrupted the beginning of the *huelga*, killing one student and silencing the tradition until 1920 when students resurrected *No nos tientes* and renewed the Huelga de Dolores parade a year later. Early in his dictatorship in 1931, Jorge Ubico outlawed the publication of *No nos tientes*. Students that persisted with the parade were beaten and shot at by the police, silencing the Huelga de Dolores until 1945. In 1962 during the Ydígoras Fuentes regime the celebration of the Huelga de Dolores ended in a rout by the security forces in which three students were killed. The subsequent military regime, headed by Enrique Peralta Azurdia, also outlawed *No nos tientes*, although it was published in El Salvador and distributed clandestinely. The Huelga de Dolores was resuscitated in 1966 but throughout the 1970s and early 1980s it continued to be a target of repression. Under the Arana dictatorship, for example, security forces prevented paraders from leaving the university. Like all other popular expressions of dissent, the Huelga de Dolores was muffled by the harsh repression of the 1978-82 period. During the 1980s the tradition gained new momentum and was incorporated into the revived popular movement.[27] In 1992 the event's organizers stressed its political character, adopting as its three themes the 500 years of resistance (since Columbus), a call for a negotiated peace, and a demand that repression of university students cease. The 1992 parade took place amid increasing repression against USAC professors and students, including on-campus bombings and assassinations. The night before the 1992 march a combined police and military unit opened fire on the students as they were preparing the floats, killing one, wounding six others, and hauling off another 14.

The Private Alternative to USAC

Prior to 1961 USAC was the country's only university. Between 1961 and 1971, however, four new private universities were established. The Rafael Landívar University, founded in 1961, is administered by the Jesuits. In contrast to Jesuit-run universities in El Salvador and Nicaragua, the Landívar University exerts a conservative influence in Guatemalan academia. The Mariano Gálvez University, founded in 1966, was established as an evangelical college although it now professes to be nonsectarian. The University of the Valley, also founded in 1966, is an outgrowth of the American School of Guatemala, and currently benefits from regular allocations of U.S.

economic aid. In 1971 the Francisco Marroquín University was formed to spread neoliberal economic thinking and neoconservative politics in Guatemala. This conservative and well-heeled university also enjoys several U.S. economic-aid programs.

The presence of the private universities did not decrease enrollment in USAC but their establishment has reduced the commitment of the national elite to maintain USAC as a source of quality higher education. The private universities serve to train a professional class in an academic atmosphere free of the leftist influence prevalent at USAC. The national university itself may eventually be privatized if a three-step privatization plan drawn up by neoliberal strategists at the Free Market Chamber is implemented. Although an expanded private role in higher education is a more recent trend, secondary education has long been dominated by private institutions. Of 459 secondary schools, the 83 percent that are private serve 55 percent of the student population.[28] Another force in the privatization of education is the business elite, which has recently begun (with U.S. government assistance) to publish and distribute textbooks promoting capitalist ideology.

Communications Media

By some very narrow standards Guatemala is said to have a free press. There is no censorship board in Guatemala, no press licensing, and the country's leading paper is even called *Prensa Libre* (Free Press)—but journalists are frequently harassed, killed, or forced into exile while their news outlets are ransacked and firebombed by masked men. Like the rest of Guatemalan society, the media is enveloped in a culture of fear.

Between 1978 and 1985, 47 Guatemalan journalists were killed and at least one hundred were forced into exile.[29] Radio commentators have tended to be the most independent voices in journalism, and consequently have suffered the highest number of assassinations.[30] One of these, popular radio commentator Mario Monterrose Armas, was gunned to death after criticizing the military government for election fraud in the 1970s. Repression of journalists continued throughout the 1980s and into the 1990s, obligating some four dozen journalists to flee the country.[31] During the first several years of the Cerezo government there were signs that the country was indeed expanding its press freedoms after years of military rule. In early 1988 two new magazines were established: *Crónica*, a weekly magazine in the style of *Newsweek*, and the short-lived *La Epoca*, which featured investigative reporting and critical political analysis. Television news took on new life, and reporters could travel to any region of the country without government permission.

In mid-1988 hopes for greater press freedom in Guatemala were dashed. Heavily armed men broke into the offices of *La Epoca* in June 1988, burglarized it, and then firebombed it. Also destroyed was the office of the news agency ACEN-SIAG (closely associated with *La Epoca*). Shortly before this attack on the social-democratic *La Epoca*, correspondents for the Cuban Prensa Latina and the Soviet Tass news agencies were forced to flee the country after receiving death threats. To many close observers of Guatemala, the forced closing of

La Epoca seemed inevitable given the restricted nature of journalism in the country. Others saw the treatment of the paper as the "litmus test" of democratic freedoms under the new civilian government.

In Guatemala, as in many other countries, reporters and editors do not criticize the military or engage in investigative reporting that would challenge established power structures. For the most part, these restrictions are understood and self-imposed. But they exist within the context of a highly repressive society, and have been reinforced by death threats, assassinations, and bomb blasts—all of which have continued into the Serrano administration. Through beatings and death threats, reporters are warned not to cover the most important human rights cases. Both the U.S. State Department and the United Nations have reported an increase in human rights violations against the press during Serrano's first year. Included in the tally of 1991 violations were the following: a noted columnist for *Siglo Veintiuno* was arrested and jailed for drug possession in an obvious case of harassment; the popular radio program Guatemala Flash received death threats after airing a paid announcement by the URNG guerrilla command; reporters for two news agencies abandoned the country after office bombings and death threats, and several journalists were beaten by members of the security forces. According to a 1991 study by the International Federation of Journalists, reporters in Guatemala continue to be terrorized into silence by a campaign of official intimidation, and this "culture of terror" intensified during the first months of the Serrano administration.[32] In 1992 the press became subject to mounting pressure by the Serrano administration to silence antigovernment criticism. The president, irate at growing press criticism, tried to stifle critical voices through gifts to the Guatemalan Journalists Association (APG). At a time when the journalistic community was facing deepening repression, including death threats and bombings, the Serrano administration failed to vigorously condemn this vigilante activity and instead urged the press to adopt a more constructive attitude in its reporting.

Besides laboring under this crude system of news censorship, reporters are also handicapped by extremely low pay scales. Beginning journalists receive under $60 a month while the best-paying newspapers offer experienced journalists $300 monthly.[33] To supplement their low pay, journalists commonly rely on bribes and other forms of payment for service rendered. This system, also common in other Central American countries, operates according to the *"fafa"* law. In his 1979 book, *The Business of the Press*, Mario Carpio Nicolle, now a *Siglo Veintiuno* columnist, explained that the law of *fafa* (apparently a bastardization of the word "half") dictates that journalists should receive at least half their income from bribes and fees. A reporter or editor, then, will often write or print a story only if a proper payment is forthcoming. To illustrate how the system works, Carpio Nicolle related a story in which the government instructed a journalist to write a front-page article on the government's 500,000-tree reforestation plan, promising him 500 *quetzales* for his effort. When the government paid him only 50 *quetzales*, the reporter wrote a piece about 50,000 trees that the government was planting.[34]

Because of the low pay and many dangers, there are no investigative journalists in Guatemala. Commenting on the current state of the trade in Guatemala, a former editor for the newsmagazine *Crónica* quipped that most reporters are simply "tape machines with legs."[35]

The Daily News

Guatemala has four daily newspapers, which in order of circulation figures are *Prensa Libre, Siglo Veintiuno, El Gráfico,* and *La Hora*. There is also a government daily, *Diario de Centro América,* which largely reproduces government notices and decrees. Print media reaches an estimated 12 percent of Guatemalan homes.[36] There are only two newspapers printed daily for every 100 inhabitants—compared to 46 in Germany.[37] Especially in *Prensa Libre, El Gráfico,* and *La Hora,* news agency reports are usually published in their entirety rather than being integrated into one report by a foreign-affairs editor. As a result, it is not uncommon to find two agency reports with essentially the same news appearing side by side. Local death and tragedy dominate newspaper headlines, particularly in *Prensa Libre* and *El Gráfico,* exacerbating the atmosphere of fear and terror that dominates the country. *Prensa Libre* and *El Gráfico* clearly favor display advertising over the presentation of news in an attractive format.

Prensa Libre, founded in 1951, is the undisputed leading daily newspaper. Owned by a diverse group of investors (including adamant Catholics and evangelicals), the paper has no identifiable political stance, although traditionally it has been closely associated with the positions of the private sector and the military. Since the mid-1980s a niche has been created in the paper for less reactionary interpretations of political and economic happenings. Columnists José Eduardo Zarco and Mario Antonio Sandoval are the paper's leading political analysts.

Siglo Veintiuno, launched in 1990, is distinguished by its professional appearance and reporting, as well as by its pluralistic approach. In contrast to the two other major dailies, *Siglo Veintiuno* is not cluttered by advertising. On its board sit members of the influential Castillo and Toriello families. Quickly becoming the country's second most important newspaper, *Siglo Veintiuno* is a voice for the modernizing wing of the private sector, frequently presenting essays about the values of privatization and free-market solutions. Its Sunday magazine offers the best social and economic reporting in the country. Overall, through its editorials and opinion surveys, *Siglo Veintiuno* actively promotes the consolidation of efficient and honest government structures.

El Gráfico, started in 1963, is owned by the boss of the National Union Center (UCN) political party, Jorge Carpio Nicolle. Party politics and news mix freely in *El Gráfico*, originally a sports weekly and still read for its sports news. At one time *El Gráfico* also published a news magazine for intellectuals, called *La Razón*, but has since dropped its pretensions to being anything other than a business venture and political instrument for the UCN. To bolster its dwindling readership *El Gráfico* began publishing regional supplements in 1991. Many still buy *El Gráfico* to read the regular columns written by political analyst Carlos Rafael Soto, which are frequently critical of government and military policies and practices.

La Hora, established in 1944, is owned by the Marroquín family. Its founder, Clemente Marroquín Rojas, served as vice-president during the government of Julio Méndez Montenegro (1966-70). Like the other dailies, *La Hora* owns its own press. Because of its small circulation (about 5,000) and its lack of advertising, it is a losing business proposition. *La Hora*, the only afternoon paper, is published not to make money but for reasons of prestige and political ambition on the part of the Marroquín family. Like the other papers, *La Hora* tends toward sensationalism and despite its pretentious intellectual style regularly publishes unsubstantiated reports.

The only other major source of written news in Guatemala is *Crónica*, a weekly magazine that began publishing in early 1988. A slick and expensive periodical, *Crónica* quickly attracted attention by the high quality of its writing and graphic presentation. Its owners represent the modernizing wing of the private sector, and the magazine has enjoyed broad private-sector support in the form of several pages of slick advertising.[38] Since 1989, when it experienced a rift between ownership and staff, *Crónica* has lost much of its stylistic flair and has slighted investigative reporting in favor of cultural news and human-interest items. It continues, however, to provide a forum for alternative political and economic views.

The Electronic Media

The electronic media, particularly radio, represent the principal means of mass communication in Guatemala. Although more Guatemalans watch television and listen to radio than read the daily papers, the general impact of the mass media is modified by the country's sharp social and cultural divisions. Disproportionately more non-indians, particularly those who are urban and educated, have regular access to the Guatemalan media.[39]

Radio reaches more Guatemalans than any other medium, and some stations are even broadcast in indigenous languages. Estimates of those who regularly listen to radio range from 50 percent to as high as 80 percent of the Guatemalan population.[40] Most radio stations belong to one of five chains that have transmitters throughout the country. Perhaps the most influential of these is Radio Fabulosa, because of its system of *radioperiódicos* or news programs. As with television, however, most radio news programs in Guatemala are produced by independent news services that buy time on individual stations. There is less military, government, or private-sector control over radio than over other media, although self-censorship reigns here as well. In the last several years, there has been a surge in evangelical radio programming.

The government, through its National Broadcasting Committee, grants broadcasting rights to four private television stations. In addition, there is one government-owned channel. Recently, cable television has burgeoned, primarily in Guatemala City. There are some 50,000 cable subscribers, virtually all of whom receive their cable television from small private companies that pirate satellite transmissions from U.S. cable companies. A 1989 survey by the ACEN-SIAG news agency revealed that 78 percent of the programming on the country's five channels is foreign-produced.[41] Mexican investors wield financial control over Channel 3 and Channel 7, while two other channels, 11 and 13, are owned, at least in part, by Honduran investors. The various news programs broadcast by the stations are in most cases owned and produced by distinct groups of investors, and are characterized by their low technical quality, although a slick TV news show (modeled after the defunct Siete Dias program of the mid-1980s) may soon be broadcast. One of the most interesting developments during the first year of the Serrano administration was the appearance of a television debate series called Libre Encuentro, associated with the Free Market Chamber (CLE), that presents opposing views on many topical issues.

The army station, Channel 5, airs many cultural programs as well as religious presentations like El Club 700, produced by Pat

Robertson's Christian Broadcasting Network. The government's news program, Hoy Lo Más Importante, is aired on all stations. There is a new UHF channel, Channel 25, which airs mostly music videos but also adds its own conservative news items. Channel 21 is the evangelical station. Though an estimated 35 percent of all Guatemalan homes have television sets, this figure drops to 15 percent in rural areas.[42]

The United States Information Service (USIS) exercises an important influence on the Guatemalan media through its many media services. Regular press bulletins are distributed to all major news media. Programs produced by the Voice of America (VOA) and the local USIS mission are also fed to local radio and television stations.

Church and Religion

Guatemala has often been described as a religious battleground—the Latin American country where evangelicalism has made the most headway against the traditional domination of the Catholic Church. From an insignificant and ostracized minority in the 1950s the evangelical churches have attained a prominent place in Guatemalan society. One-third of the society is evangelical (Protestant), and since 1982 Guatemala has had two evangelical heads of state. Considering the low rate of church attendance by declared Catholics, evangelicals already constitute the largest group of churchgoers in Guatemala, and since the mid-1970s their numbers have increased faster than the pace of population growth. Alarmed by this trend, Archbishop Próspero Penados del Barrio in 1989 targeted "foreign influence," asserting that the evangelical advance represented an imperialist conspiracy to assert U.S. economic and political dominance in the region.[43] Responding in kind, the head of the Evangelical Alliance alleged that the Catholic Church was desperately trying to "influence the state and control the population," while keeping alive "idolatry, fetishism, alcoholism, and *machismo*—all that it defends as 'tradition.' "[44]

The Catholic-evangelical contest in Guatemala is more than a battle for souls. Questions about religious persuasion often have political implications. During the height of the counterinsurgency frenzy in the highlands, Catholic clergy and catechists were identified as subversives while evangelicals were regarded as patriots and anticommunists.

The results of the 1991 election, won by evangelical Jorge Serrano, demonstrated that at least on the national level the question of religious identity is becoming less of a political issue. Whereas the religious fervor that General Ríos Montt brought to government widened the divisions between evangelicals and Catholics, the candidacy of Jorge Serrano was supported by evangelicals and Catholics alike.

Although leading elements within the Catholic Church attempted to make his religious affiliation a campaign issue, Serrano was viewed primarily as a neoconservative politician who also happened to be an evangelical.[45]

Evangelical churches experienced phenomenal growth from the mid-1970s to the mid-1980s. By the early 1990s, however, the advance of evangelicalism had lost much of its earlier momentum. Although these churches continued to expand, their rate of growth had slowed, and many that had mushroomed in the early 1980s subsequently closed down. Religion in Guatemala seemed to be approaching an equilibrium. The end of massive counterinsurgency operations in the highlands, the diminishing novelty of the evangelical style, and the shallow character of many of the new sects were some of the factors explaining the loss of momentum. Evangelical churches seemed to have won over those people most susceptible to conversion. With the marked slowdown of evangelical growth, triumphant claims that a majority of Guatemalans would be evangelicals by the year 2000 seem unwarranted. More likely a state of equilibrium will eventually be reached in which evangelicals comprise perhaps 40-50 percent of the population. Within many communities, an acceptance of religious pluralism prevails as tensions between Catholic and evangelical congregants eases. On an institutional level, however, the battle continues, with the Catholic Church desperately trying to retain its hegemony as priests and evangelical ministers maintain their hostile postures, for the most part rejecting all suggestions of ecumenism.

Entering the 1990s, both Catholics and evangelicals were much stronger than a decade before. During the 1980s the Catholic Church was invigorated as an institution under the direction of Archbishop Penados. Although continuing to lose many of its members to the evangelicals, it became more united as an institution. Its network of religious and social services also expanded after having been severely disrupted during the 1978-83 period of repression. Although the evangelical community remained fractionalized, its numbers mushroomed. No longer were evangelicals ostracized as heretics and outsiders, having at last gained their rightful place within Guatemalan society.

The Catholic Church: Power, Tradition, and Change

Despite the growth of numerous evangelical churches the Roman Catholic Church remains the country's dominant religious institution. Unlike the evangelical community, largely reticent about officially involving itself in political matters and weakened by continual splits, the Catholic Church is strengthened by a rigid unitary structure. It has also assumed a role for itself as society's moral authority. The Catholic Church plays a major role not only in the religious and cultural aspects of Guatemalan life but also in such diverse areas as politics, community development, social services, and refugee relief. Social initiatives by both Catholic clergy and lay organizations have often served as models for the development programs of many other private organizations and even a few government agencies.

Independence from Spain and the rise of a new economic elite of coffee growers in the 19th century weakened the hold of the Catholic Church. When the Liberals seized political power from the Conservatives in 1871, the church suffered an abrupt loss of power and prestige. Lands were confiscated, monasteries closed down, church control over the education system ended, and foreign clergy deported.[46] President Justo Rufino Barrios declared religious freedom while opening up the country to Presbyterian missionaries. The power and prestige of the colonial church was swept away in a new wave of liberal modernization.

Not until the Ubico regime did the Catholic Church began to recover its former position of authority. Spearheaded by Catholic Action, founded in the late 1930s, a reevangelization campaign served to reassert the institutional church in rural communities. But this effort precipitated conflicts with village *cofradías* (groups of indian elders) who had for decades assumed the role of caring for the church, organizing fiestas, and generally overseeing the social order of their communities.[47] The zeal of Catholic Action catechists to educate villagers in church dogma clashed with the religious syncretism of the indian elders. Without the regular presence of a Catholic clergy, the *cofradías* had loosely mixed Mayan and Catholic rites. In the attempt to purify the religion, those practices regarded as superstitious or magical were rejected, threatening in the process the cultural, political, and even economic position of traditional indian elites.[48] The insistence by Catholic Action cadres that church members should undergo a new personal conversion and renounce superstitious cultural practices divided communities while putting traditional leaders on the defensive.

When Ubico was overthrown in 1944 by a coalition of progressive army officers and civilians intent on modernizing Guatemala, the church felt that its own social and political power was under attack. During the next ten years the church and its lay organizations such as Catholic Action joined with the Anti-Communist Party (PUA) and other rightwing organizations to protest the liberalizing and reformist trends of the civilian governments. The church's anticommunist attacks on the Jacobo Arbenz administration contributed to the government's inability to withstand the eventual rightwing military coup. In fact, Archbishop Mariano Rossell personally cooperated in the campaign directed by the U.S. Central Intelligence Agency (CIA) to topple the democratically elected government.

The 1954 coup proved to be a blessing for the institutional church. Archbishop Rossell was awarded the Order of Liberation by the new government of Castillo Armas and the National Liberation Movement (MLN). In turn, the archbishop referred to Castillo Armas as a "legitimate saint." The new regime removed restrictions on church ownership of property, reopened the country to foreign clergy, and dropped restrictions in the public schools to religious instruction. For its part, the Catholic Church blessed the military government and echoed its anticommunist ideology, although Archbishop Rossell became increasingly critical of the violence of succeeding military regimes.

The late 1950s to the early 1960s was a period of revitalization and institutional growth for the Catholic Church. Expansion of the catechistic work of Catholic Action and the dramatic rise in the number of foreign clergy largely explain this resurgence. After 1954 priests and nuns from all over Europe and North America came to Guatemala as missionaries. Post-World War II prosperity in Europe and the United States, the expulsion of religious orders from China in the 1940s, and the call by Pope John XXIII for external help for churches in Latin America all contributed to the influx of foreign Catholic missionaries after 1954. New schools and churches were built, new dioceses and missions were opened in previously ignored areas, lay apostolic organizations were created, and church social-assistance programs were substantially expanded.

As in the rest of the world, the Guatemalan Catholic Church experienced major internal upheaval during the 1960s. Vatican Council II in 1962 and the Medellín Bishops Conference in 1968 jolted clergy and laity alike into reexamining the church's traditional place in society and politics. Even though the national church hierarchy largely resisted these liberalizing trends, many local clergy were filled with the spirit of change and transmitted that spirit to their parishioners.

Even more cataclysmic were internal factors tilting much of the church toward political dissent and support for worker and peasant struggles. For a significant minority of missionary priests and nuns, particularly those working in rural areas, the narrow anticommunist ideology with which they entered Guatemala changed dramatically: first a focus on developmentalism and self-help measures, and later to a more critical stance and an alliance with those seeking profound social and economic changes.

At the center of this changing dynamic were lay groups such as Catholic Action and Delegates of the Word, often working closely with progressive clergy. Moving beyond strictly religious functions, these lay workers began to respond to the social and economic needs of their social base by promoting the cooperative movement and popular organizing in general. No longer strident anticommunists, Catholic Action promoters began questioning the legitimacy of the military regimes, and in doing so became closely associated with rural cadres of the Christian Democratic political party. This alliance between activist church members and Christian Democrats persuaded some *cofradías* and the more conservative members of indian communities to support rightwing political forces such as the National Liberation Movement (MLN) and the Democratic Institutional Party (PID). In this way, communities became further divided between the traditionalists and economic elites on one side and the progressives on the other.[49] This confrontation went beyond differing political allegiances to include conflicts over economic survival strategies, with the cooperatives and peasant leagues promoted by Catholic Action and the Christian Democrats advocating agricultural modernization and the collective purchase of fertilizers while many traditionalists held to customary planting practices.

Increasingly, peasants gathered to share religious instruction while discussing common economic and social problems. Priests and nuns, often relying on foreign resources, encouraged the formation of savings and loan cooperatives, buying and marketing cooperatives, and the use of fertilizers. Together with lay groups, they formed peasant training centers, sponsored popular-education programs on the radio, organized literacy campaigns, and spearheaded colonization projects in Ixcán, Petén, and northern Huehuetenango. This developmentalist response ran parallel to and oftentimes overlapped with similar projects sponsored by AID and the Alliance for Progress.

In the process, lay religious leaders became community leaders and were thrust into confrontation with established local and national power structures. Catholic Action delegates, imbued with the "new Catholicism," not only broke ranks with the *cofradías* but also contested the power of local merchants and estate owners. In turn, local oligarchs and army officers began to strike out against the cooperatives and the numerous lay organizations spawned by Catholic Action.[50] From the late 1930s to the early 1970s Catholic Action went through a rapid evolution that reflected the economic and political changes experienced by the entire society. From being a strictly proselytizing church agency in its early years, the group evolved into offering ideological support for the anticommunist campaigns of the 1950s and 1960s. As its roots sunk deeper into rural communities,

Catholic Action began to sponsor cooperative economic development projects, which led to the radicalization of its members and brought on mounting repression by the state.

Both clergy and laity became increasingly radicalized as the economic elite and the army escalated their repression. Many Catholic lay leaders gradually drifted from church organizations to form peasant leagues, while others joined guerrilla movements. The traditional social doctrine of the Catholic Church was rejected in favor of the more activist "liberation theology" and class analysis. In the mid-1960s several priests also became guerrilla supporters and were expelled from the country. Former Catholic Action activists founded the Campesino Unity Committee (CUC) in 1978 to defend the interests of the peasantry on a national level. As a result, repression against the rural church intensified. By the early 1980s, the entire diocese of Quiché was closed and 13 priests had been killed.[51] In 1980 banished priests and nuns formed the Guatemalan Church in Exile, which continues to function and publishes a journal about counterinsurgency, refugees, and repression in Guatemala. Another important religious group that strongly denounces army violence is the Pro-Justice and Peace Committee, founded in the mid-1970s and later forced into exile.

Institutional Church Faces Crisis

The institutional or hierarchical church was not unaffected by the changes taking place in the rural church, particularly in the highlands. As an institution, the Catholic Church was financially and organizationally spread thin. Before the early 1960s the only official voice of the church was that of the archbishop in Guatemala City. But encouraged by Vatican Council II, bishops, priests, and nuns began creating their own associations. The first of these was the Conference of Religious Orders of Guatemala (CONFREGUA), established in 1961. A major step in the institutionalization of church structure was the 1964 founding of the Guatemalan Bishops Conference (CEG). Reacting to the increasing dominance of foreign clergy and bishops, the Confederation of Diocesan Priests (COSDEGUA) was formed in 1969.

Upon Archbishop Rossell's death in 1964, Mario Casariego assumed the archbishopric in Guatemala and was later honored by the pope as Central America's first cardinal. Casariego, like his predecessor, was an ardent anticommunist. For almost two decades, until his death in 1983, the politically adept but widely disliked Casariego strove to maintain the institutional church as a conservative institution that gave no support to the developmentalist and reformist trends emerging from the church's rural base. Despite constant repression and escalating bloodshed by the army against the highlands church, the archbishop's office enjoyed cordial and often friendly relations with the military government and oligarchy.

Although antigovernment sentiment did exist among certain sectors of the church, Archbishop Casariego managed to keep the institution largely aligned with the government and military. In spite of Casariego, the Guatemalan bishops did circulate several progressive communiqués and pastorals during his tenure. Upon Casariego's death, the military paid its respects at a ceremony in the National Palace. During the ceremony, General Héctor Mario López Fuentes eulogized: "Until his death, [Casariego] was the spiritual guide of many army officers and the confessor of the majority and he was considered the religious guide of the military institution with which he was always identified."

Following the death of Casariego in 1983, the church became a more unified institution under Archbishop Próspero Penados del Barrio. In the wake of intense persecution of the rural church in the highlands and amidst charges from the military that the church was breeding revolution, a healing process began. With the ouster of Ríos Montt—who had granted evangelical sects a prominent place in Guatemalan society—the Catholic Church hierarchy could breathe more easily. The election of a Christian Democratic president two years later also helped the church recover its strength and influence.

To a large degree, the moderate, developmentalist approach of the Christian Democratic government matched the institutional church's own social and political ideology. The church, like the Christian Democratic Party, regards its social message as a third way between communism and unbridled capitalism. By the third year of the Cerezo government, however, Catholic bishops grew more insistent that social reforms be instituted to improve the lot of the poor, whose circumstances were worsening rather than improving under the Christian Democrats.

The church under Penados del Barrio veered sharply away from the conservatism of the Casariego years. The new social voice of the institutional church became more prominent with the March 1988 release of the pastoral letter "The Clamor for Land." The pastoral letter's call for land distribution sorely angered the national elite, simultaneously lifting hopes among the poor that the church would become an ally in the struggle for justice. A year later, the Bishops Conference issued another strong statement, the Declaration of Cobán, concerning the country's deplorable economic and social conditions. In these two epistles, the bishops charged that the country's "economic structure increases the wealth of the privileged sector [while making] the majority of Guatemalans even poorer." Furthermore, they noted that "more than a few Guatemalans have lost their faith in the possibility of an authentic democratic process."[52] In even stronger language the Declaration of January 1990 criticized the army. Collectively the documents issued by the Guatemalan Bishops Conference have been the most progressive in Central America in recent years, and have highlighted the church's role as a credible and increasingly strong critic of the government's neoliberal economic policies as well as its failure to curb human rights abuses.[53]

The divisions between the church hierarchy and the radicalized clergy and laity who espoused "liberation theology" have largely been healed. Although different tendencies still exist within the Bishops Conference, Archbishop Penados has forged a new consensus among the nation's prelates around a more progressive social doctrine. In 1988 the Bishops Conference underlined the church's commitment to the "preferential option for the poor."[54] The archbishop's office has commended those within the church who have attempted to be "agents of change within the temporal structures" and has recognized popular organizations like GAM as "signs of hope."[55]

While many of the fundamental principles of the so-called "church of the poor"—including an increased recognition that the church's religious doctrine cannot be separated from the material circumstances of society—have been adopted, the church of the poor itself has been disappearing as a concept. There is a recognition even among its early advocates that liberation theology excessively politicized religion while ignoring spiritual and emotional needs. Some blame this lack of pastoral attention for creating an opportunity for the new pentecostal sects to cater to the personal needs of dissatisfied Catholics. In addition to realizing that the church has to meet the deep-felt religious needs of its adherents, there now exists a widely shared understanding that only a united church can resist threats against its members by repressive forces.[56]

The main threat to Catholic Church unity comes not from its progressive wing but from the explosive growth in charismatic communities. The "spiritualist" or "sacramentalist" tendency within the Catholic Church, as represented by the charismatic renewal movement, looms as the main obstacle to the integration of the institutional church. Like the ever-swelling evangelical churches, charismatics adhere to a pentecostal faith, with an emphasis on a direct spiritual connection between the individual and the Holy Spirit. In contrast to the more staid services of the traditional church, charismatics are very emotional in their expression of faith.

The Charismatic Renewal Movement dates back to 1974 in Guatemala, and offered a haven for many in the church who sought a purely spiritual experience in lieu of the tendency toward a mixture of religion and politics.[57] The hierarchy has been reluctant to embrace the charismatic movement fearing that charismatics serve as a bridge between Catholicism and evangelical pentecostalism. There is also concern that by stressing direct communication between God and the individual, charismatics are relegating clergy and sacraments to an almost incidental place in their faith. Thus, the Bishops Conference has warned against the dangers of the fundamentalism of the Bible and against the "division between faith and life."[58]

Over two-thirds of Catholic clerics are still foreigners, although all bishops are native Guatemalans and in some dioceses there is a majority of native clergy and nuns.[59] The church is largely centered in major urban areas, with about one-third of the total clergy based in Guatemala City.[60] Because of its precarious financial state and for fear of provoking a new wave of repression, the church sponsors few community-development or peasant training programs, focusing instead on distributive charitable programs. A countervailing trend is the *inserción* (insertion) movement of many religious orders, who are inserting their priests and nuns into poor *barrios* where they live and do pastoral work.

Part of the church's new institution-building work involves an effort to better integrate indian cultures and languages. No longer are traditional religious practices dismissed as pagan. Instead the church is adapting its own rites to indian traditions, using large stones as altars and trying to take advantage of indian spiritualism rather than criticizing it. This search for a revitalization of popular religion by bridging Mayan and Christian traditions comes at a time, however, when the *cofradías* are becoming increasingly marginalized within modernizing indian communities. Nonetheless, one sign that the legitimization of indian culture and tradition has paid off is found in the upturn in indian vocations for the priesthood—30 percent of those in Guatemalan seminaries are now indian.[61]

At the start of the 1990s, the Catholic Church had recovered the institutional stability lost during the years of extreme repression. Having recuperated its strength as an institution, the church became more forceful in its condemnation of social injustices, and former tensions between the church of the poor and the hierarchy were thus largely resolved. The added participation of lay organizations, a new openness to indian cultures, and a surge in charismatic communities all helped revitalize the church. At the same time, though, these invigorating tendencies were offset by countervailing threats to the church's stability and influence. The church hierarchy continues to lash out against the "sects," instead of addressing its own weaknesses. Strict hierarchical control, rigid dogma, and an elite priesthood limit the church's ability to respond to social needs and inhibit future growth.[62] The church's undemocratic, authoritarian structures as well as its unpopular stands on controversial issues like birth control have also undermined its credibility as a social advocate.

Even though the church hierarchy did grow more outspoken in its condemnation of economic exploitation and repression, it balked at immersing itself in the struggle for social justice. Despite calling for a more equitable land tenure system, it sought to marginalize Father Andres Girón because of his direct participation in politics and social struggles. Although the institutional church did play a critical role in facilitating national reconciliation and peace talks, it failed to give its full backing to such ecumenical groups as the Campaign for Life and Peace. Nevertheless, the Catholic Church has increasingly become an important voice for social justice, and through its Human Rights Office and its role in promoting peace negotiations it has been a key factor in the popular struggle against repression.

The Rise of the Evangelicals

Historically, Protestantism or evangelicalism has enjoyed a stronger base in Guatemala than in other Central American countries. On a visit to New York City over a hundred years ago, President Barrios requested that the Presbyterian Mission Board dispatch missionaries to Guatemala. In 1882 Presbyterian missionary John Clark Hill arrived in Guatemala City and founded the first Protestant church, which now stands in the shadow of the National Palace. In the 1890s more U.S. Protestant missionaries began arriving in Guatemala aboard U.S. banana boats.[63] Most prominent of the new mission groups at the turn of the century was the Central American Mission (CAM), a "faith mission" that brought the theology of dispensationalism to the region.[64]

In 1935 the Presbyterian Church took the lead in establishing a geographical operating agreement among the leading evangelical churches in Guatemala. The five main denominations—Presbyterians, CAM, Primitive Methodists, Church of the Nazarene, and Evangelical Quakers—agreed to divide the country into five regions.[65] The main reason for the operating agreement among the five traditional denominations was to ward off incursions by pentecostal churches, notably the Church of God and the Assemblies of God.[66] The older churches were also interested in finding better ways to coordinate their own evangelization. The early split between traditional evangelicals and pentecostals, as illustrated by the 1935 geographical divisions, was to deepen in later years, with the pentecostals and subsequently the neopentecostals coming to dominate evangelicalism in Guatemala by the 1970s.

In sharp contrast to the Catholic Church, evangelical churches recognized early on the need to preach in the numerous native languages of Guatemala and to provide translations of the New Testament. This translation work was greatly expanded in the 1950s when Wycliffe Bible Translators began sending missionaries into the country. Evangelical churches gradually whittled away at the traditional hold of the Catholic Church on the Guatemalan population. But it was not until the 1976 earthquake that the impact of evangelical churches in Guatemalan society was really significant. Along with many other nongovernmental organizations, U.S. evangelical missionaries poured into Guatemala after the earthquake. For some, humanitarianism was the main motive for coming. For others, the upheaval caused by the earthquake offered a good opportunity for evangelism. To some degree the new evangelical missionaries in the late 1970s were a reflection of the evangelical fervor taking hold in the United States.

Between the mid-1970s and late 1980s evangelical adherents multiplied at an unprecedented rate—about 12 percent a year. According to a July 1987 survey by the evangelical SEPAL, 31.6 percent of the Guatemalan population was evangelical. Within the country there are some 300 denominations and 10,000 local congregations. Even the Catholic Church has acknowledged that a third of the population is evangelical.[67] Many evangelical churches banded together in the 1980s in a national campaign, dubbed Plan '90, with two ambitious goals: to make Guatemala 50 percent evangelical by the end of 1990, and to establish an evangelical church for every community of 500 to 1,000 people. This major proselytizing effort was financed and guided by an interdenominational evangelical organization from California named OC Ministries.

March 23, 1982, is a historic date for evangelicalism in Guatemala. On that date retired General Efraín Ríos Montt assumed the presidency of the country in a military coup. Many Guatemalan evangelicals consider the coup d'état a miracle or evidence of divine intervention in human affairs. Ríos Montt, who had been a presidential candidate for the Christian Democrats in 1974, was a born-again Christian associated with a California evangelical organization called Gospel Outreach, which started a church known as "El Verbo" in Central America. Evangelicals from the United States hailed the fact that Guatemala had a "Christian" president and proceeded to organize material support for the government and to send hundreds of mission teams to the country. A White House initiative encouraged such groups as Campus Crusade for Christ, Moral Majority, 700 Club, and Youth with a Mission to support the new regime.[68]

The sudden infusion of funds and personnel from U.S. evangelical organizations, plus the free publicity provided by the Guatemalan president's public airing of his religious views, contributed to the steady growth in evangelical churches in the 1982-83 period. In the highlands, evangelical popularity was also a direct result of the army's ongoing counterinsurgency campaign. Since the late 1970s Catholic lay agents and clergy had been subject to escalating repression. Families and sometimes entire communities began attending evangelical services to protect themselves against the accusation of being sympathetic to "radical" elements in the Catholic Church.

The message of personal salvation of the evangelical churches and their often apocalyptic vision found a niche in communities beset with poverty and wracked by violence. Their strong defense of the family and attacks on drunkenness and other vices also endeared them to many in the rural communities. The emotional support provided to members by the church community plus the entertainment value generated by almost nightly activities attracted converts as well.

The evangelical community in Guatemala is far from monolithic. Instead, it is divided into a seemingly infinite number of denominations, sects, alliances, and interdenominational churches and organizations. As elsewhere in Central America, most evangelical groups have at least some association with counterparts in the United States, although as manly as 95 percent of the ministers are native Guatemalans.[69] The emphasis of most evangelicals, especially pentecostals, is on individual salvation. The individualism that distinguishes the evangelical community gives rise to myriad divisions and tendencies.

Older and largely fundamentalist churches, such as the Assemblies of God, Central American Mission, Church of God, Nazarenes, Baptists, and Primitive Methodists constitute the historical backbone of evangelicals in Guatemala. These denominations reach into the most isolated rural areas, and in the 1980s they also opened scores of new churches in poor urban *barrios*, offering ready-made communities to those who migrated to the city to escape rural violence and destitution.

The neopentecostal churches and ministries have become the most prominent in the evangelical community, owing to their presence in urban areas and their largely professional and middle-class congregations. Sects like Christian Fraternity, El Verbo, Elim, Shaddai, and Living Water Teaching comprise part of this powerful, highly conservative faction of evangelicalism. Reinforcing this trend are transnational evangelical organizations from the United States like

Campus Crusade for Christ, Full Gospel Businessmen's Fellowship International, OC Ministries, and Youth with a Mission.

Most of these groups are nondenominational and identify themselves not as "evangelical" but as "Christian" churches, thereby enhancing their appeal to Catholics and former Catholics, particularly those of "charismatic" tendencies. Neopentecostal churches, which generally embrace a "prosperity theology" (also called "name it and claim it" faith), have also attracted middle- and upper-class Catholics disaffected by the Catholic Church's social doctrine. Instead of a "preferential option for the poor," neopentecostals teach that God wants everybody to be wealthy and that people are poor because they lack faith.[70] Among former Catholics attracted to neopentecostal churches were Efraín Ríos Montt and Jorge Serrano.

In addition to local factors, the electronic ministries of such U.S. neopentecostals as Jimmy Swaggart, the Bakers, and Pat Robertson propelled the growth of this self-centered, conservative faith.[71] In 1990 Robertson's Christian Broadcasting Network (CBN) sponsored a prime-time special broadcast simultaneously on all of Guatemala's major television stations. Although originally imported and still supported (sometimes lavishly) from abroad, neopentecostalism is now largely a national movement.

Yet neopentecostalism has sown new divisions in the already deeply fragmented evangelical community. In contrast to the more traditional fundamentalist churches that have discouraged political activism, neopentecostal sects have urged the faithful to take the battle against Satan into the political arena. The neopentecostals embrace of new right politics and their equation of material wealth with faith also concern many in the evangelical community.

President Serrano is in many ways typical of neopentecostals. "In classic neopentecostal style, Serrano and his advisers are very conspicuous consumers of luxury automobiles, expensive clothing, and the finest culinary fare," observed a Presbyterian mission worker based in Guatemala.[72] In their political discourse about the need for the modernization of the state and for structural adjustment, neopentecostals like Serrano commonly emphasize the rights to life, liberty, and property—with no mention of such social rights as education, health, and proper housing. What counts is the bottom line, and humanistic principles only lead to moral and financial ruin.[73] Not unlike the way in which liberation theology reinforced peasant organizing, the neopentecostal emphasis on individualism and material success has complemented the efforts of the modernizing political and economic elite in Guatemala. Serrano himself has helped shape the political and economic ideology of the neopentecostal movement, even authoring a book on the subject.[74]

In 1975 Serrano became a Baptist while studying in the United States. Next he joined the Fraternidad Cristiana and later became a prophet in the Elim church before converting to the Shaddai sect. With the election of Serrano, Harold Caballeros, minister of the Shaddai congregation, has ascended into the limelight. Characteristic of the kind of theology that pervades the neopentecostal sector was a tract circulated by Caballeros in 1991-92 blaming Guatemala's troubles on the presence of the Serpent of the Valley. According to Caballeros, before the coming of the Spanish the native population belonged to a cult that worshiped a plumed and flying serpent—the very image of Satan. Ever since that idolatry "the land has been contaminated and the heavens closed." The Shaddai minister, who claims to have been inspired by a fellow neopentecostal prophet in South Korea, appeals for the formation of a "great army of prayer" to cast out the devil serpent and once again open the skies to God.

Evangelical churches have always incorporated a social-assistance component into their mission work in Guatemala. For example, the country's first modern hospital was established by the Presbyterians. Evangelicals set up numerous primary and secondary schools and even a university. Since the 1976 earthquake the social-service programs of evangelical churches have expanded even further. Many churches now have at least minimal day care, education, health care, or feeding programs associated with their pastoral work. With few exceptions, most social-assistance programs of the evangelical churches are characterized by their paternalistic nature—consisting of handouts accompanied by a Bible message. Virtually all the resources for these programs come from U.S. private agencies, including AMG International, CARE, 700 Club, and World Vision. To a remarkable degree, evangelical pastors credit feeding and schooling programs as a key to spreading their religious beliefs. Many invest attention in children as a way to attract parents to their churches.

Although the evangelical movement is largely conservative, certain small and relatively isolated sectors, mainly associated with traditional denominations, have adopted the social interpretations of the theology of liberation. Some are in the process of breaking with a paternalistic style of social work and encouraging development projects with a more self-determined and less dependent style. Significantly, several church-based social programs have formed an umbrella group to coordinate and further promote development projects by evangelical churches.

In early 1989 Archbishop Penados del Barrio issued a pastoral letter launching a frontal attack on the evangelicals. Associating evangelical growth with U.S. government aid, the archbishop also charged evangelical churches with undermining "the deeply communitarian feeling that exists in the Guatemalan people." In contrast, the pastoral asserted, the Catholic Church is the "only element that has managed to establish, between the diverse races and social and economic groups, a certain type of integration." Although most social commentary by the Catholic Church in other countries fits more into the ecumenical ethos of Vatican II and the Medellín Bishops Conference, the Guatemalan church's pronounced sectarianism does not. Commenting on the pastoral, one evangelical indian minister, Vitalino Similox, labeled the letter "unfortunate," parrying: "We need to talk of agreements, not differences."[75]

Refugees and the Internally Displaced

Before the 1980s most of those who left Guatemala for political reasons were *ladino* activists and politicians. In the early 1980s, however, large numbers of Guatemalan indians also began fleeing the country (Figure 5d). A people who for so long had clutched tenaciously to their land escaped on foot before the advancing terror that swept across the highlands. Since 1980 deepening economic crisis has also propelled hundreds of thousands of Guatemalans to abandon their homes to seek a better livelihood either in the cities or by leaving the country.

The counterinsurgency campaign that raged through the western highlands from 1980-83 left in its wake hundreds of destroyed indian villages. To escape this genocidal violence some 300,000 Guatemalans found new homes in the United States, 200,000 fled to Mexico, and a few thousand crossed the border into Belize or Honduras—with at least several hundred thousand remaining displaced within Guatemala.[76] The large majority who left the country in the early 1980s were never officially registered as refugees, slipping instead into the shadows of Mexican and U.S. society as undocumented residents.

Guatemalans in the United States

More than a half million Guatemalans (about 5 percent of Guatemala's population) live in the United States; at least 300,000 of them have illegally entered since 1980. To get to the United States these illegal immigrants endure graft, robbery, rape, and imprisonment in Mexico.[77] The greatest U.S. concentration of Guatemalans is found in Los Angeles, with other large communities in Houston, Washington, New York City, Chicago, San Francisco, and southern Florida. In Florida alone there are some 25,000 Guatemalans, including a large concentration of Kanjobal indians who pick vegetable and citrus crops.

Unlike Mexico, the United States has never established a refugee program for Guatemalans or other Central Americans. In the eyes of the U.S. government, Guatemalan immigrants are not political refugees deserving of special care and protection but simply economic immigrants seeking a better life. Less than 5 percent of Guatemalans who have applied for political asylum have had their petitions

Figure 5d

Refuge and Return: A Chronology

1978-80: Violent repression of popular movement, unions, church activists, and political reformists obligates many to abandon country.

1981-1983: Counterinsurgency campaign of "scorched earth" in western highlands and Franja Transversal del Norte causes massive population dislocation. Army establishes "development poles" and "model villages" to control population displaced by army offensives that destroyed more than 400 indian villages in Quiché, Huehuetenango, and Alta Verapaz. Some 200,000 refugees flee to Mexico, while several hundred thousand remain in Guatemala as "internally displaced."

1984: UNHCR and Mexican government agency, COMAR, transfer thousands of refugees living in Chiapas into camps in states of Campeche and Quintana Roo.

1986: Cerezo government establishes Special Commission for the Assistance of Repatriates (CEAR) to oversee return of Guatemalan refugees. Continuing repression and inability to guarantee security and welfare of returnees discourages massive repatriation. By end of Cerezo administration only 5,700 registered refugees had repatriated to Guatemala.

1987-88: Esquipulas II peace accords in August 1987 lead to creation of National Reconciliation Commission (CNR) and public discussion of terms for refugee repatriation through "National Dialogue."

Refugee communities in Mexico establish Permanent Commissions in December 1987-January 1988 to plan collective repatriation and present demands to government.

Army launches two major offensives in September 1987 and April 1988 in northern Quiché to force "illegal" civilian communities out of hiding in the mountains and into military/government reeducation centers. In this period, army forces 5,000, mostly Ixil indians, out of mountains with objective of isolating these communities from guerrilla forces and maintaining them under close military control.

granted.[78] Many Guatemalans living in the United States truly are economic refugees who fled a country suffering a severe economic crisis and profound social inequities.

Despite tighter border controls, the Immigration and Naturalization Service (INS) reports that Guatemalans continue to enter the United States in large numbers. Since the mid-1980s the INS has collaborated with Mexican authorities to stop the flow "in the pipeline," in other words, to prevent immigrants from ever reaching the United

---

1989: National Council of the Displaced (CONDEG) is formed by displaced groups in Guatemala City and on South Coast.

Creation in May of International Conference of Central American Refugees (CIREFCA) by regional governments and UNHCR to formulate plans for care and resettlement of refugees. Nongovernmental organizations and affected population are mostly excluded from process until follow-up meeting in 1990.

1990: In September, Communities of Population in Resistance (CPR) publicly announce their existence in newspaper ads, demanding their rights as civilians be respected and that army stop bombing their settlements.

1991: President Serrano creates National Fund for Peace (Fonapaz) to aid social reintegration and resettlement of displaced and repatriating refugees. Many suspect it is merely a disguised counterinsurgency and pacification strategy.

Over 350 Guatemalan refugees from El Tesoro refugee camp in Honduras repatriate in July, returning to new settlement in Alta Verapaz with minimum assistance from United Nations.

Permanent Commission (CCPP), mouthpiece of refugees in Mexico, continues talking with Guatemalan government over conditions for collective repatriation. Government refusal to meet refugee demands and Vice-President Espina's comment that CCPP is subversive dim hopes for repatriation in early 1992.

Mediating group chaired by head of National Reconciliation Commission and formed by Human Rights Ombudsman, Guatemala Human Rights Commission, and UNHCR established to promote dialogue between government and CCPP.

1992: Government agrees to guarantee security and legal rights of refugees and accepts principle of collective repatriation but is unwilling to allow CCPP to organize return from Mexico. UNHCR increases presence in Guatemala in preparation for massive repatriation of 30,000 refugees planned for 1992-93. Nongovernmental organizations, foreign aid agencies, and the United Nations Program to Support Guatemalan Refugees (PRODERE) also prepare plans for repatriation with guidance from CIREFCA.

States. It also launched a "public awareness blitz" in Guatemala and other Central American countries to discourage northward migration. As part of its effort to stem the tide before it starts, the U.S. government has assigned two intelligence officers, two Border Patrol officials, an immigration officer, and two antismuggling agents to Guatemala. Among other things, the agents were to "gather predictive intelligence" and work with Guatemalan law enforcement officials.[79]

Guatemalans living in the United States may have left their country behind, but between 250,000 and 325,000 of them continue to send money to family members still in Guatemala. According to recent estimates, more than $700,000 in remittances enters Guatemala every day. At least one of every ten Guatemalans benefits from remittances, with receiving families averaging $1,440 annually. As a percentage of the country's GDP, remittances doubled during the 1980s, rising from 1.4 percent in 1980 to 2.9 percent by 1989. This means that in 1989, remittances were equivalent to about one-fifth of Guatemala's export income or about half of its trade deficit. According to one survey, 55 percent of Guatemalans of working age would consider migrating to the United States if they had the financial resources to make the trip.[80]

Victims of War

During the counterinsurgency many peasants fled to squatter settlements on the outskirts of Guatemala City and other urban centers, while others headed to the South Coast hoping to find regular work on the agroexport plantations. In the most conflictive areas—northern Quiché, Huehuetenango, and the Verapaces—the army rounded up the displaced into newly created "development poles" or "model villages." Under tight military control, these dislocated villagers were "reeducated" by army civic-action teams and the adult male refugees were organized into civil patrols. About 25,000 displaced persons remained hidden in the mountains, forming new clandestine communities that evaded army forays.

Unlike neighboring El Salvador, where those uprooted by the war quickly joined new popular organizations, the masses of displaced Guatemalans remained largely unorganized. Afraid to identity themselves as displaced, many indian families began shedding signs of ethnic identity, including language and traditional dress, for fear of indicating their place of origin. Theirs became a life of "silent refuge."[81] Not until 1989 with the founding of the National Council of the Displaced (CONDEG) did refugees living in Guatemala City and the South Coast achieve any organized voice.

Those Guatemalans who fled to Mexico in the early 1980s found temporary refuge with peasant families in the bordering state of Chiapas and received assistance from the Catholic Church. With financial support from the United Nations High Commissioner for Refugees (UNHCR), the Mexican government soon established an agency called COMAR to administer the refugee population. Some 46,000 Guatemalans were granted refugee status, and in 1984 COMAR began relocating about 18,000 of them to camps in Campeche and Quintana Roo. Another 150,000 integrated themselves into Mexican society, many migrating to Mexico City but as many as 60,000 remaining in Chiapas. Among these were at least 20,000 who had historically migrated to Chiapas as seasonal laborers and simply decided not to return to Guatemala because of the repression.[82]

Repatriation and Resettlement

In the early 1980s the military vehemently denied that tens of thousands of indians were seeking refuge outside the country, charging that the reports were part of an international communist conspiracy to discredit Guatemala. For years the regime disavowed the existence of a large refugee population—much as the Honduran government denied the Nicaraguan contra bases inside Honduras. Yet while the military government was dismissing these reports, its troops crossed the Mexican border repeatedly to terrorize the refugees.

Inside Guatemala the army readily acknowledged the growing displaced population, but it charged that these victims were all fleeing from the guerrillas. Corralled in model villages and internment camps controlled by the army's civil affairs (S-5) specialists, the displaced indians themselves often reluctantly corroborated the army's version of events. In Mexico, however, the refugee population was less intimidated and offered a decidedly different version of what had caused them to flee the country.

The refugees constituted incontrovertible proof of the savagery of the country's armed forces, and their fear of returning home also demonstrated that conditions had not substantially improved under the civilian government. Finally in 1986, acknowledging that something had to be done on a governmental level to encourage the return of the refugee population, President Cerezo created CEAR (Special Commission for the Assistance of Repatriates) to work with the United Nations in facilitating the repatriation of refugees. In 1988 the commission was also authorized to oversee the resettlement of the internally displaced.

But the Cerezo government had little success in persuading Guatemalans to return home. Contrary to government promises guaranteeing their security, those refugees that did repatriate found themselves subject to army interrogation and detention. Some were killed, many others were forced into civil patrols, and the repatriated refugees were unable to recover the homes and land they had left.[83] Those who were granted land by the National Agrarian Transformation Institute (INTA) were in many cases given disputed land titles or were settled on lands subject to flooding and erosion. Promised government resettlement assistance often never materialized. Most repatriating refugees never received new citizenship documents, leaving them worried about their own and their children's future.[84] By the end of the first year of the Serrano administration only 6,700 registered refugees had returned from Mexico and Honduras. In early 1992 some 54,700 (including more than 12,000 children born in exile) remained in UN-assisted refugee camps in Mexico.[85]

Tightly organized from the beginning of their sojourn in Mexico, the residents of the refugee camps formed "permanent commissions" in 1988 in order to present their concerns and demands to the newly formed National Reconciliation Commission (CNR) in Guatemala. The Central Permanent Commission (CCPP), representing the numerous local refugee commissions, also began negotiating with CEAR, UNHCR, and the Guatemalan government about the conditions for collective repatriation. Among the conditions for reentering Guatemala, the CCPP has demanded that refugees be allowed to return to and take possession of the lands they left behind (or lands of equivalent value); their right to free association and free movement; government guarantees for their security; and a repatriation process monitored by foreign and nongovernmental organizations.

By early 1992 both the Guatemala government and the refugees found themselves under international pressure to proceed with a repatriation plan. Even before a tentative plan was adopted, the Mexican government and the United Nations were cutting back on food deliveries and other assistance to the refugee program. Short of an agreement in which their demands are met, the refugees faced the choice of returning to Guatemala without appropriate guarantees or of integrating themselves into Mexican society—an option not encouraged by the Mexican government. Many refugees, particularly those living in Campeche and Quintana Roo, have expressed interest in remaining in Mexico and applying for Mexican citizenship, although the large majority still wish to return to Guatemala. Refugee protests and international pressured eventually persuaded the Mexican government and the United Nations to soften their positions, which in turn gave the CCPP more time to consult with the refugee community and to negotiate a better reentry agreement with the government.

The main pressure on the Guatemalan government came from international funding agencies and the United Nations, which urged President Serrano to adopt a repatriation plan that would provide the guarantees demanded by the refugees. In preparation for the resettlement of refugees and the internally displaced—and to attract international funds—Serrano in 1991 created a new government agency called National Fund for Peace (Fonapaz) that will function as a branch of the presidency.[86] In addition to its resettlement duties, Fonapaz hopes to be the channel for future U.S. aid for demobilization and postwar transition in the event of a peace agreement with the guerrillas.

Although it may also manage the government's planned social-investment fund, the focus of Fonapaz is what the government euphemistically calls Zonapaz or the "peace zone." This zone covers most of the conflictive areas throughout the highlands and into the Petén, with an estimated population of 2.4 million.[87] There exists widespread concern among refugees and the displaced, however, that Fonapaz will function primarily as a control mechanism to maintain government/military supervision of nongovernmental organizations and popular refugee and displaced groups. The CCPP charged that plans for new resettlement zones smacked of creating "a logistical infrastructure for the counterinsurgency plans designed by the army, aimed at military ends and not social development."

Although the accelerated return of the refugees is probable during 1992-93, problems related to land and militarization in rural Guatemala will likely remain unresolved. Throughout the highlands the military presence was still pervasive and the system of civil patrols had not yet been dismantled by the second year of the Serrano government. Only in the Ixil triangle (comprising the towns of Nebaj, Chajul, and Cotzal in Quiché) were there unoccupied lands available for repatriates. Most of the lands left by those who fled to Mexico have long since been occupied by other peasants with government approval.

During its early years CEAR had promised to adjudicate land titles and find new lands for repatriating refugees through INTA. Early on in the Serrano administration there was also talk of purchasing lands to distribute to repatriating refugees. But the lack of available lands and the likelihood of political problems arising from any proposal that smacks of agrarian reform have given rise to backpedaling by the government to an official position of merely seeking "productive" solutions to the refugee resettlement issue. Rather than land, resettled refugees and the displaced may be offered jobs in garment plants, assuming the government is successful in attracting factories to these remote areas. According to Fonapaz President Alvaro Colom, formerly president of the Guatemalan Nontraditional Exporters Association (Gexport), several U.S. firms—particularly Liz Claiborne—have expressed serious interest in establishing *maquilas* in the Ixil Triangle.[88] In early 1992 Gexport, dependent on U.S. economic aid for virtually all its funding, set up a program to train Ixil women in garment assembly in anticipation of the government's new scheme.

Displaced Communities in Resistance

The army offensives in 1987-88, designed to ferret out the thousands of displaced people who had fled to isolated reaches of northern Quiché, forced the government refugee commission to expand its purview to the internally displaced. In 1988 CEAR, working hand in hand with the army, organized relief and resettlement operations for the some 5,000 half-starved indians that the army had managed to force out of hiding. Once out of the mountains and in army hands, these displaced indians were subjected to a three-stage "reorientation" process that included interrogation, reeducation, and relocation. Although CEAR was technically in charge of processing and caring for the displaced, it was the army's psychological operations teams that administered the temporary internment camps, the "civic and democratic education" program, the distribution of food and medical services, and the eventual relocation of these captive people.[89]

Choosing neither to flee to Mexico nor to submit to army relocation programs, thousands of indians have lived clandestinely since the early 1980s in the mountains and jungles of northern Quiché and the Petén. Survival needs as well as persecution by the military obligated these displaced communities to forge new ways of organizing and enduring, including the creation of cooperative structures and multi-ethnic communities. Pursued by the military and caught in the middle of a counterinsurgency war, these clandestine communities were subject to constant hunger and deprivation. Those who succeeded in eluding the soldiers organized themselves into Communities of Population in Resistance (CPR), and in 1990 these groups began publicly demanding that they be respected as noncombatants and that the army stop bombing their homes and fields. While acknowledging that guerrillas often pass through their communities, these indians have insisted that they themselves are not combatants, although they are committed to resisting military control over their lives.[90] The army insists that these communities are "illegal villages," whose residents are either guerrilla volunteers or have been kidnapped by the guerrillas. But CPR members contend that they are fighting to protect their inalienable right to internal refuge so "we can survive, maintain our cultures, and defend our rights as Guatemalans."[91] The CPR views its community organizations, in which numerous ethnic groups work together, as "an example for a new society of Guatemala's poor." This collective vision, shared both by the refugees in Mexico and by the communities in resistance, causes the repatriation and resettlement of these organized groups to be as much a political concern as a logistical issue for the Guatemalan government and military.

Internal Migration

Internal migration has been relatively low in Guatemala. A 1989 government survey found that only 11 percent of the population interviewed had been born outside the department in which they were presently living.[92] Guatemala City is the main destination for internal migration, although the city of Escuintla is also attracting many rural migrants. Two rural destinations of internal migration are the departments of Petén and Izabal. The largely *ladino* departments of eastern Guatemala (El Progreso, Zacapa, Chiquimula, Santa Rosa, Jutiapa, Jalapa, and Baja Verapaz, in descending order of population growth) have experienced the greatest percentage of outmigration since 1950, despite their above-average fecundity rates.[93]

Except for calamities, such as the 1976 earthquake or the massive dislocation caused by the 1981-83 counterinsurgency campaign, most internal migration is motivated by economic factors. Landlessness and increased competition for seasonal agricultural jobs are major contributors to urban migration. Poverty is nothing new in rural Guatemala, but the isolation that traditionally characterized the countryside has been rapidly disintegrating. Since the mid-1970s barriers between urban and rural Guatemala are being blurred as more roads penetrate into formerly inaccessible regions—the combined result of counterinsurgency and rural development programs.

Another major factor contributing to national integration, and thereby spurring migration, is the now pervasive presence of the electronic media. Television and radio are eroding spatial and cultural divisions between Guatemalans while elevating expectations among rural residents, who attempt to realize their dreams by migrating to the cities or, increasingly, even to the United States. In most cases, however, it is generally not the poorest of the poor who migrate. Those who leave their rural homes to seek better economic and social conditions in the cities or in the United States must first acquire the financial resources to enable them to make the big move from their ancestral village.[94]

PART 6

Society and Ethnicity

© Derrill Bazzy

Decline and Survival of the Mayan People

The vast jungle canopy of the Petén extends in all directions as you gaze from atop Tikal's Temple IV, the tallest pre-Columbian building in the Western Hemisphere. The immense stone monuments bequeathed by the people of this great city-state have survived the test of time. But the civilization that lived here had all but vanished by AD 900. No one knows for certain what combination of factors caused the collapse of Tikal and the numerous other city-states of Mesoamerica. It seems, however, that the waning of the Mayan civilization was the result of internal weaknesses and imbalances rather than uncontrollable geological or climatological factors.

Linked only by commerce and lacking any political cohesion, the Mayan civilization was a collection of separate (and usually warring) city-states not unlike those of ancient Greece. Beginning around AD 250 the method of warfare turned more gruesome. No longer was the objective simply to capture one or two nobles from the enemy camp. Instead, massive assaults were launched with the aim of spilling as much blood as possible, capturing large numbers of slaves, and taking sacrifice victims. This escalation of war paralleled the rise of a top-heavy class of nobles and priests who measured their worth in jewels, quetzal feathers, animal furs, temples, and retinues.

Archeologists speculate that as tribute demands escalated and temples rose higher, the caloric needs of the overworked peasant and worker class increased. This mounting caloric demand stressed the environmental sustainability of the society's food production system while placing new burdens on the peasantry. The changing nature of war required the construction of expansive fortifications, more troops, and a bloated military budget. Based on recent archeological findings, it is estimated that as much as 75 percent of the income of city-states such as Tikal were channeled into military expenditures.[1] Under this strain, the societies and the environment that supported them began to disintegrate. Nobles that were formerly revered became viewed as oppressors and warlords. One archeologist working in Guatemala described post-Classical Mesoamerica as resembling something out of the postapocalyptic movie "The Road Warrior."[2]

When the Spanish arrived in Guatemala, there were about one million native people and the major groups were locked in bitter rivalry, facilitating their colonization. There was no one decisive conquest, simply because there was no single indian civilization to subdue. Descendants of the classical Mayan city-states were the most numerous of the native groups, which also included the Pipil Aztec indians (South Coast and in the East) and the Xinca indians (East). By 1650, disease, war, and exploitation had nearly obliterated the native population, until they numbered only about 200,000. The breeding of the Spanish and creole classes (direct descendants of colonizers) with the indians created an expanding *mestizo* (mixed race) sector.

Existence on the Margin

Today, indians are relegated to the margins of Guatemalan society. Isolated in terms of language and politics, their exploitation is a cornerstone of the national economy. Guatemala's agroexport system has been built on the backs of cheap indian labor. Tourism, the country's second largest source of foreign exchange, is also largely dependent on the image of the indigenous culture for attracting foreign visitors.[3]

Describing the ethnic composition of present-day Guatemala is a sociological challenge due both to the lack of good census data and the difficulty of defining who is indigenous. In addition, there is the related problem of deciding what terms to use.

Most native people define themselves by their home village and by their language group. Other terms such as "indio," "indigena," "natural," and "nativo" have been used largely by non-indians to classify non-Spanish language speakers, with "indigena" (indigenous) generally considered the least deprecating and most acceptable. Beginning in the 1970s many self-identified native people began to call themselves Mayas, a term that has also been appropriated by the nationalistic and culture-centered movement that emerged in late 1980s. But the term "Maya" is also problematic since not all of the indigenous people have Mayan roots and there never existed a self-identified Mayan civilization. Neither is there any close identification between the indigenous people of today's Guatemala with the societies that built the grand monuments and temples. Although some self-designated Mayas feel strongly that all other nominations are deprecatory, many other native leaders prefer the term "indigena" or "indio."

Estimates of the indigenous population vary greatly. Government censuses reveal a dwindling concentration of native peoples, sliding from 78 percent in 1778 to 65 percent in 1893 to 54 percent in 1950 to 43 percent in 1973 to 42 percent in 1981. In contrast, the Maya Language Academy (ALMG) estimates a current native population of 70 percent, while the Council of Mayan Organization (COMG) claims that 65 percent of Guatemalans are indian. Sociologists, journalists, and anthropologists generally play it safe by considering about half the Guatemalan population as indigenous. Estimations often vary according to the political sympathies of the observer, with those leaning toward the left often asserting that a clear majority of Guatemalans are indians.

One problem in gauging the indigenous population is the weak methodology of the national census, which defines whether one is indian or not primarily by language and dress. Mayan nationalists and some anthropologists charge that government statistics are designed to minimize the native population in the interests of promoting national integration.[4]

Another difficulty in calculating the proportion of indigenous people in Guatemala is that the generally accepted dividing line is not race but culture and language. Guatemalan society is divided into two main categories: indian and *ladino*. The term *"ladino"* previously referred to the creole class but in common usage now simply means non-indian. It includes a small Caucasian elite, a large *mestizo* sector, and even counts those indians who no longer wear *traje* (traditional dress), speak a native language, or consciously identify themselves as indigenous people. Also often considered *ladinos* are other minorities such as blacks, Chinese, and Middle Easterners.

There is little dispute that culture rather than race is the better indian-*ladino* criteria since the entire Guatemalan population shares the same gene pool.[5] The critical issue here, however, is that *ladinización* is a socialization process heavily influenced by the fact that *ladinos* control the nation's politics and economy as well as determining its social norms.[6] Furthermore, to be accepted outside one's own indian community one has to look, act, and talk like a *ladino*. Imitation is a tactic to evade pervasive discrimination.

Ethnic discrimination permeates Guatemalan society. To be an *indio* is to be dumb, lazy, crude, backward, and altogether less civilized in the stereotypical view of many *ladinos*. In fact, *indio* is a common term of insult in *ladino* society. Within the narrow bounds of indian communities, one can advance economically and socially while maintaining traditional dress and language. But to succeed in the dominant society, or even simply to get a decent job, an indian is pressured to shed her or his cultural identity and assume *ladino* dress and behavioral patterns. For these reasons, low estimations of the indigenous population are sometimes questioned; and it is argued that without societal pressure and discrimination the numbers of self-identified indians would be much greater.

Although discrimination against Mayas is a powerful social determinant, it is not the only reason why indian people are shedding their dress, language, and culture. As indian communities become less isolated due to an expanded transportation infrastructure, a more integrated national economy, and the influence of mass communications (particularly television), young indian women and men see little advantage in maintaining traditional ways. In fact, many reject aspects of their culture as being personally constraining. Yet it has been said both by Maya nationalists and some foreign anthropologists that for an indian woman to wear *ladino* clothes is like being stripped of her entire identity, to feel naked in a world of strangers. This is undoubtedly true in many cases, such as when urban employment necessitates a change in one's style of dress. It is also true that wearing—and not wearing—*traje* is highly significant and symbolic for most indian women.

According to Demetrio Cojtí, leader of a seminar on ethnic questions at San Carlos University and sometimes described as the first self-identified Maya nationalist: "*Traje* is an identity. *Traje* is an ethnic reaffirmation of a people."[7] Anthropologist Carol Smith asserts: "Modern Maya women wear their woven garments with pride as a statement that they belong to particular Maya communities—into which they were born and into which they will marry. When such women put on *ladino* garb, they are stating that they are available for the conquerors rather than for the men of their own community."[8]

Yet the decision not to wear the traditional *corte* (skirt) and *huipil* (blouse) is increasingly a personal choice of indian women who want to *modernizarse* so as not to remain trapped in what they see as a confining and oppressive past. For reasons of comfort, style, vanity, and especially economy, many indian women are turning toward *ladino* styles of dress and appearance. Many would also rather listen to Michael Jackson than to traditional marimba music. Asked whether they still consider themselves indian, women frequently respond: "No soy de traje" or even "No soy indigena de trenza" (I am no longer the kind that wears traje . . . or uses braids). Wearing *traje*, though it continues to be a source of cultural affirmation for many indian women, represents an economic burden. It costs at least $75 to make a complete outfit—about a quarter of the annual per capita income for most Guatemalans.

The more contact an indian community has with non-indian society and economy, the less traditional it remains—not only due to prejudice, but also out of valid personal choices. In many areas of the country, indian men, usually more exposed to the dominant economy and society, have acquired the dress and behavior patterns of their *ladino* counterparts. This has left indian women as the primary bearers of cultural identity—explaining why the decisions of many young women to cut their hair, not to arrange their hair in braids, to wear make-up, or to no longer wear *traje* is viewed by Mayan cultural nationalists as so threatening to the survival of indian traditions.

There is also the underlying issue of patriarchal control. Once a young women decides not to wear the *traje* of her community, she becomes more of a free agent, instead of the exclusive property of the men of her village. It is common for indian men to adopt *ladino* lifestyles or even North American ones (in the case of immigrants to the United States) while insisting that their daughters and wives maintain the traditional culture and all its personal manifestations. The same is true for most Maya nationalists, who look on with horror as indian women cut their hair or wear lipstick, but who are not in the least bit critical of men who have by their appearance completely crossed over to *ladino* styles.

The indian people have long been eclectic in their adoption of foreign customs, beliefs, and technologies. Yet the pace of change and adaptation is occurring now at unprecedented rates. The more isolated an indian community is from *ladino*-dominated society and the closer it is to the subsistence culture of the peasantry the more likely it is to have maintained its language, dress, and customs. The process of assimilation and acculturation has been spurred on by the penetration of traditional societies by economic, religious, cultural, political, and military influences. Thus, while a decision to adopt *ladino* styles or to drop traditional customs and dress may be personal, the choice occurs in an oppressive environment where indigenous ways are disparaged. When an indian man or woman decides, for example, not to wear *traje* to avoid attracting military attention or to improve his or her chances for landing a job, the choice is hardly a free one.

Facing Extinction

Certain events in Guatemalan history have been defining moments for its indian population. Among the most decisive have been: the economic, labor, and political reforms of the 1944-54 period of progressive government; the outreach work of Catholic Action and the resulting conflict with the *cofradías* (traditional indian leaders); the cooperative movement and other developmentalist programs of the 1960s and 1970s; the rise of the popular movement in the 1970s and the coalition building between indian and *ladino* activists; the revolutionary concepts popularized by leftist guerrillas especially in the 1975-81 period; the breakdown of the traditional dual structure of agriculture and the accompanying problems of landlessness and rural-to-urban migration; the militarization of the highlands in the early 1980s; the massive displacement of indian population caused by the counterinsurgency war; the extension of the country's transportation network into formerly inaccessible regions; gradual economic integration, illustrated chiefly by the rise of nontraditional export production; the explosive growth of evangelical churches; and the extension of electronic media into indian homes.

These factors—combined with the absence of organized efforts to promote and preserve indian languages and culture—are contributing to the rapid demise of ethnic diversity in Guatemala. Some observers even predict that the 1990s will be the last decade in which Guatemala's distinctive ethnic and cultural diversity will be evident. The loss of languages and culture is lamentable, but even more ominous is the erosion of the traditional land base and economy of the indian people. Without adequate land and the resources needed for the land to produce, indian communities will continue to disintegrate in the face of landlessness, environmental crisis, and the deteriorating terms of trade for peasant agriculture. The breakdown of the rural economy is especially devastating for cultural survival in Guatemala where indigenous identity emanates primarily from local communities rather than from a broader sense of tribe or of a "Maya nation."

There are four main indigenous languages: Quiché (spoken in the village of Mazatenango as well as Quiché, Quetzaltenango, Sololá, Retalhuleu, and Totonicapán departments); Mam (Huehuetenango, San Marcos, and Quetzaltenango); Cakchiquel (Antigua village and the departments of Sacatepequez, Chimaltenango, Sololá, and Guatemala); and Kekchí (Alta Verapaz, Izabal, and Petén). Several languages are in immediate danger of extinction. An estimated 30 people, all more than 50 years of age, speak Itzá in San José, Petén. Chortí, spoken in several municipalities of Chiquimula, is also on the verge of disappearing. The same is true with Xinca, with only a dozen adherents in Santa Rosa. Pocomám (used in the villages of Palín, Chinautla, Mixco, and San Luis Jilotepeque) and Mopán (spoken only in San Luis, Petén) are also endangered, though native speakers have taken steps to preserve and revive these languages. Most of the 19 native languages are linguistically distinct, hampering cross communication (Figure 6a).[9]

As of 1981 government census statistics, the departments with a majority indian population were Totonicapán (97 percent), Sololá (94 percent), Alta Verapaz (89 percent), Quiché (85 percent), Chimal-

Figure 6a

Ethnic Regions in Guatemala

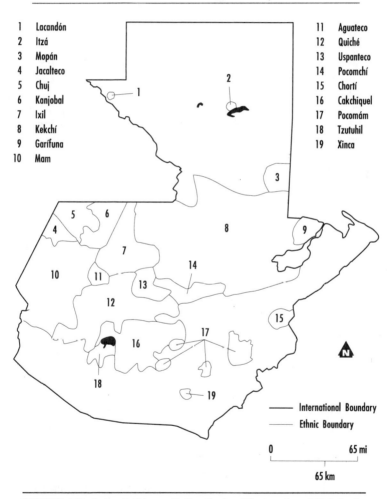

1	Lacandón	11	Aguateco
2	Itzá	12	Quiché
3	Mopán	13	Uspanteco
4	Jacalteco	14	Pocomchí
5	Chuj	15	Chortí
6	Kanjobal	16	Cakchiquel
7	Ixil	17	Pocomám
8	Kekchí	18	Tzutuhil
9	Garífuna	19	Xinca
10	Mam		

International Boundary
Ethnic Boundary

0   65 mi

65 km

SOURCE: Lilly de Jongh Osborne, *Indian Crafts of Guatemala and El Salvador* (Norman: University of Oklahoma Press, 1965), p. 70.

tenango (80 percent), Huehuetenango (66 percent), Quetzaltenango (61 percent), Baja Verapaz (57 percent), and Suchitepequez (56 percent). The departments that experienced the most rapid abatement in the percentage of indigenous population between 1950 and 1981 were San Marcos, Chiquimula, Jalapa, Retalhuleu, Jutiapa, Santa Rosa, Zacapa, and El Progreso. Loss of land and language among the indian people in the eastern departments has led to a dramatic *ladinización* of this region. Such was also the case in San Marcos (where the percentage of indian population slipped from 72 percent to 48 percent), particularly along the coast and in the volcanic uplands, though the more isolated highlands villages have maintained high percentages of indians.

Migration to the cities has historically been a mainly *ladino* phenomenon, but during the 1980s there was an upsurge in indian urbanization as well. Guatemala City growth is far outpacing the overall national rate of population increase, and the capital currently accounts for about one-quarter of the nation's population. Once in the city, the cultural identity of an indian migrant dissolves quickly. According to a 1991 evaluation of population patterns by the AVANCSO research institute in Guatemala City, the nation no longer has an indian majority because of the continuing process of *ladinización*. It was estimated, however, that outside of Guatemala City the population is still divided about evenly between indian and *ladino*.[10]

Departments with the highest concentration of indians are among the poorest in Guatemala, experiencing the worst education and health indicators. Only departments in the eastern region, especially Jutiapa, Jalapa, and Chiquimula, suffer similar indignities.

The Garifuna Community

The Garifuna, formerly called Black Caribs, are Guatemala's smallest ethnic group, and are centered around Livingston on the Bay of Honduras. They descend from a mixture of African and Carib peoples on the island of St. Vincent in the Lesser Antilles. Resistance to British encroachment of their land base led to the Carib War of 1795. After the British prevailed in 1796, the entire Black Carib population was deported to Roatan Island off the coast of Honduras. The slightly more than 2,000 who survived the deportation soon dispersed along the Atlantic Coast of Central America from present-day Belize to the Misquito Coast of Honduras and Nicaragua.[11]

The 4,500 Garifuna in Guatemala represent less than 1 percent of the population, and have largely escaped the violence that has afflicted other indigenous groups in the country.[12] While some Garifuna support themselves by fishing and farming, wage labor in the logging and shipping industries has historically predominated. Since the 1960's a great many Garifuna have migrated to the United States, and remittances from these migrants are a major source of income. Since the mid-1980's Livingston has become a popular tourist destination, and service-sector jobs in the tourist industry are a major source of employment.[13] The recent popularity of Garifuna music and dancing holds the potential to either reinforce Garifuna cultural identity or reduce it to a sideshow, depending on how it is promoted. Large-scale permanent migration in the face of limited economic opportunities is the greatest threat to the survival of the Garifuna as a distinct ethnic group.

Indian Organizing

Until the past few decades indian organizing has been limited largely to the management of their own communities and to religious activities. The agrarian reform program and the labor code introduced in the 1944-54 period opened up unprecedented opportunities for popular organizing around economic issues. It was not until the 1960s, however, that indians began to organize themselves in cooperatives, self-help associations, peasant leagues, and educational groups, mostly as a result of Catholic Church outreach programs such as Catholic Action. Out of catechistic and literacy programs a young indian leadership emerged that was attracted by new economic development schemes initiated by foreign missionaries, U.S. economic aid projects, international nongovernmental organizations, and the Christian Democrats. This new progressive thinking challenged the traditional indian elites clustered around the *cofradías* (brotherhoods established by the Spanish that cared for the "saints" of the Catholic Church while also performing other religious and political functions). In fact, the very act of promoting cooperatives and other economic development projects targeted the organizers for repression by the local economic power structures and the military.

This new activism centered around Santa Cruz del Quiché and north into the Ixil Triangle. In this region repression against the indian popular movement first surfaced, triggering political radicalization that eventually led to a merging with leftist guerrillas. The indian bourgeoisie of Nebaj, spawned largely by the labor-contracting business trade and the use of communal lands, was alarmed at the growing popular activism of the early 1970s. The head of the local *cofradía*, Sebastián Guzmán, wrote a letter to General Carlos Arana Osorio, then president of Guatemala, in which he solicited Arana's direct intervention because "a bad seed is now among us, the communists, and they are fighting among us with cooperatives, and other foolish notions."[14] Two years later Guzmán petitioned the army commander of Santa Cruz del Quiché to "come to finish off the guerrillas" because "they are Cubans through and through." According to the EGP, in December 1975 Guzmán, together with other members of the traditional indian elite in Nebaj, met at Guzmán's home to draw up what became the first black list of "subversives" and their supporters in Nebaj. The list was handed over to army intelligence, and in March 1979 the army occupied Nebaj following the appearance of the EGP in the town and began its scorched-earth counterinsurgency campaign.

During the 1970s links steadily developed between the indian popular movement and their *ladino* counterparts. The earthquake that shook the highlands in 1976 catalyzed interethnic cooperation and organizing. Not only did earthquake reconstruction unite indians and *ladinos* in a common purpose, but it also brought together different indian communities for the first time. Also fostering indian-*ladino* popular coalitions was the organizing and support work related to the march to Guatemala by the miners of Ixtahuacán, Huehuetenango in 1977. With the founding of the Campesino Unity Committee (CUC) in 1978, the indian popular movement began to spread rapidly through all parts of the highlands. CUC soon became a prominent member of the National Committee for Labor Unity (CNUS), marking a new stage in the swelling indian-*ladino* alliance. The indian popular movement reached its apex in 1980. Gathering clandestinely at the Iximché ruins in February 1980, just after the burning of the Spanish embassy with CUC activists inside, indian leaders from throughout the nation issued what became known as the Declaration of Iximché, in which they proclaimed: "We have to fight together with workers, peasants, students, squatters, and other democratic popular sectors."[15] As a result of their common adversities, CUC and other indian groups sought closer ties with the *ladino* popular movement. Soon thereafter the distinction between the rural popular movement and the guerrillas all but vanished as mounting repression persuaded entire indian communities to cast their lot with the armed resistance. Passive support of the guerrilla movement suddenly transformed into massive incorporation in a surge of leftist triumphalism in 1980-81.

Another current of indian activism also emerged in the early 1970s focused more on cultural than on political or economic issues.[16] In 1973 the recently founded Indigenous Association for Maya/Quiché Cultural Preservation protested the unequal treatment toward the indian beauty queen of Quiché, who had not received the same monetary reward as the *ladino* queen. The Indigenous Seminars sponsored by Catholic Action also provided a forum for the incipient cultural-nationalist movement, centered in Quetzaltenango. However, the Maya nationalist movement, which criticized indian-*ladino* coalitions and the emphasis of class over cultural divisions, never took root among the wider indian populace and had faded away by the late 1970s.

The debate between Maya nationalism and leftist social activism was fueled by the publication of two major books in the early 1970s. Severo Martínez Peláez in his *La patria del criollo* posited a class-based interpretation of ethnic divisions, contending in typical marxist fashion that today's indigenous peoples were products of colonial means of production and, as such, stood as obstacles to economic and social progress. In contrast, Carlos Guzmán Bockler and Jean-Loup Herbert tendered a cultural interpretation of Guatemalan history.[17]

Embracing the cultural nationalism philosophy, some Mayan leaders encouraged separatism and viewed all contacts with *ladinos* as suspicious. As part of a backlash at the failure of the guerrilla insurgency of the early 1980s, a new class of Mayan intellectuals and teachers revived Maya nationalism, uncovering new sources of support in the United States and Europe. Several U.S. indian groups, such as the National Indian Youth Council and the Indian Law Resource Center, that were supporting the Miskito counterrevolutionaries in Nicaragua also promoted an "indian alternative" for Guatemala, encouraging cultural, political, and economic autonomy.[18] Criticizing the revolutionary and socialist ideas of the URNG, Maya nationalists and their foreign supporters recommended the creation of a Popular Maya Republic. This separatism was denounced by other indian groups, including the International Indian Treaty Council, as unwittingly bolstering the counterrevolutionary objectives of U.S. foreign policy.

Counterinsurgency Invades Indian Communities

In the late 1970s the army suddenly realized that the indians of the highlands were quickly becoming an insurgent population. Socioeconomic conditions —particularly the land crisis—certainly provided cause for rebellion. But it was a combination of the new social teachings of the church, the focus on cooperative formation by many foreign development groups, and the popular-education programs of the guerrillas that sparked what the army considered to be a widespread indian revolt. What was so threatening, from the army's point of view, was the way whole communities suddenly seemed to adopt an organized posture in the face of deteriorating socioeconomic conditions.

The terror unleashed by the military was designed to undercut this wave of popular organizing and to force the indian population to submit to military control. In the process, hundreds of villages were razed, tens of thousands killed, and hundreds of thousands displaced. The level of devastation was unprecedented. It represented the culmination of a campaign of repression dating back to the early 1970s and first directed against indian cooperative organizers, literacy workers, catechists, and other social activists.[19] As the popular movement expanded, so did the intensity of repression. Perceiving no alternative to armed revolution, indians swelled the ranks of the guerrilla forces in 1980-81, at which point the army responded with its scorched-earth counterinsurgency effort. Although the military's campaign of terror was ghastly, it would be a historical error to conclude that only indians suffered from military attacks on rural civilian populations. In the 1966-68 period more than 6,000 peasants (mostly *ladinos*) died in a ruthless army campaign to wipe out the guerrillas and their *campesino* supporters.

In 1984 the World Council of Indigenous Peoples accused the military of pursuing a "policy of systematic extermination of the indian population of Guatemala." In response to these ethnocide accusations, the military justified its counterinsurgency focus on the highlands as a campaign against the stronghold of guerrilla support. Critics, however, charge that only the racism of Guatemalan society can explain the wholesale extermination of over 400 indian villages.[20]

Massacres of indian communities thought to be sympathetic to leftist guerrillas (themselves largely indian) constituted only one element of this ethnocide. As part of its pacification plan, the army attempted to restructure and reprogram indian communities. Development poles, model villages, strategic reeducation camps, penetration roads, obligatory civil patrols, and the encouragement of evangelical proselytizing were all part of the army's overall plan to undermine the indian community and to assert the dominance of "the national identity." As a psychological action plan for the Ixil Triangle disclosed, the purpose of pacification was "to capture the mentality of the Ixils to make them feel part of the Guatemalan nation."[21]

The army's National Security and Development Plan for the highlands brought popular organizing to a halt by mid-1980. But in the latter part of the 1980s, independent grassroots groups once again began to emerge among Indian communities. Most members of the GAM human rights group are indian women; the same is true for CONAVIGUA, founded in 1988 by indian widows in Chimaltenango. Among its objectives are confronting the "abuse, rape, and exploitation which we suffer at the hands of soldiers, civil-patrol leaders, and military commissioners," and helping Guatemalan women, particularly rural indian women to "become conscious and active in the struggle for the well-being of the community."

A courageous indian-based group, the Runujel Junam Council of Ethnic Communities (CERJ), also organized in 1988. The first activity by this Quiché group was a march in Guatemala City denouncing civil-patrol abuses. Its director, Amilcar Méndez, is *ladino* but its membership is virtually all indian. The Campesino Unity Committee (CUC), forced underground during the scourge of blood-shedding in the early 1980s, resumed organizing in 1988. CUC leaders declare that they are now working "to have one more *tortilla* for our children." Another indian organization, the Highland Campesino Committee (CCDA) formed in 1982, operates mainly in Sololá and Chimaltenango.

Temporarily pacified by a combination of military repression and psychological operations, indian communities demonstrated new signs of resistance by 1990. Following an army massacre that left 13 dead in the Tzutuhil indian village of Santiago Atitlán in December 1990, virtually the entire community organized a successful campaign to expel the army outpost. Similar organizing also occurred in two other towns on the shores of Lake Atitlán. Also impressive was the organizing that resulted in the Second Encounter of the 500 Years of Indigenous and Popular Resistance in October 1991 in Quetzaltenango. At that conference, however, a rift between Maya nationalists and the popular movement hinted at future strains. The group hosting the international conference, Majawil Q'ij or New Dawn, is a coalition of grassroots indian organizations including CUC, CONAVIGUA, CONDEG, and CCDA. The climax of the international conference was a massive march of 25,000—95 percent indigenous and two-thirds women—through the streets of Quetzaltenango, highlighting the growing importance of popular organizing among the nation's indian communities.[22] The leaders of the conference were criticized, however, by Maya nationalists for too closely associating with the nonindigenous popular movement and *ladino* leftists.

To some degree, the resurfacing of indian nationalism has been a product of the disillusion, deception, and betrayal that many Guatemalan indians felt after the counterinsurgency campaigns of the early 1980s. In large part, this feeling of betrayal by the guerrillas was fostered by the military in its attempt to lay full blame for the violence on the guerrillas. At the same time, though, many indians felt they had been used as pawns and sacrificial lambs by the *ladino* guerrilla leadership. It is alleged that guerrilla leaders abused indian communities, establishing bases for a marxist revolution but then retreating in the face of the army's counteroffensive, leaving supportive indigenous communities exposed and without armed protection. This perspective is propagated by a new wave of Maya nationalists (such as Demetrio Cojtí) affiliated with the Maya Language Academy (AMLG) and with ethnic studies programs at the San Carlos and Rafael Landívar Universities.

One current of indian nationalism, known as the "fourth world" theory, contends that indians have little in common with *ladinos*, even poor ones. Indians are considered inherently different from non-indians, who, spoiled by Western industrialized culture, will never understand or respect indian lives and culture. Indians in Guatemala live in such a "fourth world."[23] They are "caught in the middle, and are being moved around like pawns on a chessboard."[24]

Within Guatemala, indian nationalism draws resonance and definition from the teachings of the controversial anthropologist Carlos Guzmán Bockler, who in various books has encouraged the revival of a Mesoamerican indian nation. In seminars that he leads for indian university students, Guzmán argues that indian problems are race-rooted rather than of a class nature. He feels that an "indian war" may be necessary to protect indian rights and assert indian culture. Like other "fourth world" advocates, Guzmán believes that Western culture and civilization have been forcibly imposed on indian communities and need to be discarded. Thus Guzmán lumps leftist guerrillas with other racist "Westerners."[25]

In contrast to this cultural-nationalist analysis, Ja C'amabal I'b, a collective of Guatemalan indians living in Mexico, countered: "We are opposed to those theories which, through a desire, whether sincere or not, of preserving what is indian from all 'contamination of the West,' in reality imply renouncement of the knowledge that we need to make our struggle for liberation effective. This would condemn our struggle to romanticism and failure."[26]

Since the mid-1980s the main focus of Mayan cultural nationalism has been the preservation and regeneration of native languages, which are vanishing at an accelerating pace.[27] Some efforts to revive indian languages and to promote indian culture through bilingual instruction and higher-education programs are funded by the U.S. government. Hatching from these U.S.-funded programs have emerged many of the new sector of Maya nationalists, such as those directing the Maya Language Academy (AMLG). The principal idea of the AMLG is to create a unified written alphabet for the diverse Maya languages, but longer-term goals include affording indigenous people "greater say over their destiny, access to state funds for indian-controlled projects, and greater autonomy in the educational, political, social, and economic spheres."[28]

Founded in 1987, the AMLG was formally incorporated in 1990 as a semi-autonomous state entity, at which time the Guatemalan government granted it funding. The AMLG's total financial dependence on the government and strong U.S. support for such programs have resurrected concerns about connections between Maya nationalism and attempts to undermine and divide the popular movement.

These suspicions have been heightened by the manner in which Maya nationalists define their movement as nonpolitical, yet direct all their criticism at the popular and guerrilla movements rather than at the government and military.[29]

Revolutionary Movement: The Indigenous Question

The leftist revolutionary movement has struggled with questions regarding ethnicity and revolution since the early 1960s. At first, indian issues and the role of indigenous people in the revolution were interpreted solely in terms of the marxist doctrines of the Guatemalan Workers Party (PGT) and the country's first guerrilla front, Rebel Armed Forces (FAR). Indians were considered to be unorganizable and too passive to play a critical role in revolutionary struggle. This reasoning partly explains the decision to focus the first guerrilla *foco* in an area of northeastern Guatemala populated mostly by *ladino* peasants.

Not until the late 1960s did Guatemalan insurgents recognize the revolutionary potential of the indian population. When guerrilla forces resurfaced in the late 1970s, the focus of their organizing was among the indian communities of the *altiplano*. The three major rebel groups—Guerrilla Army of the Poor (EGP), which targeted northern Huehuetenango and Quiché; Revolutionary Organization of People in Arms (ORPA), which organized in Sololá and San Marcos; and FAR, which established its base in Petén—took more care this time in promoting indian leadership and presenting the revolutionary struggle in terms of indian interests. The URNG claims that 70 percent of its combatants, collaborators, and social base are indigenous people.[30]

Although more conscious of racism and the need to integrate indians into the struggle, the guerrilla leadership has not, however, fully developed an analysis of ethnic issues. The Guatemalan National Revolutionary Unity (URNG), the guerrilla coalition, places high priority on what it calls "ethnic-national questions," while cautioning against the dangers of indian nationalism. In 1985 the EGP asserted: "The situation of the indian as both oppressed and exploited, in which class contradictions are linked to ethnic-national contradictions is what gives the Guatemalan revolution its special character."[31] Further clarifying this commitment to resolving ethnic-national questions, the URNG declared: "The revolutionary movement must respect, with great dedication, the legitimate rights of the ethnic-national groups, creating economic and political bases which will allow them real access to the entire society. The participation at the directorate and every level of the guerrilla movement, as well as full participation at the national level after we take power, is the pre-requisite for all possible change."

Both from within and outside the guerrilla forces, Guatemalan indians themselves, like Rigoberta Menchú, are trying to determine the extent and nature of ethnic-national questions in Guatemala. As Domingo Hernández, a member of Ja C'amabal I'b and former CUC leader, reflected: "[We] Indians are just now beginning to analyze for ourselves our vision for the society to which we belong, what we think of the new society, what we think of our own culture and identity, of our particular needs and desires." Hernández credited the URNG with being one of the few groups to seriously address ethnic issues in Guatemala, adding:

> "Despite errors and insufficiencies, the revolutionary organiza-
> tions have played a decisive role in helping the indian people
> develop a systematic critique of their problems [by providing the
> people] with a revolutionary perspective, explaining the class
> nature of the state, the government, and the army, explaining
> the profound causes of the exploitation, oppression, and social
> discrimination and suggesting the need for unity between poor
> *campesinos* and workers, and between indians and *ladinos*."[32]

Despite the advances made by URNG leaders, many indians feel that the guerrilla leadership, composed entirely of *ladinos*, still clings to old models. As one critique proposed: "The revolution must be a political method, through which the popular masses decide their destiny, not an already decided system. The indian must play a protago-nist role, a role not won as a concession, but rightfully owned."[33]

As the debate about the role of indians in the guerrilla movement and in defining its goals evolved, Guatemalan indian organizations rose to the forefront of the popular struggle by the early 1990s. Indian leaders and groups became protagonists in determining the scope of the grassroots movement and in establishing its goals and strategies. The rise in indian consciousness and activism was reflected in the ex-alted importance of indian popular organizations, in the re-emer-gence of the Maya nationalist trend, and in seemingly spontaneous grassroots, indigenous protests in places such as Santiago Atitlán (antimilitary and pro-local control), San Jorge la Laguna (land occu-pation), and Totonicapán (antimilitary recruiting). Tensions between Maya nationalists and social activists have stimulated essential de-bate about the identity and character of the Guatemalan nation. Such debate has resulted in a stronger URNG position with respect to in-digenous rights, including items in its May 1992 peace proposal de-manding that historic indian land rights be respected and that economic development programs be drawn up and administered by indian communities.[34] Indian activism within both the guerrilla and popular movements is slowly leading to a new realization of the importance of resolving ethnic issues in the struggle for peace and justice in Guatemala.

The awarding of the 1992 Nobel Peace Prize to Rigoberta Menchú focused international attention on the oppression of indigenous people in Guatemala. The Continental Campaign of 500 Years of Indigenous and Popular Resistance had nominated Menchú at the its 1991 assembly celebrated in Guatemala. The peace prize served to highlight the central role that Menchú and other indian activists associated with the Majawil Q'ij coalition are playing in rebuilding the popular movement in Guatemala.

The Environment

© Derrill Bazzy

Nature and Environmentalism

Slowly Guatemala is waking up to the environmental crisis created by its wasteful and unequal patterns of resource use. As yet there is little popular consciousness about the unsustainability of resource-use practices in the countryside. But in the Guatemala City metropolitan area—home to 25 percent of the population—there is a new awareness of the environmental limitations of unregulated growth. It is a consciousness born of the travail of daily life—the lack of water, the thick diesel fumes that smother the city, the hazards of living on the sides of precipitous ravines, and the stench rising from the mountains of unprocessed garbage accumulating in the city dumps.

Outside the country's urban center the environmental crisis is equally severe. For the most part, though, it takes the form of a deepening conflict over the use and control of land. Decades ago the country had enough land to sustain, albeit unequally, a dual system of agriculture in which peasants relied on small plots for at least part of their subsistence while landed oligarchs, agribusinesses, and ranchers expanded across the country's best terrain. This dual structure is being threatened on both sides by such symptoms of environmental degradation as massive erosion and depletion of the soil, drying up of rivers and streambeds, and the lack of land resulting from the loss of agricultural frontiers.

Although environmental deterioration is only now threatening human society and economy, the country's flora and fauna have long suffered from human activities. From the cloud forests of the highlands to the mangrove coastal swamps, Guatemala (which means the "land of trees") has been steadily losing much of its animal and plant life over the last four decades of economic modernization.[1]

Biodiversity and Extinction

The quetzal, the resplendently plumaged creature few have ever seen, is the national bird of Guatemala. It has lent its name to the national currency and to the country's second largest city. The quetzal is the symbol of Guatemala.

One of the few places you can hope to see a quetzal is at the Quetzal Reserve (Biotopo del Quetzal) on the road to Cobán in Alta Verapaz. The lush green of the reserve stands in tragic contrast to the deforested country that surrounds the national bird's final sanctuary. It is a creature of the cloud forest—a misty jungle of deep-green ferns and impenetrable foliage that once covered the mountains of the Guatemalan highlands. Today, the range of the quetzal is only 2,500 square kilometers. By the year 2000 the Guatemalan quetzal might be extinct, leaving only the few stuffed birds one sees in the National Palace and in dusty museums to accompany the images of the fabled creature woven into the *huipiles* and blankets of the native people of this deforested land.

Despite the extent of environmental degradation, Guatemala is still an enchantingly beautiful country. As the northernmost point of the isthmian bridge between the two American continents, the country hosts an extraordinary ecological diversity (Figure 7a). Its vertebrate fauna selection is the most diverse and the second most numerous in the region (after Costa Rica) with 45 endemic vertebrate species. But Guatemala's list of 133 endangered species also ranks a close second to Costa Rica's 138.[2] Besides the quetzal, other species on the endangered list include howler and spider monkeys, pumas, ocelots, jaguars, tapirs, harpy eagles, scarlet macaws, and two species of crocodiles.[3] Guatemala hosts the richest and most diverse flora in Central America, with some 8,000 species of vascular plants. Such food crops as maize, runner beans, tomatoes, and cocoa originated in the historic Mayan civilizations of Mexico and Guatemala, emphasizing the importance of preserving this genetic base.[4]

There are four basic physical regions in Guatemala: the Pacific coastal plain, the Pacific mountain chain, the interior highlands, and the Petén-Caribbean lowlands.[5] The general ecological zones that spread across these geographical regions are the lowland tropical and subtropical rainforests, the seasonally dry forest of northeast Petén, the highland oak and pine forests, tropical savannas, and mangrove forests (Figure 7b).

Fifty years ago the Pacific coastal plain looked far different from its appearance today. Only the occasional ceiba tree reminds one that this land of pasture, canefields, and swamps was once densely forested and uninhabited. Post-World War II expansion of the cotton, sugar, and cattle industries together with numerous colonization programs leveled the ancient subtropical forests of the Pacific lowlands. With the trees went most of the animal life, including the bears and ocelots that used to roam these lands. Threatened species such as crocodiles, caimans, iguanas, and fresh-water and marine turtles are still found along the beaches and in the mangrove forests, but they are rapidly disappearing.

Paralleling the coastal plain is the spectacular Pacific mountain chain, which encompasses both the cloud forests of the higher elevations and the volcanic uplands or *boca costa*. Thirty-three volcanos, including the highest peak in Central America (Volcán Tajumulco), divide the coastal plains from the interior highlands. Most of the volcanos are biotic islands that host their own communities of flora and fauna, much of which could not survive elsewhere. Although a federal law prohibits economic activity on the folds of the volcanos, fuelwood gathering and farming are common even on the steepest inclines. Deforestation of these high elevations is not only threatening native species but is also destroying the watershed for the country's largest cities.

To the east of the Pacific mountain chain lie the interior highlands or *altiplano*—an extraordinary mix of mountains, mesas, volcanos, and valleys. Covered by highland oak, pine forests, and tropical savannas, these highlands extend from the southern reaches of the Pacific chain to the foothills north of the three mountain ranges: Sierra de los Cuchumatanes, Sierra de Chama, and Sierra de las Minas. These mountains provide the most important source of tropical pine germ plasm in the world, with seeds from the Cuchumatanes having been used in reforestation programs in Africa and Asia. The pine forests found in the central highlands of Guatemala are largely secondary growth, which has occurred after the original hardwood trees were cut.[6] The complexity of this area's geology and topography, including 11 of the country's 14 ecological zones, give rise to diverse microclimates of wind, temperature, rainfall, and humidity.

The Petén-Caribbean lowlands are situated along the country's Caribbean coast, in Petén department, and in the isolated northern stretches of Huehuetenango, Quiché, and Alta Verapaz. Hot and humid, these mostly subtropical flatlands host a small section of tropical rainforest near the Caribbean as well as extensive broadleaf forests including such tropical trees as Spanish cedar, mahogany, and *chicle*. The region surrounds Lake Izabal and the Dulce River, which provides a critical habitat for the endangered sea mammal, the manatee. Half of Guatemala's 664 species of birds are found in these lowland forests, as well as a rich array of wildlife including jaguars, pumas, monkeys, peccaries, and tapirs.

Because of the lack of scientific surveys little hard information is available on the status of endangered species in Guatemala. Destruction of habitats is the principal threat facing wildlife, but the trafficking in exotic birds and animals as well as the export of animal skins also endanger the country's remaining animal diversity. The export of monkeys, jaguar skins, macaws, and other exotic "products" of the tropics is a big business, with most legal and illegal export going through Honduras or Mexico. Guatemala does have laws protecting its flora and fauna, but these laws are routinely flouted and the government has shown little political will to end such practices. Both commercial and personal hunting also threaten many species. Particularly harmful is the continued practice of hunting females during periods of reproduction. Iguanas, whose meat finds a market in both rural and urban communities, are hunted precisely when the females are bloated with eggs.[7]

Figure 7a

Environment in Statistics

Land Use

Total land area	42,040 sq. miles
Land tenure	2% of population owns 65% of land
Cultivated land	17% (1980)
Permanent pasture	8% (1980)
Forest and woodland	42% (1980)
Protected Areas	54 areas under public and private control

Deforestation

Deforestation rate	265,000-395,000 acres/yr.
Forest cover as % of national territory in 1959	67%
in 1990	35%
Projected loss of all forest cover	25-40 years

Use of deforested wood: Lumber (4%); Fuel for industries (5%); Fires and disease (9%); Domestic firewood (26%); Cleared for other purposes, mainly agriculture and ranching (56%).

Erosion

Land at high risk of erosion	30%
Land already seriously eroded or degraded	25-35%

Biodiversity

Plants	8,000 species
Orchids	527 varieties (57 endemic)
Vertebrates	1,500 (45 endemic)

Deforestation Advances

At current rates of deforestation, Guatemala will completely lose its forest cover in 25-40 years. Its estimated rate of deforestation is 1,080-1,620 square kilometers annually.[8] Some 65 percent of the country's original forest cover has been destroyed, most in the last three decades. Since 1980 Guatemala has lost more than 5,000 square kilometers of dense forests, not counting mangrove forests and forests of secondary growth. Reforestation efforts, although now under way, are minimal—at most only 10 percent of what is cut is reforested.[9]

Cutting firewood is the leading cause for deforestation—directly accounting for about one-quarter of deforestation in Guatemala.[10] Two of every three Guatemalans do not have electricity in their homes, and as many as three of every four rely exclusively on wood

Mammals	250 species
Birds	664 species (including 184 migratory)
Reptiles	231 species
Amphibians	88 species
Fish (fresh-water)	220 species
Endangered or threatened animals	133 species

Forests

Species of coniferous trees	17
Species of broadleaf trees	450

Water and Sanitation

% of towns with municipal water systems (not including Guatemala City) with treated water	24%
% population without easy access (in house or community spigot) to potable water	39%
% population without sewage service	41%
% homes in Guatemala City metropolitan area without water service	54%
% homes in Guatemala City metropolitan area without sanitary service	27%

SOURCES: H. Jeffrey Leonard, *Natural Resources and Economic Development in Central America: A Regional Environmental Profile* (Washington, DC: International Institute for Environment and Development, 1987); James Nations et al., *Biodiversity in Guatemala* (Guatemala City: AID, December 1988); *Perfil Ambiental de Guatemala* (Guatemala City: Produced for the U.S. Agency for International Development by Universidad Rafael Landivar, 1984); UNICEF, *Situación de pobreza: Guatemala* (Guatemala City: May 1991).

for cooking. An extremely inefficient form of combustion, the burning of firewood not only is deforesting Guatemala but also constitutes a major cause of maladies such as pulmonary and cardiovascular problems as well as eye irritation.

Figure 7b

Guatemala's Ecological Zones

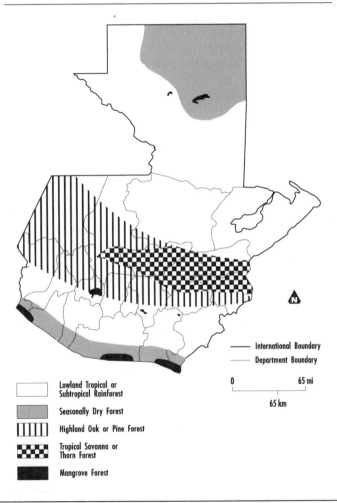

International Boundary
Department Boundary

0   65 mi

65 km

Lowland Tropical or
Subtropical Rainforest

Seasonally Dry Forest

Highland Oak or Pine Forest

Tropical Savanna or
Thorn Forest

Mangrove Forest

SOURCE: Florence Gardner, "Guatemala:A Political Ecology," Green Paper #5 (EPOCA: October 1990), p. 2.

The country's rich mangrove forests, a bountiful source of shrimp and fish, are rapidly being lost to reckless development. An estimated 40 percent of the mangrove forests have been seriously degraded or lost since 1965.[11] Each year many acres of mangroves are cut to produce fuel for drying salt from sea water—a process that could more easily and economically be achieved using accessible solar methods. Mangroves are essential for coastal preservation and provide a crucial component in the life cycle of a surprising amount of marine life. Some marine biologists believe that up to 90 percent of commercial fish in Guatemala's coastal waters spend at least part of their life cycle in the mangrove forests.[12] Considered economically worthless by most local residents and developers, the mangrove swamps actually provide an important foundation for the shrimp and fishing industries as well as for tourism.

The rapid pace of deforestation is most visible in Petén, where as much as 120,000 acres are deforested annually. Until the early 1970s, when colonization programs expanded and military influence increased, Petén was one of the few places in Guatemala where one could escape the kinds of vicious economic exploitation and repression common elsewhere in the country. Peteneros, until recently, used to describe life in this province using two maxims: "The forest is rich and provides for us," and "Petén is more democratic and tranquil than the rest of Guatemala."[13]

Population pressures explain part of this devastation. In the two decades following the 1970 opening of an all-weather road linking central Petén to southern Guatemala, the population of this remote region skyrocketed from 15,000 to 260,000—far above the 150,000 that the government thought the region was capable of sustaining when it first began studying Petén's development in 1958. Besides the new road that joined the region to the rest of Guatemala, another factor leading to the area's population explosion has been a series of colonization programs since the 1960s sponsored by the government and collaborating church agencies. Particularly since the 1970s, Petén has also been the refuge of Kekchís pushed off their lands by an invasion of corporate investors, ranchers, and generals interested in profiting from the relatively unexploited region of Alta Verapaz. Most of the new Peteneros are, however, poor *ladinos* who migrated to Petén to escape landlessness and economic deprivation.[14]

Despite new government regulations, logging continues to denude Petén of precious hardwoods.[15] Even within so-called protected areas, lumberjacks, counting on the cooperation of local military commanders, cut mahogany and cedar trees for export to Mexico and thence to other foreign destinations. Virtually none of the hardwood cut in Petén undergoes value-added processing before leaving the country. Bootlegging lumberjacks working within protected reserves receive as much as $2,000 each for the large trees, which require 50-100 years to regenerate if reforested properly. In the search for the lucrative hardwoods, hundreds of thousands of lesser value trees are also cleared. According to one estimate, for every salable tree cut, 20 others are destroyed in timbering.[16]

Firewood collection also threatens hardwoods, one study having estimated that 95 percent of households in rural Petén depended exclusively on hardwoods for domestic fuels.[17] Another environmental pressure stems from peasant farmers who practice slash-and-burn agriculture, which after several years leaves land suitable only for pasture. By 1985 nearly 40 percent of Petén forests had been cleared by a combination of loggers, ranchers, and peasants practicing slash-and-burn agriculture. More recent estimates revise that figure upward to as much as 60 percent. Up to 5 million cubic meters of wood, much of it tropical hardwood, are wasted each year in the Petén region as a result of clearing and burning.[18]

Oil exploration and drilling also threaten Petén, the location of most of the country's 26 million barrels in proven reserves—with probable oil reserves of up to one billion barrels. Since 65 percent of the national territory is covered by sedimentary rock, geologists predict that oil reserves could be found throughout the entire country. Guatemala consumes an average of 26,500 barrels of petroleum a day, nearly two-thirds of which is satisfied by Mexico and Venezuela under the San José Accord.[19]

Guerrilla sabotage, the isolation of the region, and the low quality of the country's petroleum (high-sulphur) have been among the factors that have slowed development of these reserves. Basic Resources International (Bahamas) has been operating in Guatemala for 15 years, producing about 3,500 barrels daily, most of which is exported for refining. Guerrillas, largely of the FAR contingent, have repeatedly sabotaged oil operations in Petén, forcing Amoco to abandon its drilling in 1988. With prospects of the guerrilla war ending, international firms have expressed renewed interest in exploiting the country's oil reserves—an interest the government has actively encouraged.

Guerrilla threats to the oil industry persist, however, and the government and oil companies also face mounting local and international concern about the effect of proposed drilling and refining on the fragile ecosystem of the area. Such concern was instrumental in stopping Exxon's 1989 plans to drill for oil on the protected archeological site of El Ceibal. In late 1990 the government signed a 25-year drilling contract with Royal Dutch Shell, which hopes to be extracting oil from Lake Izabal and its perimeter by 1996.

In 1991 Venezuela also entered into a joint oil-exploration project with Guatemala. The agreement was signed under the rubric of the 1983 Hydrocarbons Law, which governs foreign exploitation of natural resources. The law grants 70 percent of all profits to the oil companies, but stipulates that developers may recuperate "exploration costs" before Guatemala gets its share. In December 1990, the Hydrocarbons Law was amended; red tape to obtain permits for petroleum exploitation was greatly simplified, and regulations were relaxed in order to promote foreign investment.[20]

In its eagerness to exploit the country's oil reserves, the Guatemalan government will have to come to terms with competing pressures to preserve Peten's more than 70 archeological sites and with efforts to foster ecotourism. In 1990 the government did set aside a 3.5-million-acre reserve in the Petén, but oil drilling will be permitted in some areas. In fact, the government itself plans to begin refining operations in Petén in 1992.[21]

Erosion Follows

Deforestation, especially when combined with the unsustainable agricultural practices common in Guatemala, leads inevitably to eroded soils, clogged waterways, and flooding. In many areas there are also rising complaints that the climate is turning hotter and drier.

Increasing population pressures and inequitable patterns of land tenure contribute to the alarming erosion problem facing the country. In Guatemala City the homeless are squatting on steep terrains and along the edge of deep ravines. Hundreds of thousands of land invaders are carving out settlements in areas previously regarded as unlivable and are clearing off the little vegetation left on these barren spaces. When the rains come, the sides of the ravines inevitably give way and floodwaters devour parts of these shantytowns. In the countryside peasants farm seemingly impossibly steep volcanic slopes—often tying themselves to rocks and small trees to maintain an upright posture.

The poor, pushed onto the most unstable lands and living in the most unstable structures, are the main victims of the country's earthquakes. After the devastating 1976 earthquake, Guatemalans, resorting as always to black humor, likened the earthquake to a cowboy movie in which all the indians die.[22]

An estimated 25 to 35 percent of Guatemala's land cover is considered eroded or seriously degraded.[23] About two-thirds of the Guatemalan land mass is highly susceptible to soil erosion because so much of the soil is unconsolidated volcanic ash located on fragile slopes. The high population ratio—469 persons for each square kilometer of cultivated land— represents a serious threat to soil stability. Annual soil runoff in Guatemala is estimated to range from 20-300 metric tons per hectare in areas still under vegetative cover to 700-1,100 metric tons per hectare in unforested areas.[24] Little is being done to halt the advance of erosion. Government programs to promote soil conservation practices, never wielding much impact, have been trimmed even further by recent budget-cutting measures.

Extensive soil erosion resulting from deforestation and hillside farming has led to serious silting of rivers and lakes. The carrying capacity of the Motagua River was reduced by 50 percent between 1960 and 1980 due to sedimentation, a process causing flooding and threatening irrigation projects. Agricultural development on steep slopes is also contributing to the rapid siltation of Lake Atitlán, while mining and lumber operations are causing major sedimentation in Lake Izabal.[25] Some of the country's smaller lakes are almost completely eutrophic, such as Lake Ocubilá (near Huehuetenango), whose surface is 95 percent covered by algae and vegetation. Not too long ago Guatemalans could enjoy the sight of clear water rushing down streams and riverbeds during the rainy season. Now those waterways are clogged with silt from eroded banks and foaming with detergents and other human products.[26]

The extreme depth of Lake Atitlán and its isolation from large urban centers have protected this spectacular area from rapid deterioration. Nonetheless, the lake and its natural life are endangered. In the past thirty years the variety of fish in the lake has declined from 18 to seven species. Erosion caused by increased cultivation and home construction on the lakefront and in surrounding hills has led to a dramatic loss of vegetation around the lake. In 1956 the government declared the area a national park with multiple uses, but it has never been managed as such. In 1960 there were 28 chalets fringing the water; in 1991 there were 501 second homes cluttering the shore.[27]

Hydroelectric power, too, has brought ecological, financial, and human catastrophe to Guatemala. Financed by the World Bank and the Inter-American Development Bank (IDB), hydroelectric projects like the infamous Chixoy Power Plant have forced thousands of peasant families off their lands, leaving in their wake massive deforestation, heavy reservoir siltation, and evaporative water loss without providing the promised cost-efficient energy. These projects also account for about half the country's external debt.

Counterinsurgency war and related road-building programs have been other major factors in the accelerating deterioration of the environment. Scorched-earth tactics and aerial bombing have left scars across the face of the highlands and the Petén region. In conflictive

areas, the army, using local civil patrols as "voluntary" labor, deforested large swaths of forest on both sides of new and existing roads in
order to avoid ambushes. The counterinsurgency campaign of the
1980s sparked new interest in road-building efforts in isolated areas
frequented by guerrilla forces. Although funded by the United States
and other foreign donors for the purposes of promoting rural development, the so-called farm-to-market routes also served as penetration
roads that linked remote areas to military bases.

The Plague of Pesticides

Excessive pesticide use renders farm labor on agroexport plantations dangerous work. Along the littoral highway fringing the fertile
coastal plain, billboards advertise chemicals that are banned in the
industrial world. The chemical fog that clings to these flatlands
leaves your eyes smarting and your lungs gasping for breath.

It used to be that the chemical war against the environment was
confined to the hot and humid coast. In the last 20 years, however,
chemicals have been integrated into the agricultural practices of
small peasant farmers in the *altiplano* as well, thanks to promotion
by extension agents and foreign development agencies. In recent
years, chemical use has soared due to programs to promote the production of blemish-free nontraditional agroexports. Even in the
United States, the production of spotless produce necessitates frequent sprayings. In tropical climates like that of Guatemala, almost
constant pesticide application is needed to grow fruits and vegetables
acceptable for the U.S. market. This new focus on nontraditional
agroexports has resulted in a rash of health problems and threatens
the environmental balance of the *altiplano*. At least 1,000 Guatemalans are treated annually for pesticide poisoning.[28] In one recent survey, more than half of the small farmers interviewed reported
knowing one or more people who had collapsed, been taken to the hospital, or died from pesticide poisoning.[29]

Another sinister problem is that produce rejected by U.S. buyers
due to excessive chemical input is sold on the local market to unsus-
pecting customers. According to an official at the country's Social Security Institute: "In Guatemala, food can have all the insecticides in
the world, and still be sold on the local market."[30] Adulteration of
milk, cheese, and meat products is common in Guatemala, yet the
government does little to guarantee that consumers get safe food
products. Worm-infested and bacteria-laden meat represents a major
threat to public health, but when a veterinarian recently spoke out
about the dangerous quality of meat on the market, he was assassinated a few days later.

Among the pesticides with unrestricted use in Guatemala that the Pesticide Action Network (PAN) has labeled "the Dirty Dozen" (most dangerous pesticides to human health and to the environment) are Aldicarb (Temik), Paraquat, and Methyl Parathion.[31] So unregulated and careless is pesticide use in Guatemala that growers often spray already harvested products before sending them to market to keep the bugs off their vegetables. Besides the health threats arising from pesticide use, there are also growing economic concerns that the cost of chemical imports undermines the benefits of increased exports (see The Agricultural Economy).

Another aspect of the chemical threat comes in the form of the U.S.-sponsored "war on drugs," which involves widespread spraying of vegetated areas with such glycophosphate herbicides as Round-Up. The spraying, which targets marijuana and poppy-growing areas, has elicited protests from affected communities, which report deaths, illnesses, and nondrug crop losses as a result of the program. In early 1988, the decimation was briefly halted after reports of more than a dozen related deaths in San Marcos and Petén. However, the spraying soon resumed. Critics in Guatemala claim that in addition to Round-Up, such restricted-use chemicals as paraquat, malathion, and EDB have also been reportedly used in the defoliation campaign.

Like many other third world countries, Guatemala has been targeted as a cheap place to dispose of hazardous wastes produced in the industrial world. Various proposals to ship toxic wastes to Guatemala have generated heated debate in the national legislature regarding the extent to which the country should allow the dumping or recycling of these wastes. Greenpeace's office in Central America has encouraged the country to adopt strict laws regulating the import of all industrial and toxic wastes.

The Urban Nightmare

The environmental destruction triggered by rapid and uncontrolled urbanization has not been quantified or scientifically assessed. But there is little doubt that urbanization, particularly in sprawling Guatemala City, is laying waste to the environment while slowly choking the life out of city residents. Home to some two million persons, the metropolitan area is expected to swell to 3.5 million residents by the end of the century.

Smoldering garbage in city dumps emits an acrid odor that blankets Guatemala City during the night and is perhaps the most repulsive symptom of this urban nightmare. Every day Guatemala City produces 1,400 tons of garbage—only three-quarters of which is collected. Since the city has no facilities to treat this waste, it is simply burnt and used as landfill. Since garbage is undifferentiated, the hundreds of people who make a livelihood sorting through the city dumps find everything from discarded bottles to body parts from hospitals. Especially during the dry season the dumps smolder and occasionally flare up, with winds spreading the stench throughout the city. Simply passing near the dumps can induce headaches and nausea. Both treated and untreated sewage is dumped into the waterways, and as much as 70 percent of this sewage eventually reaches Lake Amatitlán south of the city. Once a favorite recreation center, the lake has degenerated from its former deep blue to a brownish green. Besides being a receptacle for urban sewage, the lake also collects the chemical wastes dumped by the some 270 industries located near its shoreline.[32]

Diesel fumes clog both the city's air and the lungs of its inhabitants. Street vendors report high incidences of lung and heart diseases. So thick are the fumes that the faces of pedestrians are uniformly covered with a thin dark coat of carbon and chemicals. Owing to the rapid deterioration in city air quality, vehicle pollution—what Guatemalans call *humo negro* (black smoke)—emerged as more of a public issue in the early 1990s. Laws do exist to regulate the emission of black smoke, but these laws are not enforced. In fact, diesel fuel consumption is encouraged in Guatemala by low diesel fuel prices (about 40 percent less than regular gasoline). Buses are the main culprits. Despite government subsidies to support the public transportation system, bus owners install old and inefficient diesel engines in their vehicles, ignoring the public hazard they constitute. Low diesel prices and the unavailability of unleaded gasoline also encourage individuals to purchase diesel-fueled vehicles, In Guatemala, car dealers remove catalytic converters—and frequently even seat belts—before putting cars on the market. Aggravating the lack of local controls and enforcement is the low quality of imported fuels from suppliers in Mexico, Venezuela, and other countries.

The city's water agency assures residents that their water quality is one of the best in Central America. However, the city's treatment plants are inefficient and do not provide potable water of acceptable standards. In addition, the city's wells are drying up, and the streams that traverse the larger metropolitan area are badly polluted. In fact, these waterways could more aptly be called sewage channels. Underground reserves are dropping sharply—due both to overexploitation and to a decline in the replenishment rates as a result of advancing erosion and deforestation. The city's water system is badly designed, having no infrastructure to capture rain waters and losing (through leaks) 35 percent of what it does pump. Unregulated well drilling and the unpaid use of both city-piped and nearby stream water for irrigation purposes also undermine the city's ability to meet the basic water demands of the citizenry.

It is not the quality of water that residents are most concerned about; it is the increasing lack of it. In the early 1980s the capital city began rationing water in largely poor zones that had sprung up on the area's outskirts. As demand has risen and production rates have dropped, rationing has constricted use sharply, with some areas not receiving water for days at a time. More than one-fifth of the city's residents are not served by city water and have to search each day for their own sources. The lack of water even in areas reached by the city's system has forced tens of thousands of desperate residents to resort to buying from water merchants, who often sell them barrels of bacteria-infested liquid.

The water the city does provide is unmetered, so billing does not reflect usage. Given this loophole, residents of wealthy areas generally continue to enjoy as much water as they need to soak lawns, wash cars, and fill swimming pools. In early 1992, due to drought conditions affecting much of Central America, the lack of water in Guatemala became so severe that public hospitals had to curtail their already limited services for lack of water. In 1991 alone the production capacity of the city's water system dropped by 10-15 percent.

Only a few decades ago the department of Guatemala was nearly 90 percent forested. Today less than 30 percent remains under forest cover, with the urban center completely stripped of vegetation. Parks and outdoor recreation areas are extremely scarce. For each city resident, there is only 2.3 square meters of green space. Besides the process of urbanization itself, the continuing deforestation of surrounding areas is the result of the ever-growing demand for firewood. No other Central American city is so dependent on wood for household cooking and heating. Guatemala City in the space of a few decades has evolved into an urban jungle—almost devoid of greenery, beset by air and water pollution, and a breeding ground for crime.

The environmental crisis in Guatemala City affects all its residents, but it hits the poor hardest. Wealthy areas are generally removed from the city's main business centers and transportation arteries and are thus not as directly affected by vehicle emissions. Not having to ride the buses or walk the streets, the rich also avoid the common experience of being enveloped by suffocating clouds of "black smoke." So too the monied classes do not have to subject themselves to the risks of eating at one of the 7,000 street stands in the city, where the food is exposed to contamination by airborne fecal matter and chemical contaminants. More than 45 percent of Guatemala City residents live in marginal areas without paved streets, garbage services, or sufficient water.

Protecting the Environment

It was not until the late 1980s that environmentalism and conservation began to take hold in Guatemala. The first protected areas were set aside in 1882, but for recreational, not conservation, objectives. In 1955 Guatemala established the first national parks, including Tikal and the Dulce River area. But it was not until the Cerezo administration that the state enacted its first environmental protection laws. Through the Environmental Protection and Improvement Law, the government formed the National Commission for the Environment (Conama) to coordinate all national environmental policies and programs. With the increasing importance of ecotourism, the country has declared new protected reserves and has begun to regulate timbering operations in Petén. A landmark 1990 decree set aside a 3.5-million-acre Mayan Biosphere Reserve in the northern Petén, managed by a dedicated team of conservationists working for the newly created National Council of Protected Areas (Conap).[33] Conap has faced strong opposition from Peteneros, not only the timber industry but also peasant communities, who charge that Conap has illegally deprived them of their lands. Although the government has made some advances in environmental protection, it has failed to integrate environmentalism into its economic and social development strategies, nor has it demonstrated much political will to enforce environmental standards to the detriment of immediate economic interests.

Guatemala does not have a viable environmental movement, but merely fledgling conservationist groups such as the Environmental Defense Association (Aprodem) and Defenders of Nature that make few links between conservation, economic sustainability, and social justice. This is due to the class character of these elite groups as well as their fear that linking their work with socioeconomic issues would expose them to repression and endanger their environmental activism. Within the popular movement, environmental issues and demands have not yet been incorporated into other social struggles. To a large extent, environmentalism is seen as an issue for the privileged elite rather than as a critique of inequitable patterns of resource ownership and use. Compared to its neighboring countries of El Salvador, Nicaragua, and Costa Rica, environmentalism in Guatemala is still in its incipient stages. Hopeful signs include the creation of numerous environmental groups at the national university; new environmental research efforts by FLACSO, ASIES, and AVANCSO; and budding environmental awareness among many nongovernmental organizations.

PART 8

U.S. Influence

© Derrill Bazzy

U.S. Foreign Policy

Between Guatemala and the United States there has existed a long-term sharing of political, economic, and foreign policy interests. This alliance has been, in part, the natural result of the historic predominance of U.S. trade and investment in the Guatemalan economy. Historically, Washington's foreign policy toward Guatemala has also been guided by the perceived Monroe Doctrine prerogative to manage the politics of countries considered to be in the backyard of the United States and, more specifically, by U.S. concerns that a leftist challenge in Guatemala could spread north to Mexico.

Describing U.S. foreign policy interests in Guatemala and arguing for a resumption of U.S. military aid in 1982, Lt. General Wallace Nutting, chief of the U.S. Southern Command, noted: "The population is larger, the economy is stronger, the geographical position is more critically located in a strategic sense. The implications of a Marxist takeover in Guatemala are a lot more serious than in El Salvador."[1] For its part, the U.S. Agency for International Development (AID) also commonly justifies U.S. commitments of "development" assistance in strategic terms, telling the U.S. Congress in 1989: "In terms of U.S. interests in Central America, Guatemala occupies a key position because it has the largest population and strongest economy in the region and has only recently returned to democratic government. The success of democracy and of free-market-based economic reform will have a profound effect on the entire region and act as a brake on Marxist-Leninist expansion."[2]

Since the late 1980s the aggressive anticommunism of U.S. foreign policy in Guatemala has given way to a strategy guided by regional trade and investment concerns, specifically an interest in creating a hemispheric free trade zone. In an effort to forge a more economically and politically stable Guatemala, U.S. criticism of the nation's human rights record, the military, and the extremist right-wing sectors has increased.

Relations Sour and Sweeten

Relations between Washington and the nation's military regimes were shaken in 1977 by the Carter administration's insistence that Guatemala improve its human rights record. Between 1977 and 1983 government-to-government links between the two nations were strained, obligating Guatemala to solicit aid from other countries including Israel, Taiwan, South Africa, and the military regime in Argentina. Nevertheless, U.S.-Guatemala relations were never completely severed, as indicated by the continuing flow of U.S. economic aid.[3]

Relations began to warm again after President Reagan took office. New commercial arms deliveries were approved by the White House, which also attempted to persuade Congress to boost economic aid and renew direct military aid.[4] As the Guatemalan army began to wind down its campaign of terror and the country moved toward civilian rule, the Reagan administration found the U.S. Congress more receptive to its requests for military aid. Although the failure of the Cerezo administration to support the contra war against the Sandinista government in Nicaragua resulted in deteriorating relations with the Reagan administration by the mid-1980s, Guatemala's foreign policy of "active neutrality"—nonintervention in the internal affairs of other Central American countries—found favor among congressional Democrats.[5] To demonstrate this support, the Democrat-controlled Congress approved even more military aid than that requested by the administration for Guatemala, while stipulating that it be of a "nonlethal" nature—meaning military vehicles and equipment rather than guns and ammunition.

Between 1981 and 1988 Washington whitewashed Guatemala's human rights record, apparently feeling that harsh critiques of the security forces would serve to bolster the position of the guerrillas and weaken the stability of the government.[6] Several months after Ríos Montt took power, Assistant Secretary of State Thomas Enders argued that Guatemala's new dictator had "improved the human rights situation and opened the way for a more effective counterinsurgency."[7] Although Washington recognized that human rights abuses did exist in Guatemala, it was not until late in the Cerezo administration and after the arrival of U.S. Ambassador Thomas Stroock in 1989 that the United States publicly began to acknowledge the pattern of human rights abuses. In a major break with the past, the State Department, starting with the publication of its 1990 annual report on human rights, began to accuse the military of being the main perpetrator of these violations (see Lawlessness and Human Rights).

A combination of factors explain this more critical U.S. posture toward Guatemala. By the late 1980s Washington became less preoccupied with Central America as global trade issues and developments in the Soviet Union and Eastern Europe demanded more attention. The transfer of the presidency from Reagan to Bush also shifted the focus off Central America. As the United States became less concerned about military threats to its hegemony in the region, given the collapse of the socialist bloc and the electoral defeat of the Sandinistas in Nicaragua, economic and human rights considerations began to influence U.S. foreign policy posture toward Guatemala. No longer did the concern about Soviet/Cuban/communist penetration in the U.S. "backyard" dominate the U.S. foreign policy agenda.

In Congress attitudes about supporting Guatemala also began to change. With the contra war in Nicaragua over, congressional liberals no longer felt the need to uncritically back Guatemala's "democratic" government. Unlike Cerezo, Serrano did not enjoy a strong base of support among congressional Democrats. Both in Congress and in the administration there also emerged a realization that a civilian government alone did not ensure an improved human rights climate.[8] During most of the Cerezo administration, U.S. and other international support flowed into Guatemala based on the widespread belief that the military was finally subject to civilian control. However, escalating human rights abuses toward the end of the Cerezo years and the continued impunity of the security forces from prosecution led to skepticism about the ability and the will of civilian leaders to assert their control over the military. Promises from politicians and generals that Guatemala was moving toward an *estado de derecho* (rule of law) no longer sufficed. Increasingly, the United States and other foreign donors demanded a substantially improved human rights climate and an end to military and police impunity. To a lesser degree, pressure was also brought to bear on the government for a successful conclusion of peace talks with the URNG guerrilla forces.

Levels of U.S. foreign assistance tumbled as President Serrano was not extended the benefit of the doubt that Cerezo had enjoyed. From a high of $193 million in combined economic and military aid in 1987, the amount of foreign aid dropped to $85 million by 1992, with further decreasing sums scheduled for future years. Budget cutbacks, competing requests for U.S. aid, human rights questions, and fading foreign-policy concern with Central America resulted in the declining U.S. aid commitments. In December 1990, President Bush preempted a congressional initiative against further aid to Guatemala by suspending military assistance.

Although U.S. economic aid has decreased, it still provided significant support for the country's economic stability, especially in balance-of-payments assistance; and Washington continued to exercise considerable influence in Guatemala. Playing on its connections with such multilateral lenders as the World Bank and the Inter-American Development Bank (IDB), the United States stepped up pressure for increased trade liberalization and fiscal reform. Giving in to U.S. pressure, Guatemala in late 1991 joined the General Agreement on Tariffs and Trade (GATT) and signed a "framework agreement" for trade and investment negotiations with the United States. Along with the other Central American nations, Guatemala has moved steadily toward adopting free trade policies in line with President Bush's Enterprise for the Americas Initiative (EAI).

Rather than focusing on new commitments of foreign aid, as the National Bipartisan Commission on Central America (Kissinger Commission) suggested in the 1980s, the EAI addresses trade, external debt, investment, and environmental concerns. Under the EAI, Guatemala benefits by having its bilateral debt with the U.S. government reduced and restructured. The initiative allows countries to pay interest on restructured debts in local currency into national "environmental funds" to be administered by a joint commission of national, government, nongovernmental, and U.S. representatives. Yet another component of the EAI is the creation of a Multilateral Investment Fund (MIF) to be administered by the IDB to promote privatization, provide technical assistance, finance studies researching ways to boost investment, and pay for retraining of workers whose jobs are eliminated due to industrial restructuring. To be eligible for EAI benefits, Guatemala must prove its willingness to comply with the structural adjustment programs recommended by the World Bank and the International Monetary Fund (IMF), and will be required to demonstrate its commitment to promoting foreign investment.

Unlike in the recent past when geopolitical concerns dominated the U.S. foreign policy agenda in Guatemala, the promotion of free trade and export-oriented investment now shapes bilateral relations. The neoliberal imperative, prioritizing economic concerns over political ones, has nudged Washington toward adopting new postures with respect to human rights, demilitarization, and democratization. Although the United States has not yet clearly established policies concerning domestic political and military affairs in Guatemala, the liberalization of the economy and the promotion of its free trade agenda have become its main concerns.

Using bilateral and multilateral funding as leverage, Washington has pressured Guatemala to adopt economic reforms that further its neoliberal goals. A strong critique of human rights abuses, support for efforts to guarantee the "rule of law," suspension of military aid, public support for the peace negotiations, and a focus on antinarcotics operations all indicated a changing U.S. posture toward the Guatemalan military. Washington has called for the downsizing of all Central American armies and the strengthening of civilian police. The military, once regarded as a key U.S. ally in the fight against communist subversion, is now seen as somewhat of a destabilizing force. In an attempt to relegate the army to its proper place in the neoliberal order, Washington has become an advocate of demilitarization and the ending of military impunity. Although Washington has yet to take a clear position with respect to the role of the Guatemalan army, U.S. embassy and government officials would like to see a military both subordinate to and accountable to civilian rule and one that can function as a reliable local partner in the fight against narcotrafficking.

Washington, however, appeared unwilling to make a clear break with past allies and policies. Although the condemnation of human rights abuses and the suspension of military aid were steps in that direction, the United States has declined to condition its entire bilateral aid package (both economic and military) and its support for multilateral assistance to a substantial improvement in the human rights climate and the end to military impunity. Furthermore, U.S. concern for human rights abuses emanated primarily from cases involving U.S. or prominent local citizens cases while failing to address the systematic repression of the popular movement and the structural injustices that deprive Guatemalans of their most basic rights.

U.S. Trade and Investment

No other Central American country, with the exception of Panama, has attracted so much U.S. trade and investment. The United States is Guatemala's leading trading partner, purchasing 41 percent of its exports and providing 37 percent of its imports in 1991.[9] Principal U.S. imports from Guatemala include coffee, sugar, fruits and vegetables, and garments, while the chief U.S. exports to Guatemala are machinery and electronics goods, petroleum and petroleum products, chemicals, vehicles, plastics, and paper products. According to the U.S. Department of Commerce, trade and investment guarantees provided by the U.S. Export-Import Bank (Eximbank) and the Overseas Private Insurance Corporation (OPIC), as well as incentives offered by the Caribbean Basin Initiative (CBI), accelerated U.S. trade with Guatemala in the late 1980s. Most new investment has been in export-oriented manufacturing operations, primarily clothing assembly plants, and in nontraditional agricultural ventures.

Except for a few years in the early 1950s when an agrarian-reform program affected the vast uncultivated lands of United Fruit, U.S. investors have always enjoyed a highly favorable business climate in Guatemala. Some 400 U.S. firms have investments in the country, ranging from small tourist businesses to large transnational corporations like United Brands and RJ Reynolds. Ninety of these companies are among the top 500 corporations in the United States. According to the Commerce Department, the top U.S. investors in Guatemala are Castle & Cooke, Goodyear, and Texaco.[10]

Investors in the agricultural sector are mostly small U.S. agribusiness companies involved in the production and processing of nontraditional agroexports. Among the better-known U.S. corporations operating in Guatemala is RJ Reynolds, which owns the Del Monte banana plantations near Puerto Barrios on the Atlantic Coast. Goodyear cultivates rubber plantations, and Ralston Purina runs a variety of agroindustries including a feed mill. Other food-processing giants in the country include Warner Lambert (gum manufacturing), Beatrice (snack foods), Coca-Cola (instant coffee), and Philip Morris (cigarettes).

Seventeen of the top 20 U.S. pharmaceutical firms are active in the country, as are the top ten U.S. chemical firms, which manufacture pesticides. Three hotel chains—Sheraton, Ramada Inns, and Westin Hotels—help tourists feel at home in Guatemala. Shell, Texaco, and Exxon are the main gas distributors. The State Department once referred to Guatemala as "the plum of Central America" because of its potential oil reserves. The slow rate of extraction and guerrilla sabotage dampened initial enthusiasm, although such companies as Exxon and Royal Dutch Shell have either signed or plan to sign new exploration contracts with the Guatemala government (see Nature and Environmentalism).[11] More than 70 percent of the garments assembled in the some 400 *maquiladoras* are shipped to the United States. Most of the garment production is managed by local or Korean investors on contract with such U.S. firms as Montgomery Ward, J.C. Penney, Target, K-mart, Liz Claiborne, Sears, Gap, Gitano, H. Collectibles, and Tot Trends. More than 15 U.S. companies also have direct investments in Guatemala's garment industry.[12]

In October 1991, on the heels of its accession to the multilateral General Agreement on Tariffs and Trade (GATT), Guatemala signed a framework accord for discussion in Washington of trade and investment issues. A similar accord between the United States and Mexico set the stage for free trade negotiations in 1991-92. Washington has little complaint with Guatemala's investment climate and is increasingly pleased with its liberalization of foreign trade. Besides nudging Guatemala closer to a free trade stance, as advocated by President Bush's Enterprise for the Americas Initiative, the framework agreement also gives Washington more leverage over the country's economic policy. A major area of U.S. concern has been the lack of protection of intellectual-property rights (patents and copyrights) in Guatemala. Leading the private-sector attack on this front is the Motion Picture Export Association, which in 1991 singled out Guatemala as one of the world's major abusers of intellectual-property rights (by showing films and renting videos without paying fees or royalties).

Economic Aid

Although U.S. military aid was halted in 1977, modest levels of U.S. economic aid continued to flow into Guatemala during the Lucas García and Ríos Montt regimes. In the early 1980s, this aid—averaging about $15 million a year—was an important, and in some cases the only source of support for military-sponsored development programs in the western highlands.[13] As Guatemala moved toward civilian rule in the mid-1980s, the Reagan administration successfully pressured Congress for a rapid ascent in economic aid. By 1989 Guatemala had become the seventh-largest recipient of U.S. economic aid in the world.

Assistance Strategy in the 1980s

During the 1980s U.S. foreign policy toward Guatemala was simply a variation on its overall Central American policy. Like its neighbors Honduras and El Salvador, Guatemala was regarded by the U.S. government as a success story in "democratization." Support for the transition from military to civilian rule was accompanied by a program of economic stabilization and private-sector support. According to Washington, the economic salvation of Guatemala, as with other Central American countries, depended upon efforts by the government and AID to promote private-sector investment and nontraditional exports, which would spur economic growth while uplifting the poor via the magic of the marketplace.

Unlike in El Salvador, where Washington wholeheartedly and unabashedly supported the counterinsurgency war, the U.S. embassy tried to maintain some public distance between itself and the Guatemalan military. Nonetheless, military aid edged upward in the late 1980s, supplemented by indirect military aid through civic-action and drug-enforcement programs and by the approval of new commercial military sales. During the 1980s Guatemala received increasing allocations of all forms of U.S. economic aid, ranging from food aid and trade credits to economic support funds and an expanded Peace Corps program. The main instrument for the delivery of U.S. economic aid is the Agency for International Development (AID), which is an agency of the U.S. State Department and thus directly reflects U.S. foreign policy goals.

Beginning in 1983 the United States sponsored a program of political and economic stabilization. Among the elements of this plan were the following:

– Large injections of balance-of-payments economic assistance.

– Development assistance and local-currency funding to support the military-controlled pacification campaign in conflictive areas.

– An economic-growth strategy based on the promotion of private-sector investment, particularly in nontraditional exports.

– Military aid, training, and arms sales to support the army's counterinsurgency efforts and to link it more firmly to the United States.

– Support for the "democratization" process through economic-aid programs that finance electoral processes, policy think tanks, police training, judicial reform programs, and new business associations.

– Financial and diplomatic backing for multilateral aid lending from such institutions as the Inter-American Development Bank, and support for related efforts to improve the international standing of Guatemala.

From 1985 to 1990, Guatemala received more than $800 million in AID funding (Figure 8a). Five out of every eight dollars came in the form of balance-of-payments support either through Economic Support Funds (ESF) or the Title I food-aid program. This downpour of U.S. dollars provided crucial foreign financial support for the institutional reordering and stabilization plan initiated by the military high command in 1984. The ESF and Title I programs were used by the U.S. embassy to back an economic-stabilization program for the Cerezo government and to push through such structural-adjustment measures as currency devaluation and price liberalization. Besides ESF and food aid, Washington funds Development Assistance projects and even specifies in ESF agreements just how the Guatemalan government must expend the local currency generated by U.S. balance-of-payments support.

Aid for Counterinsurgency

During the 1980s AID program summaries, strategy statements, and congressional budget presentations made little or no mention of the fighting in Guatemala. There were no references to the fact that the army's multifaceted counterinsurgency campaign focused on the very same parts of the country where AID's own rural development programs were concentrated. There was no discussion of the degree to which the military determined the development priorities for the highlands and other conflictive areas. Nor was there any mention of the dominance that the military exercised (through the military-controlled interinstitutional councils) over the financial resources of other government agencies.[14]

Initially, AID contributed directly to the model village programs initiated by the military regimes of Ríos Montt and Mejía Víctores. After a congressional resolution in 1984 expressly prohibited such direct aid, indirect funding from AID continued to contribute to the military's "development" plans for the conflictive areas. Apparently,

Figure 8a

U.S. Economic Aid to Guatemala

In millions of U.S. $.

Year	DA	ESF	PL480 I	PL480 II	Peace Corps	Total
1977	14.3	0	0	4.5	1.5	20.3
1978	4.5	0	0	4.6	1.5	10.6
1979	17.4	0	0	5.3	2.0	24.7
1980	7.8	0	0	3.3	1.8	12.9
1981	9.1	0	0	7.5	2.0	18.6
1982	8.2	0	0	5.6	1.7	15.5
1983	12.3	10.0	0	5.4	1.9	29.6
1984	4.5	0	6.7	6.5	2.6	20.3
1985	63.2	12.5	20.0	8.2	3.0	106.9
1986	37.0	52.8	18.1	5.9	2.9	116.7
1987	38.0	115.5	22.7	8.5	3.1	187.8
1988	30.1	79.4	13.2	5.4	4.1	132.2
1989	34.2	80.0	17.1	11.5	4.2	147.0
1990	29.5	56.5	17.1	9.0	2.6	114.7
1991	29.4	30.5	18.0	10.0	2.6	90.5
1992*	28.2	30.0	15.0	10.2	2.7	86.1
1993**	21.0	10.0	15.0	9.8	2.7	58.5

*Estimated.
**Proposed.
SOURCES: U.S. Overseas Loans and Grants: Obligations and Loan Authorizations July 1, 1945–Sept 30, 1978, 1981, 1983, 1985, 1987, 1989, 1991; AID, FY 1993 Summary Tables; TJ Morgan DOD Interamerican Region, June 1, 1992.

the U.S. embassy made no attempt to restrict the Guatemalan government agencies that it funded from using this money to advance military-directed development projects. Examples of the ways in which indirect AID funding complemented counterinsurgency objectives abound:

– AID was the main supplier of food and money for World Food Program (WFP) activities in Guatemala, which provided the underpinnings both for the infamous "Beans and Guns" pacification project and for the food-for-work programs that built model villages and army barracks in the highlands.

– AID was the main source of funds for rural roads projects at a time when the army considered the construction and maintenance of penetration roads to be critical to its counterinsurgency efforts.

– Direct AID funds as well as local-currency funds generated by Title I and ESF programs flowed into the military-controlled relief organizations of the National Reconstruction Committee (CRN) and the National Emergency Committee (CNE).

– Many of the government agencies funded by AID—including INAFOR, Ministry of Education, National Cooperative Institute, Ministry of Health, Rural Roads, INDECA, National Agrarian Transformation Institute (INTA), Agricultural Development Bank (BANDESA), National Housing Institute (BANVI), and the National Electricity Institute (INDE)— were ordered to give priority attention to the development poles and model villages.

In these and other ways, AID-financed community-development promoters, agricultural credit, technical assistance, housing, and cooperative formation indirectly served to support the army's National Security and Development Plan.[15] Although AID is prohibited from using economic aid to support military programs, the provision of U.S.-donated food and housing supplies for model villages in the early 1980s clearly violated this regulation.

Assistance Levels Drop

From an average yearly assistance level of $135 million in the 1985-90 period, Guatemala's allocation of economic aid funds fell to less than $90 million annually in 1991-92. Most severely cut have been Economic Support Funds, dwindling to $30 million a year in 1991-92 (with just $10 million requested for 1993) from a $66 million annual average in the 1985-90 period.

Although Washington's funding objectives remain basically the same, there have been some important changes. The overall economic thrust of the AID program continues to be support for economic stabilization, structural adjustment, and export-oriented investment by the private sector. On the political front, Washington funds various "democracy strengthening" programs aimed at bolstering the institutional infrastructure of civilian government. Reflecting the waning counterinsurgency campaign in the highlands, the United States has also reduced its commitment to economic development and social service programs in this poor region. An ascending funding priority for AID is conservation, such as support for the newly created Maya Biosphere Reserve in Petén. In 1992 AID also launched a six-year $37 million family-planning project.

Private-Sector Support

In its support for the private sector in the 1980s, Washington was caught in a contradiction. On the one hand, it acknowledged that the conservative elite continually blocked fiscal and agrarian reforms necessary for the country's economic and political stability. On the other hand, the United States remained committed to the private sector as source of economic growth.

To resolve this dilemma AID funding has, since the mid-1980s, supported the development of the "modernizing" wing of the private sector through the creation and financial backing of a variety of new business organizations such as the Enterprise Chamber (CAEM), Free Market Chamber (CLE), Guatemalan Nontraditional Exporters Association (Gexport), and the Guatemala Development Foundation (Fundesa). Through these and other business associations, Washington has encouraged the emergence of a less reactionary business elite that fully supports neoliberal economic restructuring and is willing to consider measures designed to strengthen social stability, such as the creation of a social investment fund, increased minimum wages, and tax reform (see The Business Lobby). It was not until the Serrano administration that the growing influence of this modernizing sector became readily apparent, as illustrated by the lack of strong business opposition to the fiscal reforms of early 1992.

Since 1983 the United States has tried to prop up and stimulate the private sector with a dizzying array of AID-funded development programs, including Agribusiness Development, Private Sector Development Coordination, Private Enterprise Development, Private Sector Education Initiatives, Micro-Enterprise Development, Micro-Enterprise Promotion, and Entrepreneurial Development. The private sector also stands first in line to receive local currency funds generated by the Title I and ESF programs. AID's Private Enterprise Development project (1987-91) illustrated the agency's top-down approach to international development by channeling $10 million to the

AID-created CAEM and several other business organizations as part of its ongoing "Strengthening the Private Sector" action plan.

Washington's private-sector support projects have succeeded in their goal of injecting a strong modernizing element into the business elite while reducing the influence of the most reactionary sectors. At the same time AID support, combined with such U.S. trade initiatives as the CBI, helped spark the impressive explosion in nontraditional exports, mainly garments, fruits, and vegetables. In terms of economic stabilization and restructuring, Washington can also point to its influence in slashing the government's budget deficit, coaxing through a new tax bill, liberalizing trade regulations, and nudging Guatemala toward free trade. But serious economic development problems—including expanding poverty and landlessness, insufficient productive investment, vastly inadequate social services, and lack of public-sector investment—persist. Both Washington and the modernizing private sector will have to address these issues if economic and political stability are to be achieved.

Democracy Strengthening

As a specific project, "democracy strengthening" is relatively new, dating back to the mid-1980s. But the United States has long disbursed economic aid in Guatemala for the stated objective of building democracy. In 1954 Washington directed a coup that overthrew a democratic government and installed a rightwing, military-controlled one. It followed the coup with extensive economic aid programs, intending to remake Guatemala into "a showcase for democracy." Until the mid-1980s, however, democracy strengthening meant little more than ridding the country of communists, leftists, and guerrillas.

With the encouragement of Washington, the post-1954 military regimes set out to dismantle the social reforms of the 1944-54 period, in the process killing or arresting hundreds of suspected communists while sending nearly 800 Guatemalans into exile. From the U.S. embassy's perspective, the wave of repression unleashed by the Armas regime was not as efficient or complete as it could have been, despite the fact that there were at least 200 extrajudicial executions at the time of the coup and that all farmworker and labor organizations were dismantled.[16] Just a month after the June 1954 coup, the U.S. embassy regretfully informed Washington that, although "the overt Guatemalan Communist apparatus" had collapsed, "the Communist conspiracy has yet to be totally destroyed" because of the "ineptness and laxity" of the new government.[17]

Although it boasted of supporting democracy and the "free Western system," the Eisenhower administration regarded the democratization and social reforms initiated during the Arévalo-Arbenz years as a threat to its own interests and those of the economic elite. Col. Carlos Castillo Armas was chosen as the "liberator," although the U.S. ambassador complained in January 1955 that "there are moments when he seems almost pathetic. He must literally be led by the hand step by step."[18] Unable to find an acceptable alternative to Armas, the U.S. embassy gave its blessing to sham elections in which the government itself entered ballots for Armas and his handpicked congressional candidates on behalf of illiterate peasants. Armas was subsequently assassinated by rightwing political opponents, but Washington's fixation on erasing the communist threat in Guatemala continued. In 1957 the State Department presented the new junta with a list of 500 "dangerous" and "undesirable" exiles who should not be allowed to return to Guatemala, noting that "many of the important non-card-carrying communist and noncommie exiles are as dangerous or more so [than the communists themselves] and can further the interests of international communism."[19] With the help of Washington, the Guatemalan military soon developed its own intelligence capabilities enabling it to formulate its own lists of "undesirables" slated for removal by death squads.

Almost three decades after it first intervened in Guatemala, Washington in 1983 began using its economic aid to support a democratic transition strategy backed by the army (see Armed Forces). With the guerrilla threat diminished and the economy in crisis, U.S. politicians felt it was time to encourage the transfer of government from the military to civilians. Two years after the military regime of Mejía Víctores began the democratization process, the Reagan administration touted Guatemala as "the most recent democratic success story in Central America." The United States provided essential support for the transition process, sponsoring get-out-the-vote campaigns and helping to create an electoral system in 1985. A succession of assembly, municipal, and presidential elections were held, with the promotional and logistical aspects of this process paid for largely by AID and the USIA. In 1990 U.S. assistance similarly aided the electoral process, including more get-out-the-vote drives.

During the Cerezo administration, U.S. aid for democratization included subsidizing a variety of think tanks and public forums to discuss national issues, training legislators in sessions (run by the U.S.-based Center for Democracy), promoting U.S. scholarships and civic-education programs, upgrading and financing the country's judicial system, and training police. Yet despite efforts to improve the nation's judiciary and the quality of police work, Guatemala's courts and police remained corrupt, inefficient, and reluctant to pursue human rights cases (see Lawlessness and Human Rights).

U.S. support for "democracy strengthening" stems from a variety of sources. Although AID is the central fount, most money comes not through the agency's local office in Guatemala but from its national and regional offices. Democratization aid also passes through the National Endowment for Democracy (NED), which receives these funds from AID and the USIA. Both NED and AID have been instrumental in the formation and development of several nongovernmental institutes that help shape government policy.

These organizations include the following:

The **Center for Political Studies (CEDEP)** is the most liberal of the study and policy centers funded by the United States. It began with polling and get-out-the vote projects in 1985 and has sponsored a series of forums on such issues as the peace process and the Caribbean Basin Initiative. CEDEP has close links to the Christian Democratic party and has come under attack by the extreme right wing.

The center-right think tank **Association of Social Studies and Research (ASIES)** receives most of its funding from the Konrad Adenauer Foundation, a branch of the conservative Christian Democratic Party of Germany. ASIES is pluralistic in the sense that it attempts to bring together a wide range of perspectives. The goal of ASIES is the stabilization of democracy within the context of a joint military-government project of national stability. The largest of the country's think tanks, ASIES sponsors forums and publishes bulletins to enhance popular education on such themes as the environment and elections. Although public education is the most visible focus of ASIES, its main efforts go into behind-the-scenes formulation of policy for government and the modernizing sector of the military. ASIES, which includes retired military officials in its directorate, cosponsored a forum at American University in Washington in 1988 with ESTNA, a studies center closely associated with the military.

The Center for Strategic Studies for National Stability (ESTNA) was founded in 1988 by then Minister of Defense Gramajo. Housed in the military's old Polytechnical Institute, ESTNA has received AID and NED funds to sponsor policy forums and training seminars for the country's leading businessmen, politicians, academics, and military officers. Because of ESTNA's ability to bring together many of the nation's most influential leaders, its forums are regarded as highly influential in shaping government policy. Although few dispute the need for all sectors to exchange ideas, the institute has been criticized for its role in continuing the military's influence in governance and for bolstering the political ambitions of military officers, particularly its founder.[20]

Founded in the 1960s, the **Economic and Social Studies Center (CEES)** is the oldest think tank in Guatemala. It is linked to the extreme political right and serves as a mouthpiece for conservative economic theories. Its Alfa and Omega Studies Collection publishes pamphlets promoting the causes of anticommunism, neoliberal economics, and the primacy of the private sector. CEES is closely associated with the AID-funded Francisco Marroquín University.

In addition to supporting these policy institutes, the U.S. government is also a main source of income for study and propaganda centers serving business and conservative labor in Guatemala. Since 1983 AID and NED have provided primary funding for the conservative Confederation of Guatemalan Trade Union Unity (CUSG) and its study center. CUSG, founded in 1983, is closely linked with the AID-funded and AFL-CIO-sponsored American Institute for Free Labor Development (AIFLD).[21]

Washington has also financed political training programs for the country's business sector and political parties. Through NED, for example, U.S. funds have been channeled to the Academy for Liberty and Justice, closely associated with the Solidarity Action Party (MAS) of Jorge Serrano.[22] The AID- and NED-funded Center for Democracy supports the U.S.-government's democratization program from its offices in Guatemala City.

AID chose the Association of the Friends of the Country (Amigos del País), a 200-year-old organization of the traditional oligarchy, to implement its popular-education project for rural Guatemala. This Private Sector Education Initiative Project publishes a newspaper called *Roots: The Friendly Voice of the Campesino* (produced in cooperation with the Chamber of Industry). The new AID-funded Highlands Institute, based in Quetzaltenango, is one of several AID projects designed to educate the most promising indian youth. The Central America Peace Scholarship program does its part by bringing young Guatemalans to the United States to acquaint them with the "American Way." Although neither AID nor NED fund popular organizations or progressive institutes, NED has financed the National Reconciliation Commission (CNR), the nongovernmental commission created in compliance with the Esquipulas II accords.

With the reduced emphasis on combating military threats in Central America, AID's Democracy Strengthening Project has gained new prominence in the U.S. foreign policy agenda. Despite the conclusion by Harvard University, a previous co-sponsor of AID's judicial-reform project, that the Guatemalan government lacked the political will to prosecute human rights abuses, the United States continues its program to strengthen the Guatemalan judiciary. In addition, U.S. democratization funds are flowing into the government's Human Rights Ombudsman's office as well as supporting the Guatemalan Human Rights Commission (see Lawlessness and Human Rights).

AID defines its democracy initiative in economic as well as political terms, claiming that "democracy is an economic development issue" since open and accountable governments provide better opportunities for economic growth. AID asserts that it is committed to the establishment of political systems that "extend the rights of citizenship and political participation throughout the population; respect civil and human rights; maintain effective, responsive, and accountable government institutions; and allow genuine political debate and competition, culminating in free and fair elections and the continuity of civilian rule."[23]

Since late 1990 Washington has suspended direct military aid due to human rights concerns, but it has balked at using its more substantial economic aid package as leverage to ensure that its stated democratization standards are enforced. The Bush administration declined to link the release of ESF allocations to human rights, although in 1991-92 it did make release of the ESF contingent on the Guatemalan government's approval of a fiscal reform package. In mid-1992 the Western Affairs Subcommittee reinstated more restrictive language for the proposed 1993 foreign aid authorization that would link continued ESF funding to progress on particular human rights cases.

Military Aid

Strong bilateral ties were established with Guatemala's security forces as a result of the U.S.-sponsored coup in 1954. Support for the army's civic-action programs and its counterinsurgency campaign in the 1960s further strengthened this relationship. With the advent of the Reagan administration, Washington steadily solidified its links to the Guatemalan military. Although U.S. funding never approached the levels received by Honduras or El Salvador, Guatemala did receive some direct U.S. military assistance and substantial other military-related aid in the 1980s (Figure 8b).

The country's police forces have also benefited from extensive U.S. aid and training. Before AID's Office of Public Safety was closed by Congress in 1974 owing to human rights violations associated with the police-training program, the U.S. government had trained over 32,000 Guatemalan police—the largest such effort in Central America. The program also sponsored the establishment of a joint police-military intelligence and communications center, branded a "computerized death squad" by human rights monitors.

The security-assistance termination provisions of the Foreign Assistance Act were never formally applied to Guatemala. The State Department did not officially identify the country as having demonstrated "a consistent pattern of gross violations of internationally recognized human rights." Nonetheless, the Guatemalan military regime in 1977 objected even to considerations by the Carter administration to apply such restrictions, and declined to sign further military-aid agreements with the United States. It was the position of the Guatemalan military that drastic counterinsurgency measures were needed and it could not afford to be restricted by international human rights monitoring.

Instead, it began to seek aid and training from other sources, including Israel, Argentina, and Taiwan. Not until 1982, when Ríos Montt seized power, did official relations with the United States once again begin to warm. The Reagan administration sought congressional approval for renewed military aid in 1983, but not until fiscal year 1985 was military training renewed and not until 1986 did military aid begin flowing to Guatemala. Although U.S. military assistance was discontinued between fiscal 1978 and 1985, Guatemala continued to buy arms and other military supplies from the United States during this period. During the aid hiatus, Commerce Department licenses were issued for over $100 million in military or dual-use supplies, including such items as aircraft, pistols, shotguns, and military vehicles.

After 1986 direct U.S. military aid and training steadily increased, but always with the congressional restriction that the assistance be of a nonlethal variety. Recognizing that the U.S. Congress would only support military aid if couched in the language of democ-

Figure 8b

U.S. Military Aid to Guatemala

In millions of U.S. $.

Year	IMET	FMF/ FMS	MAP	Total
1977	0.5	0	0	0.5
1978	0	0	0	0
1979	0	0	0	0
1980	0	0	0	0
1981	0	0	0	0
1982	0	0	0	0
1983	0	0	0	0
1984	0	0	0	0
1985	0.5	0	0	0.5
1986	0.4	0	5.0	5.4
1987	0.5	0	5.0	5.5
1988	0.4	0	9.0	9.4
1989	0.4	0	9.0	9.4
1990	0.5	3.7	2.8	7.0
1991	0.4	0	0	0.4
1992	0.2	0	0	0.2
1993*	0.4	0	0	0.4

*Proposed.
SOURCES: U.S. Overseas Loans and Grants: Obligations and Loan Authorizations July 1, 1945–Sept 30, 1978, 1981, 1983, 1985, 1987, 1989, 1991; USA Congressional Presentation for Security Assistance Programs FY 1991, 1992, 1993; Luz Hartly, Comptrollers Office, Department of Defense, September 8, 1992.

racy strengthening, both the civilian government and the military high command of Guatemala have reworded their pleas for U.S. aid to emphasize preserving the country's democratic process. Cerezo, for example, told U.S. lawmakers that he needed U.S. military aid not so much to fight the counterinsurgency war but to demonstrate to the military that the civilian government was on their side. Military leaders, in turn, told Congress that U.S. military aid strengthened the hand of those within the armed forces who supported civilian rule and the United States.

Won over by these arguments, Congress approved higher levels of military aid. For 1988 and 1989, Congress approved $9 million—up from the $5 million level in 1986-87—on the condition that the army respect human rights, even though human rights violations were clearly rising at the time. The appropriated level of military aid dropped to $6.5 million in 1990, and in December 1990 the Bush administration suspended further assistance because of U.S. dissatisfaction with Guatemala's "lack of commitment to protect human rights" and in particular with its failure to prosecute those members of the Guatemalan army responsible for killing U.S. citizen Michael Devine.[24] Washington's suspension of direct military aid to Guatemala was supported by Congress in strong language in the proposed foreign assistance appropriations bill for 1993, which will continue the suspension of direct military aid and condition delivery of ESF money until such time that the president determines that there has been an improvement in the human rights climate. If military aid is renewed, it will be used to facilitate the reintegration of soldiers and guerrillas into civilian life in the event of a peace accord.

For its part, the Department of Defense (DOD) has continued to argue for congressional approval of FMF assistance to Guatemala on the grounds that the "Guatemalan armed forces desperately need repair parts to keep existing equipment working, military equipment and materiel stocks are dangerously low, U.S. equipment is old and needs replacement, the air force's fixed-wing aircraft and helicopters have a low operational readiness, many military vehicles need replacement, and the army's communication system is not secure and cannot support units in the field." The DOD justifies continuing IMET training of Guatemalan officers, contending that it "exposes Guatemalans to U.S. traditions of democracy, human rights, and civilian-government control of the military."[25]

Overall, the objectives of the U.S. security-assistance program in Guatemala are to: "foster respect for human rights and the rule of law; encourage civilian control of the armed forces and better civilian-military relations; encourage downsizing the military and its assumption of nation-building roles; prevent development of narcotrafficking;

and enhance stability and foster a climate conducive to foreign investment."[26]

The termination of direct U.S. military aid was an important indicator of U.S. displeasure with the military's human rights abuses,
especially those affecting U.S. citizens. But the United States has
thus far still refrained from taking more serious action, such as a cutting off ESF aid or voting against multilateral financial support for
Guatemala. Human rights organizations have long pointed out that
Section 502B of the U.S. Foreign Assistance Act prohibits all security
assistance, including economic support funds, to countries with a consistent pattern of gross human rights violations. The termination of
all military and police training as well as military/civic-action programs has also been recommended by these human rights groups.

Other Military-Related Aid

At the same time that pressure was building in the U.S. Congress
to suspend military aid because of continuing human rights abuses
during the Cerezo administration, the Pentagon was lobbying for
closer relations with the Guatemalan military. The first sign of this
new relationship was the $13.8 million sale in early 1989 of 16,000
M-16 assault rifles to the Guatemalan army by Colt Industries.
Closely following the highly controversial M-16 deal, the State Department authorized the sale of an A-37B counterinsurgency plane
for a nominal sum, which observers called a giveaway. Defense Minister Héctor Alejandro Gramajo purchased these items in an effort to
modernize Guatemala's military with U.S.-manufactured arms and
equipment. Although critics noted that the sales violated both congressional restrictions and the Pentagon's own stated commitment to
provide only nonlethal training and aid to the country's armed forces,
closer military bonds continued to be sought. The presence of General
Fred Woerner, then commander of the U.S. Southern Command, as
an honored guest at the Guatemalan Army Day celebrations in mid-
1989 indicated the degree to which Washington was eager to enhance
its influence and contacts with the Guatemalan armed forces. Woerner presided over a ceremony in which 32 U.S. trucks were deliv-
ered to the country's Ministry of Defense.

Aside from direct military aid and renewed commercial sales, the
Pentagon found a variety of other ways to support the Guatemalan
military in the 1980s, including road-building and other mili-
tary/civic-action programs as well as critical air-transport support.
Logistical air support, supplied mainly from the Palmerola Air Base
in Honduras, began in 1987 and repeatedly provided assistance to
counterinsurgency operations and military-controlled refugee reset-

tlement activities in Petén and the northern reaches of Quiché. At least one U.S. pilot has died and nine airmen have been injured in several crashes resulting from these logistical operations.[27]

The United States gradually expanded its military/civic-action programs during the 1980s. The first signs of this nonlethal but counterinsurgency-related activity were medical programs sponsored by the Tropical Medicine Program of the Jungle Warfare School in the Panama Canal Area. Three months after the November 1988 Aguacate massacre (in which 21 *campesinos* were killed by the army), uniformed and armed members of the U.S. National Guard participated in a civic-action program in Chimaltenango only a short distance from Aguacate. The program, jointly sponsored by AID and the Ministry of Health, was largely a public relations effort that involved teeth-pulling and aspirin distribution by U.S. soldiers. With the Guatemalan military providing transportation and translation services, the operation was judged a success by the National Guard. Before heading back to Honduras in a Black Hawk helicopter, a U.S. trooper wrote, in English, "Happy Day" across the wall of a village shack.

Shortly after this civic action in Chimaltenango, 40 U.S. army engineers arrived in the increasingly conflictive Sololá area to direct a major road-building project designed to afford the Guatemalan army access to the isolated areas where guerrillas operated around Lake Atitlán. Other civic-action programs in Guatemala have involved the 475th Mobile Army Surgical Hospital and the 973rd Dental Detachment. The 1990 suspension of U.S. military aid did not terminate military/civic-action projects, in which U.S. National Guard and Army Reserve units supplement the Guatemalan army's public-relations work. These programs do not seek out or train civilian health promoters and are not part of any long-term health care strategy. Instead, the intended beneficiary of these "hearts and minds" civic-action programs seems to be the Guatemalan army. As the Washington Office on Latin America noted: "The effort visibly places Guatemalan troops alongside U.S. guardsmen, linking the United States to local army efforts in the eyes of the population."[28]

Although on a much smaller scale than in the 1960s and early 1970s, the United States resumed training Guatemalan police forces in the 1980s. The police forces, under de facto control of the military, are trained through State Department and Drug Enforcement Administration (DEA) programs. Despite the continued implication of the police forces in serious human rights violations, U.S. aid pays for a variety of police-training programs both inside Guatemala and in the United States, designed to improve police efficiency in criminal investigations and antinarcotics operations.[29]

Antinarcotics Operations Stepped Up

Since the late 1980s, U.S. antinarcotics operations in Guatemala have greatly expanded, with the DEA's country budget soaring from $350,000 in 1987 to more than $2.5 million in 1992. Guatemala, the cardinal transshipment location for Colombian cocaine, is the location of DEA's Central American Drug Enforcement Center (CADENCE). At the U.S. embassy in Guatemala City, the State Department also maintains a Narcotics Affairs Section (NAS) office with four agents who work closely with the dozen DEA agents in Guatemala.

At first U.S. antinarcotics operations focused almost exclusively on curbing marijuana and poppy production in the departments of San Marcos, Huehuetenango, and Petén. Working closely with the Guatemalan police and military, the DEA has organized aerial spraying and small-scale ground eradication operations that, while crimping marijuana and poppy cultivation, have simultaneously angered many small farmers who complain that their traditional crops have also been contaminated and destroyed. As U.S. radar and other antinarcotics efforts have gradually made drug-smuggling efforts more difficult in other Central American countries, smugglers have stepped up transshipment and drug-money laundering operations in Guatemala. The country's meager radar capacity, its location midway between Colombia and the United States, and the presence of hundreds of unmonitored airstrips render it an ideal location for drug smuggling.

At U.S. prompting, the Guatemalan police and military have established a Joint Information Collection Center and a Joint Anti-Narcotics Squad that consolidate the intelligence and interdiction operations of the Treasury Police, National Police, and military police. Guatemalan police and military are trained and equipped for antinarcotics activities and participate jointly with DEA agents in drug eradication and interdiction campaigns. With U.S. support, the Treasury and National Police have both formed specially trained drug-interdiction units. Besides the DEA (a division of the Department of Justice) and the State Department, other U.S. agencies involved in antinarcotics efforts with the Guatemalan police and military are the U.S. Customs Service and the United States Information Agency (USIA). The U.S. military is also assuming an increasingly direct role in antinarcotics activities. The U.S. Navy, Coast Guard, and Marines have all participated in joint training exercises in drug interdiction with the Guatemalan navy. The United States also pays for joint communications and coordination of narcotics intelligence between the Guatemalan security forces and those of other Central American nations.

According to a *Los Angeles Times* report, the CIA has also deepened its involvement with the Guatemalan army's G-2 intelligence division. The CIA is paying retainers to relatively high-ranking G-2 officers for information on regional matters as well as for help in fighting drug trafficking. The *Times* quoted a local source confiding about the G-2: "As long as they keep doing good work, you don't ask about involvement in the killings and disappearances so often attributed to them." According to the *Times* report, the CIA has "challenged the DEA for control of the war on drugs in Guatemala."[30] Human rights concerns have prevented the United States from advocating a greater and more public role for the military in antinarcotics operations, but progress on the most prominent human rights cases, particularly those involving abuses toward U.S. citizens, might open the door for expanded cooperation between the Pentagon, the DEA, and the Guatemalan military.

Reference Notes

Introduction

1. H. Jeffrey Leonard, *Natural Resources and Economic Development in Central America* (New Brunswick, NJ: Transaction Books, 1987).
2. United Nations, *Prospects of World Urbanization* (New York: 1988).
3. Ibid.
4. David Stoll, "The Land No Longer Gives: Land Reform in Nebaj," *CS Quarterly* 14, 1990.
5. Jim Handy, *Gift of the Devil: A History of Guatemala* (Boston: South End Press, 1984). Handy's book provides an excellent history of Guatemala.
6. A fascinating new study of the background for the 1954 coup is found in Piero Gleijeses, *Shattered Hope: The Guatemalan Revolution and the United States* (Princeton: University of Princeton Press, 1991).
7. Good sources on modern Guatemalan history and political developments include: Susanne Jonas, *The Battle for Guatemala: Rebels, Death Squads, and U.S. Power* (Boulder: Westview Press, 1991); Stephen Schlesinger and Stephen Kinzer, *Bitter Fruit: The Untold Story of the American Coup in Guatemala* (Garden City, NY: Doubleday, 1982); Susanne Jonas and David Tobis, eds., *Guatemala* (New York: North American Congress on Latin America, 1981); James Painter, *Guatemala: False Hope, False Freedom* (London: Catholic Institute for International Relations/Latin America Bureau, 1989); Jonathan Fried, Marvin E. Gettleman, Deborah T. Levenson, and Nancy Peckenham, eds., *Guatemala in Rebellion: Unfinished History* (New York: Grove Press, 1983).

Part 1: Government and Politics

1. The 1991 abstention rate compares with a 37 percent rate in the first-round vote in November 1990 (with an additional 7 percent in null or blank votes) and a 34 percent rate in the 1985 election of Vinicio Cerezo. In the 1991 run-off vote 1,275,379 valid votes were cast; there were 75,000 null or blank votes; and 1,753,994 of the more than 3 million registered voters failed to vote. At least 600,000 eligible citizens (over 16 years of age) are not registered to vote.
2. See Tom Barry, *The Politics of Counterinsurgency* (Albuquerque: Resource Center, 1986); and Kjell Enge and Chris Krueger, *Security and Development Conditions in the Guatemalan Highlands* (Washington: Washington Office on Latin America, 1985).
3. Rachel Garst and Tom Barry, *Feeding the Crisis: U.S. Food Aid and Agricultural Policy in Central America* (Lincoln: University of Nebraska Press, 1990).
4. "National Reorganization Presidential Address to the Guatemalan Nation," March 19, 1987. Cited in Guatemalan Church in Exile, *Guatemala: Security, Development, and Democracy* (Managua: 1989), p. 23.

5. David Stoll, "Guatemala: Why They Like Ríos Montt," *NACLA Report on the Americas* XXIV, No. 4, December/January 1990/91.

6. The members of the president's Cabinet include the ministers of foreign relations, finance, economy, public works and communications, education, culture, agriculture, health, labor, energy and mines, defense, development, and interior. There is also a minister without a specific portfolio and the director of the Central Bank.

7. "La Perestroika Llega a los Marxistas Guatemaltecos," *Crónica*, February 23, 1989.

8. Interview with Mario Solórzano, May 8, 1987; Partido Socialista Democrático, *Construcción del Partido Socialista Democrático y Desarrollo del Proceso de Democratización* (no date).

9. "Las Dos Alas del PSD Luchan por Llevarse la Rosa," *Crónica*, May 12, 1988.

10. For an excellent and more thorough description of the origins of the Christian Democratic Party, see: Painter, *Guatemala: False Hope, False Freedom*, pp. 58-78. Much of this section on the DCG is based on information and analysis in the Painter book.

11. Vinicio Cerezo, *The Army: An Alternative*, as cited in Painter, *Guatemala: False Hope, False Freedom*, p. 72. Cerezo's essay was not the first time this road to political power was outlined by the DCG. In 1974, party leader Danilo Barillas authored a small book entitled *Christian Democracy and its Position on the Army: A Call for an Historic Compromise*.

12. A commentary by the now-defunct *Siete Días* television news program, cited in *Report on Guatemala*, Guatemala News and Information Bureau, November 1988.

13. Raul Marin, "Guatemala: Sin Lugar Para La Paz," *Pensamiento Propio*, April 1990.

14. The withdrawal of Juan Carlos Simons, Oliverio García Rodas, and Jorge Skinner Klée also weakened the party.

15. Mulet's father, Augusto Mulet Descamps, was press secretary under General Miguel Ydígoras Fuentes and later founded what was perhaps the most reactionary newspaper ever to exist in Guatemala, *Alerta*. After being ejected from the MLN, along with Alvaro Arzú and other members of the professional wing, Edmund Mulet and his cohorts commandeered the PNR. In the 1985 campaign, the PNR and the PR initially formed an alliance with the UCN, and Mulet decided to remain with the UCN when the alliance fractured.

16. *Prensa Libre*, April 12, 1992.

17. See, for example, *La Hora*, March 25, 1992.

18. There have, however, been some rare cases in which victims have survived torture and disappearance, subsequently providing testimony about the detention centers and torture methods of the security forces. One such case involved the kidnapping and torture in 1990 of U.S. Ursuline Sister Diana Ortiz, who in 1992 returned to Guatemala to mount a legal case against former Defense Minister Gramajo.

19. Americas Watch and Physicians for Human Rights, *Guatemala: Getting Away with Murder* (New York: August 1991), p. 3.

20. Americas Watch, *Closing the Space: Human Rights in Guatemala, May 1987-October 1988* (New York: 1988), p. 1.

21. *Insight*, March 13, 1989.

22. *Report of UN Special Observer* (Geneva: United Nations Human Rights Commission, 1989).

23. Myrna Mack was an anthropologist who co-founded the Association for the Advancement of the Social Sciences (AVANCSO), and before her death had been researching the conditions of the internally displaced, including those of the communities in resistance in the Ixcán.

24. Jean-Marie Simon, *Guatemala: Eternal Spring, Eternal Tyranny* (New York: Norton, 1987), p. 227.

25. Americas Watch, *Messengers of Death: Human Rights in Guatemala, November 1988-February 1990* (New York: March 1990).

26. Inaugural address reprinted in *Foreign Broadcast Information Service*, January 16, 1991.

27. *Human Rights Watch Annual Report 1991* (New York: 1992). Human Rights Watch said that Serrano's statements were without foundation to its knowledge and such characterization was "tantamount to a death sentence for CERJ activists."

28. Ibid.

29. *Christian Science Monitor*, July 9, 1991.

30. Penados was echoing a November 29, 1991, statement by the region's bishops which observed that Central Americans had "entered a culture of death. We are now so accustomed to living

in the midst of such horrible violence and dreadful massacres and crimes that we have been left insensible." *Central America Report*, December 6, 1991.

31. U.S. embassy, *The U.S. State Department Human Rights Report: Guatemala*, (Guatemala City: February 1992).

32. Bonnie Tenneriello, "Military Prosecutions and Other Human Rights Developments in Guatemala," Washington Office on Latin America, June 5, 1992.

33. *Crónica*, July 27, 1991, asserted that the charges made against ex-Defense Minister Gramajo at his graduation from Harvard "could be the result of a coincidence of interests among human rights groups in the United States, the Democrats in Congress and the URNG."

34. *La Hora*, March 25, 1992. Appointed as Human Rights Ombudsman near the end of the Cerezo administration, Ramiro de León Carpio, cousin of Jorge Carpio Nicolle and vice-presidential candidate on the UCN ticket in 1985, openly accused the army of being the main human rights violator and took the Serrano government to task for failing to control the abuses.

35. Americas Watch, *Persecuting Human Rights Monitors: The CERJ in Guatemala* (New York: May 1989), p. 43.

36. See Americas Watch, *The Group for Mutual Support* (New York: 1985).

37. See Americas Watch, *Persecuting Human Rights Monitors*.

38. Human Rights Watch, *The Persecution of Human Rights Monitors, December 1989 to December 1990, A Worldwide Survey* (New York: December 1990), p. 2.

39. Americas Watch, "Guatemala: Slaying of Rights Activists, Impunity Prevail Under New Government," *News from Americas Watch*, April 14, 1991.

40. Americas Watch and Physicians for Human Rights, *Getting Away with Murder*, p. 12.

41. See Washington Office on Latin America, *The Administration of Injustice: Military Accountability in Guatemala* (Washington, DC: December 1989) and International Human Rights Law Group, *Maximizing Deniability: The Justice System and Human Rights in Guatemala* (Washington, DC: July 1989).

42. Americas Watch, *Messengers of Death*.

43. Statement by Philip B. Heyman in a hearing before the Subcommittee on Western Hemisphere Affairs of the Committee on Foreign Affairs, House of Representatives, *Options for United States Policy Toward Guatemala* (Washington, DC: U.S. Government Printing Office, July 17, 1990)

44. As Americas Watch noted in 1991: "The police, although nominally under the jurisdiction of the Interior Ministry, remain effectively under army control, making them unwilling to investigate cases where the army is implicated." Americas Watch and Physicians for Human Rights, *Guatemala: Getting Away with Murder*.

Part 2: Military and Insurgency

1. See Gabriel Aguilera Peralta, "Terror and Violence as Weapons of Counterinsurgency in Guatemala," *Latin American Perspectives* VII, 1980 and James Dunkerley, *Power in the Isthmus* (London: Verso, 1988).

2. For an excellent overview of the dimensions of this repressive apparatus see Michael McClintock, *The American Connection: Vol. II State Terror and Popular Resistance in Guatemala* (London: Zed Books, 1985).

3. Piero Gleijeses, *Shattered Hope: The Guatemalan Revolution*, p. 386.

4. Ibid. Gleijeses citing a Guatemalan intellectual, p. 386.

5. Economist Intelligence Unit, *Guatemala, El Salvador, Honduras: Country Profile 1991-92* (London), p. 11.

6. Colonel Enríquez, in Guatemalan Church in Exile, *Guatemala: Security, Development and Democracy*, p. 6.

7. The IPM also owns a cement company in the department of El Progreso that is not currently operative.

8. International Institute for Strategic Studies, *The Military Balance 1990-91* (London), p. 196.

9. A Guatemalan general interviewed by journalist Allan Nairn described the G-2 as "an apparatus dedicated to finding and eliminating people of the left. Furthermore, there are three op-

tions: disappear them, eliminate them in public, or simply invite them to leave the country." Remarks made at Brown University (Providence, RI), April 11, 1991.

10. Enrique Ortego, "Los hilos del crimen," *Siglo Veintiuno*, February 2, 1992.

11. *Guatemala: Elections 1985*; Gabriel Aguilera Peralta and Jorge Romero Imery, *Dialéctica del Terror en Guatemala* (San José: Editorial Universitaria EDUCA, 1981).

12. "Above the Law? Civil Patrols in Guatemala," *Central America Report*, May 18, 1990.

13. Ibid.

14. Painter, *Guatemala: False Hope, False Freedom*, p. 50.

15. *Guatemala: Elections 1985* (Guatemala City: Inforpress Centroamericana, October 1985); *Democracy or Deception? The Guatemalan Elections 1985* (Washington: Network in Solidarity with the People of Guatemala, 1985).

16. For a more complete description of the PNSD, see: *La Política de Desarrollo del Estado Guatemalteca 1986-1987* (Guatemala City: AVANCSO, 1988), pp. 4-5. Also see: George Black, "Under the Gun," *NACLA Report on the Americas*, November 1985.

17. This concept of "national-security civilian governments" was articulated by Franz Hinkelammert, director of the Department of Ecumenical Investigations (DEI) in Costa Rica. Cited in Guatemalan Church in Exile, *Guatemala: Security, Development, and Democracy*, p. 16.

18. Guatemalan Church in Exile, *Guatemala: Security, Development and Democracy*. This is a valuable analysis of the military's national-stability project.

19. For a discussion about rifts within the army see: Allan Nairn, "Guatemala During the Cerezo Years," *Report on Guatemala*, September 1989.

20. National Forum speech, August 12, 1987.

21. *Central America Report*, June 19, 1992

22. Sheldon B. Liss, *Radical Thought in Central America* (Boulder: Westview Press, 1991), p. 33.

23. Timothy P. Wickham-Crowley, *Guerrillas and Revolution in Latin America: A Comparative Study of Insurgents and Regimes since 1956* (Princeton: Princeton University Press, 1992), p. 17.

24. Norman B. Schwartz, *Forest Society: A Social History of Petén, Guatemala* (Philadelphia: University of Pennsylvania Press, 1990), p. 249.

25. URNG, *Proclamación Unitaria de la Unidad Revolucionaria Nacional de Guatemala* (January 1982).

26. By 1990 the URNG had a presence in the departments of Petén, Alta Verapaz, Quiché, Huehuetenango, San Marcos, Quetzaltenango, Totonicapán, Sacatepéquez, Sololá, Suchitepéquez, Escuintla, Chimaltenango, and in Guatemala City.

27. *Central America Report*, September 13, 1991.

28. *La Jornada* (Mexico City) interview with Pablo Monsanto reprinted in *Report on Guatemala* 12, No. 3., Fall 1991.

29. Ibid.

30. For a critique of the National Dialogue see: "National Dialogue: Reconciling the Poor to their Poverty," *Entre Nos*, April 1989; Guatemala Human Rights Commission—USA, *Information Bulletin*, September 1989.

31. *Siglo Veintiuno*, May 8, 1991.

32. *Miami Herald*, February 16, 1992.

33. Interview with Pablo Monsanto, *Report on Guatemala*, Fall 1991.

34. Quoted in *La Jornada*, June 21, 1991.

35. In its annual report for 1991, the Office of the Human Rights Ombudsman claimed that it investigated and verified 71 cases of "political assassination," kidnapping, or disappearance by the URNG.

36. The list of violations of humanitarian standards included the kidnapping of two UN officials, the 1968 assassination of an ex-U.S. ambassador, the 1970 kidnapping of a West German ambassador, and the 1967 assassination of a *Prensa Libre* journalist. *Central America Report*, February 28, 1992.

37. Edgar Gutiérrez, "Guatemala ¿en la ruta de la paz?" *Siglo Veintiuno*, January 19, 1992.

38. Because of their weak negotiating position, it could be that the URNG would attempt to prolong the talks until such time that events turned more in their favor, via renewed rebel military strength, new divisions within the armed forces, or a broadened popular movement.

Part 3: Economy

1. Measured by 1990 per capita GDP, Nicaragua ($505) is the poorest country in the region, followed by Honduras ($880), Guatemala ($892), El Salvador ($1,091), Belize ($1,637), Costa Rica ($1,677), and Panama ($1,938). The per capita GDP of Mexico was ($1,980). Inter-American Development Bank (IDB), U.S. embassy Business Fact Sheets, *Economic and Social Progress in Latin America: 1991 Report* (Washington: 1992), p. 273.
2. These figures according to SEGEPLAN, INE, and World Bank estimations.
3. U.S. embassy, *Guatemala: Economic Trends* (April 1992).
4. Bank of Guatemala figures cited in CEPAL, *Guatemala: Situación de 1990* (Mexico City: October 1990), Table 14.
5. The distribution of the tax burden was as follows in 1991: 44.1 percent from sales tax (IVA); 25.4 percent import taxes; 15.3 percent corporate income tax; 9.6 percent export tax; 3.4 percent personal income tax; and 2.6 percent real estate taxes.
6. For an analysis of Serrano's attempt to secure a social pact see "La disputa entre el pacto socialy las movilizaciones populares," *Perspectiva* (AVANCSO), January/March 1991.
7. In relative terms, the private sector and the public sector each accounted for 50 percent of total investment in 1981, but the private sector's share rose to 77 percent by 1990.
8. INE-FUNAP, *Perfil de la pobreza en Guatemala* (Guatemala City: 1991).
9. Ibid., p. 1.
10. World Bank, *Guatemala: Country Economic Memorandum* (April 1991), p. 87.
11. Average real wages refer only to those covered by the Guatemalan Social Security Institute (IGSS), which keeps data on 28 percent of the economically active population. IGSS wages are generally higher than the wages in the rest of the economy.
12. World Bank, *Guatemala: Country Economic Memorandum*, p. 84.
13. Based on statistics from INE, cited in *Siglo Veintiuno*, March 16, 1992.
14. World Bank, *Guatemala: Country Economic Memorandum*, p. 152.
15. CEPAL, *Bases para la transformación productiva y generación de ingresos de la población pobre de los países del istmo centroamericano* (Mexico City: January 1992), p. 32.
16. World Bank, *Social Investment in Guatemala, El Salvador, and Honduras* (New York: 1991), p. 2.
17. UNICEF, *Situación de pobreza: Guatemala* (Guatemala City: May 1991), p. 17.
18. *Cronica*, March 14, 1992, citing SEGEPLAN statistics.
19. *OMNI*, November 1991.
20. Thomas Melville, "Land Tenure in Guatemala," *Report on Guatemala*, November-December 1986; "Girón Lights the Fuse: Land Problem in Guatemala," *Central America Report*, July 11, 1986.
21. U.S. Agency for International Development, *Land and Labor in Guatemala: An Assessment* (Washington: Development Associates/U.S. Agency for International Development, 1982).
22. The agricultural GDP is composed of export crops (28.3 percent), crops for domestic consumption (20.7 percent), industrial use crops, such as sugar (12.2 percent), livestock and poultry (30.4 percent), and forestry and fishing (8.4 percent). World Bank, *Guatemala: Country Economic Memorandum*.
23. James F. McSweeney, *El subsector café de Guatemala: Una evaluación* (Guatemala City: AID, 1988).
24. Ibid.
25. Painter, *Guatemala: False Hope, False Freedom*, p. 36.
26. "Government Measures Bail Out Coffee Trade," *Central America Report*, September 28, 1990.
27. "Una República Bananera que Ha Dejado de Serlo," *Crónica*, April 7, 1988.
28. Julio Figueroa, *El Cultivo Capitalista del Algodón* (Guatemala City: San Carlos University, September 1980).
30. Robert Williams, *Export Agriculture and the Crisis in Central America* (Chapel Hill: University of North Carolina Press, 1986), pp.77-94; Tom Barry, *Roots of Rebellion* (Boston: South End Press, 1987), pp.35-39.
30. "El Oro Verde," *Crónica*, December 17, 1987.

31. Polly Hoppin, *Pesticide Use by Growers of Non-Traditional Crops in Guatemala: Implications for Residues* (Guatemala City: AID/ROCAP, April 1989).

32. Polly Hoppin, *Pesticide Use in Four Non-Traditional Crops in Guatemala* (Guatemala City: AID/ROCAP, June 1989).

33. U.S. Department of Agriculture, "Guatemala: Agricultural Situation" (Washington: March 1, 1989).

34. Ibid.

35. World Bank, *Guatemala: Country Economic Memorandum*, p. 52.

36. Ibid., p. 56.

37. See Rachel Garst, "El ocaso del trigo nacional," *Siglo Veintiuno*, March 10, 1992.

38. Economist Intelligence Unit, *Guatemala, El Salvador, Honduras: Country Profile*, p. 20.

39. The Guatemala-Mexico trade balance in 1991 was a negative $60 million.

40. CITGUA, *La maquila en Guatemala* (Mexico City: 1991).

41. Luis Everado Estrada Vázquez and Francisco Leonel Santizo González, *La industria maquiladora en Guatemala: Perspectivas y efectos económicos y sociales* (Guatemala City: Universidad de San Carlos de Guatemala, 1989), p. 68.

42. Scott Norvell, "Guatemala Lures Apparel Firms in Effort to Quash Civil War," *Journal of Commerce*, October 23, 1991.

43. Shelley Emling, "Guatemala Offers New Perks to Investors in Rural Areas," *Business Latin America*, May 11, 1992.

44. INDE is in charge of the production and distribution of electricity in all departments except Guatemala, Sacatepequez, and Escuintla where the Guatemalan Electricity Enterprise (EEGSA) distributes electricity produced by INDE.

45. World Bank, *Guatemala: Country Economic Memorandum*, p. 75.

46. Ibid.; Economist Intelligence Unit, *Guatemala, El Salvador, Honduras: Country Profile*. All figures are 1990.

47. According to 1990 Inguat figures, 26 percent of the country's visitors came from either the United States or Canada, 26 percent from El Salvador, 18 percent from other Central American nations, 15 percent from Europe, 6 percent from Mexico, 5 percent from South America, and 3 percent from all other countries.

48. According to figures provided by the U.S. embassy, combined antinarcotics operations eradicated an estimated 576 hectares of opium poppy cultivation in 1991, leaving harvestable cultivation at an estimated 1,145 hectares for a potential yield of 17.2 metric tons.

49. Lee Hockstader, "Drug Trade Routed Through Guatemala," *Washington Post*, May 25, 1991.

50. For an overview of cocaine smuggling in Guatemala, see "Narcotrafico," a special report published by *Siglo Veintiuno*, November 11, 1991.

Part 4: Social Forces

1. For a description of this period see Edelberto Torres Rivas, "The Origins of Crisis and Instability in Central America," in Susanne Jonas and Nancy Stein (eds.), *Democracy in Latin America: Visions and Realities* (New York: Bergin and Garvey, 1990), pp. 53-64.

2. Susanne Jonas, *The Battle for Guatemala*, p. 124. Jonas appropriately calls the 1976 earthquake a "class-quake" because it left the wealthy, who lived in better constructed homes in less precarious terrains, largely unaffected.

3. More than 400 cooperatives still exist in Guatemala, mostly in the fishing and agricultural sectors, but they only rarely play a role in the popular movement. Instead they are largely limited to commercial dealings, and since 1979 the some 50,000 coop members have been under the supervision of the government agency INACOP.

4. Unions such as the General Confederation of Guatemalan Workers (CGTG)—not related to the confederation with the same name founded in the 1980s—attempted to unify industrial and agricultural workers during the 1944-54 period.

5. Julio Cambranes, *Democratización y movimientos campesinos pro-tierras en Guatemala*, Cuaderno 3 (Guatemala: CERCA, 1988).

6. For additional reflection on this new social phenomenon see Edgar Gutiérrez, "La democracia local," *Siglo Veintiuno*, August 18, 1991.

7. For a more complete treatment of NGOs in Guatemala see: *Análisis del Fenómeno de las ONGs* (Guatemala City: IDESAC/SERJUS/SOJUGMA, 1988); *ONGs, Sociedad Civil, y Estado en Guatemala*; and Resource Center, *Private Organizations with U.S. Connections in Guatemala*.

8. Miguel Angel Reyes and Mike Gatehouse, *Soft Drink, Hard Labor: Guatemalan Workers Take on Coca-Cola* (London: Latin America Bureau, 1987).

9. For a valuable critique of the repression of labor organizing during the Cerezo years see James A. Goldston, *Shattered Hope: Guatemalan Workers and the Promise of Democracy* (Boulder, CO: Westview Press, 1989). A summary of the repression against labor during the first six months of the Serrano administration is found in David Loeb, "Labor Movement Faces Escalating Repression," *Report on Guatemala* 12 (2), Summer 1991. Also see International Labor Rights Education and Research Fund et al., "Petition and Request for Revision of the Status of Guatemala in the GSP," June 1, 1991.

10. A history of recent unionization in Guatemala is found in two reports by CITGUA: *El movimiento sindical en Guatemala 1979-85* (Mexico City: 1989) and *El movimiento sindical en Guatemala 1986-88* (Mexico City: 1990).

11. For a description of unions at the start of the Cerezo administration see Gerald Michael Greenfield and Sheldon Maram, eds., *Latin American Labor Organizations* (Greenwood Press, 1987).

12. Goldston, *Shattered Hope*, p. 148. This book gives a thorough discussion of the labor code and the bureaucratic obstacles facing labor unions in Guatemala.

13. Using AID funds, AIFLD covers CUSG's $267,000 annual budget while USIA monies, channeled through AIFLD and the Free Trade Union Institute (FTUI), support CUSG's Study Center, established in 1985 to support the democratization process. The AID Mission in Guatemala supports AIFLD through its Agriculture Production and Marketing Service Project, which aims "to strengthen the capacity of farm unions to furnish needed service to their members."

14. *Central America Report*, June 22, 1990.

15. Interview with Ismael Barrios, February 27, 1989.

16. In 1991 Gexport reported that as many 70,000 workers were employed in 250 *maquiladoras*, but such high estimates of the number of factories and employees seemed designed to boost artificially the economic importance of the *maquila* industry.

17. An excellent overview of the *maquila* industry is *La maquila en Guatemala* (Mexico City: Ciencia y Tecnología para Guatemala, December 1991).

18. A 1991 study by Kurt Petersen of the Schell Center for International Human Rights at Yale University found that 12 attempts to form unions in the *maquila* sector were all crushed by selective or massive firings of the work force.

19. This campaign was sponsored by the U.S./Guatemala Labor Education Project in Chicago. See, for example, "The Phillips-Van Heusen Campaign: A Struggle for Justice and Basic Rights in the Global Economy," (1991), by the U.S./Guatemala Labor Education Project.

20. Cindy Forster, "Organizing in the Maquila Factories," *Report on Guatemala* 12 (1), Spring 1991.

21. *Central America Report*, December 13, 1991, citing CUC leader Sebastión Morales.

22. Ibid. Pay estimate from Vice-Minister of Labor Carlos Contreras.

23. For a history of *solidarismo* in Guatemala see Alfredo Anckermann Sam, "El solidarismo en Guatemala," *Cuadernos de Investigación* (San José: CSUCA, 1989).

24. Unverified figures from Guatemalan Solidarista Union (GSU), which also provided the following percentage breakdown of *solidarista* associations: industry (40 percent), agriculture (25 percent), services (12 percent), commerce (11.5 percent), agro-industry (6.7 percent), ranching (1.4 percent), lumber (1.4 percent), finance (1 percent), and mining (1 percent). As of early 1991, *solidarismo* as an alternative form of worker organization had not achieved an official stamp of approval by the government, but strong business support for the associations ensures that the government will not hinder the growth of this anti-union movement and may spell imminent official recognition.

25. For an overview and analysis of *solidarismo* in the 1990-91 period see: "Solidarismo: Anti-Unionism in Sheep's Clothing," *Envio*, Vol. 10, No. 119, June 1991; Daniele Rossdeutscher, "Solidarismo Challenges the Labor Movement," *Report on Guatemala* 12 (1), Spring 1991.

26. AID has financed *solidarista* training programs at the John XXIII Social School in Costa Rica and founded a regional business association, FEDEPRICAP, which promotes *solidarismo* throughout the region. Leading the campaign in the 1980s in Guatemala was a group of Guatemalan businessmen and U.S. consultants, many of whom are closely associated with the Management Association of Guatemala (AGG). They include Enrique and Ricardo Arenas, owners of the La Perla *finca* in Ixcán; José Rolz, owner of the CONAPEL paper mill; and Joseph Recinos, managing director of the Equity Expansion consulting firm.

27. Interview with Joseph Recinos, May 1987; Curtin Winsor, "The Solidarista Movement: Labor Economics for Democracy," *The Washington Quarterly*, Fall 1986.

28. One of the earliest works to analyze the oligarchy was Richard Adams, *Crucifixion by Power* (Austin: University of Texas Press, 1970). More recent works include Rene Poitevín, *El proceso de industrialización en Guatemala* (San José: EDUCA, 1977); Benjamin Crosby, *Crisis y fragmentación: Relaciones entre los sectores publico-privado en America Central* (Miami: Florida International University, 1985); and Marcie Mersky, *Empresarios y Transición en Guatemala* (San José: CSUCA, 1989). Also see CACIF, *Guatemala: Pasado, presente y futuro* (Guatemala City: 1988), and Inforpres Centroamericana, *Los empresarios ante la crisis* (Guatemala City: 1988).

29. Cited in Mersky, *Empresarios y Transición en Guatemala*.

30. The Unagro coalition fell apart in 1991 because of differences between the General Association of Farmers (AGA) and the Agricultural Chamber.

31. See, for example, Carmen Sofia Brena, "Completa la vista," *Cronica*, April 3, 1992.

32. The term "new right" is taken from the provocative "Central America's Left, Right, and Center," *Envío* 11, No. 128, 1992.

33. For a detailed study of business chambers see Rachel Garst, *La organización de la estructura gremial empresarial en Guatemala* (Guatemala City: FLACSO, forthcoming in 1992)

34. The CCG became the Chamber of Commerce and Industry in 1933, and during the Arbenz administration led private-sector opposition to agrarian and social reforms. In 1960 industrialists formed their own chamber. The CCG is the business association with the widest base, boasting branches in each department and with plans under way to establish municipal affiliates. A less belligerently conservative organization of merchants is the Association of Guatemalan Business Owners (Acecogua), founded in 1953.

35. According to Dunkerley, "the fact that a broad section of the local bourgeoisie was strongly and directly tied to U.S. capital . . . impeded the development of an industrially based modernizing 'national bourgeoisie.' " James Dunkerley, *Power in the Isthmus* (London: Verso, 1988), p. 464.

36. The six main member organizations of CACIF are the Chamber of Commerce, Agricultural Chamber, Chamber of Finances, Guatemala Chamber of Tourism, Association of Sugar Producers, and the Chamber of Industry. In addition, specially invited members include Guatemalan Chamber of Builders (CGC), Association of Gasoline Distributors, and the National Transport Industry Coordinator. In addition to these groups, the Greater Association of Presidents includes the presidents of Funtec, Fundesa, Fafides, Fundap, AGA, Friends of the Country, CAEM, and CLE.

Part 5: Social Sectors and Institutions

1. Ana Isabel García, *Mujeres Centroamericanas*, Vol. 2 (San José: FLACSO, 1989).

2. Ibid.

3. *Prensa Libre*, November 25, 1991.

4. Iduvina Hernández, "Para romper el silencio," *Siglo Veintiuno*, May 24, 1991.

5. Ibid. Also see CITGUA, *La Maquila en Guatemala*.

6. Tracey Dewart, "Reproductive Risks," *Links*, Spring 1992, p. 13.

7. APROFAM, *Encuesta de planificación familiar y salud materno infantil* (Guatemala City: May 1985).

8. CITGUA, *Situación de la mujer en Guatemala IV* (Mexico City: Ciencia y Tecnologia para Guatemala, September 1989). p. 28.

9. Ibid., p. 25-33.

10. *Informe de La Cuarta Conferencia Regional Sobre la Integración de la Mujer* (CEPAL, October 31, 1988); *Situación de la Mujer en Guatemala* (Ciencia y Tecnología para Guatemala, March 1987).

11. *Encuesta de Empleo* (Guatemala City: FLACSO, 1989).

12. *Análisis de la situación: Guatemala* (Guatemala City: UNICEF, May 1991).

13. Tracy Bachrach Ehlers, "Debunking Marianismo: Economic Vulnerability and Survival Strategies Among Guatemalan Wives," *Ethnology* XXX (1), January 1991.

14. Ibid. In her study of two highlands communities (San Antonio Polopó and San Pedro Sacatepequez), Ehlers found that "women's productive contribution has been devalued and marginalized, exacerbating female economic vulnerability and creating worrisome implications for gender relations in the future."

15. *Propuestas de ley en relación a la condición de la mujer guatemalteca III* (Guatemala City: Oficina Nacional de la Mujer, July 1990).

16. *Análisis de la situación: Guatemala.*

17. *Situación alimentaria nutricional de Guatemala* (Guatemala City: INCAP and OPS, March 1991)

18. World Bank, *Social Investment Funds in Guatemala, Honduras and El Salvador* (1991).

19. Guatemala Health Rights Support Project, *Reading the Vital Signs: Report of the 1988 Health Delegation to Guatemala* (Washington: October 1988).

20. Painter, *Guatemala: False Hope, False Freedom*, p. 4. Child mortality has been steadily dropping in Guatemala, although still considerably above regional averages. Child mortality per 1000 children under five dropped from 128 in 1980 to 113 in 1985 to 102 in 1990.

21. *Crónica*, October 20, 1988.

22. World Bank, *Social Investment Funds.*

23. *Siglo Veintiuno*, January 29, 1992.

24. *Central America Report*, August 9, 1991.

25. Guatemala Health Rights Support Project, *Reading the Vital Signs.*

26. *No nos tientes* was originally an antigovernment periodical published by the School of Medicine at the University of San Carlos.

27. Ana Fresse, "La Huelga de Dolores," *Siglo Veintiuno*, April 6, 1992.

28. *Central America Report*, August 4, 1989.

29. Report by International Federation of Journalists and the Canadian Committee to Protect Journalists, 1991, cited in *Mesoamerica*, June 1991.

30. Ibid.

31. "Guatemala: Repression and Self-Censorship, Sign of the Journalistic Profession," *CERIGUA Monthly Glance*, 1988.

32. *Miami Herald*, June 30, 1991.

33. Report by International Federation of Journalists and the Canadian Committee to Protect Journalists, 1991, cited in *Mesoamerica*, June 1991.

34. Interview with Mario Carpio Nicolle, March 1989.

35. Interview, May 15, 1987.

36. *Análisis de la situación: Guatemala* (Guatemala City: UNICEF, May 1991).

37. Report by International Federation of Journalists and the Canadian Committee to Protect Journalists, 1991, cited in *Mesoamerica*, June 1991.

38. *Crónica* owners include: Francisco Pérez de Antón (a Spanish-born businessman with wide cultural and intellectual interests who is associated with the CAEM business chamber and is an owner of the Pollo Campero fast-food chain), Juan Fernando Quezada Toruño (an important lawyer and brother of Bishop Quezada Toruño), Rodolfo Gutiérrez Machado (an investor and well-known publicity agent), and Juan Caso Fanjul (a Spanish-born investor).

39. See Nancy Morris, Broadcast Media Use and Social Structure in Guatemala, Working Paper 116 (University of Pennsylvania, September 1989).

40. *Análisis de la situación: Guatemala*. UNICEF estimated that 80 percent of Guatemalan families had radios, while Morris (in *Broadcast Media Use*) reported that 50 percent of those surveyed listened to the radio.

41. *Central America Report*, August 4, 1989.

42. *Análisis de la situación: Guatemala*.

43. *La Iglesia Católica en Guatemala: Signo de verdad y esperanza*, Pastoral letter of Archbishop Penados (Guatemala City: January 1989).

44. Brook Larmer, "Religious Row Endangers Guatemala," *Christian Science Monitor*, March 10, 1989.

45. Dennis A. Smith, "Coming of Age: A Reflection on Pentecostals, Politics, and Popular Religion in Guatemala," (Guatemala: CELEP, 1991).

46. José Luis Chea, *Guatemala: La cruz fragmentada* (San José: Department of Ecumenical Investigations, 1988).

47. F. Rosa Lima, *La cofradía: Reducto cultural indígena* (Guatemala: 1988).

48. For a detailed description of this period see Ricardo Falla, *Quiché Rebelde* (Guatemala: 1978).

49. Luis Samuadu, Hans Siebers, and Oscar Sierra, *Guatemala: Retos de la Iglesia Católica en una sociedad en crisis* (San José: DEI, 1991), p. 31. Another book-length but less insightful history and analysis of the Catholic Church is Chea, *Guatemala: La cruz fragmentada*.

50. For a history of this period see: Phillip Berryman, *The Religious Roots of Rebellion: Christians in Central American Revolutions* (New York: Orbis Books, 1984) and A. Opaz Bernales, "El movimiento religioso en Centroamérica: 1970-1983," in Daniel Camacho and Rafael Menjívar, eds., *Movimientos populares en Centroamerica* (San José: DEI, 1985).

51. It is interesting to note that one priest was killed on the last day of the Laugerud government, 11 during the Lucas García regime, and one during the Mejía Víctores government. Paradoxically, there were no priests killed during the Ríos Montt regime, although a few dozen evangelical pastors suspected of harboring leftist sympathies were murdered during his short tenure.

52. *The Clamor for Land: A Collegial Pastoral Letter by the Guatemalan Bishops Conference* (Managua: Guatemalan Church in Exile, May 1988); Penny Lernoux, "Bishops Take Courageous Stand," *National Catholic Reporter*, October 7, 1988.

53. "Guatemala: Challenges to the Military Model," *Envío* (Managua), May 1990.

54. *Plan Gobal de al Conferencia Episcopal Guatemalteca para 1988-92* (Guatemala City: 1988).

55. *Plan pastoral arquidiocesano 1986-88* (Guatemala City: 1986).

56. Ibid.

57. For an analysis of the U.S. origins and conservative implications of the charismatic movement see M.D. Díaz, *El Movimiento de la Renovación Carismática como un proceso de socialización adulta* (Mexico: 1985).

58. *Plan Gobal de al Conferencia Episcopal Guatemalteca para 1988-92*.

59. Bruce Calder, "Historical Patterns of Foreign Influence in the Guatemalan Catholic Church," (manuscript) Forthcoming in *Historia General de Guatemala*, No. 5.

60. The Catholic Church is divided into 12 administrative units: Archdiocese of Guatemala, dioceses of Jalapa, Zacapa, Verapaz, Quiché, Huehuetenango, San Marcos, Quetzaltenango, Sololá, and the apostolic administrations of Petén, Izabal, and Escuintla. Esquipulas, part of the Zacapa diocese, has the special status of prelature.

61. Interview with Archbishop Penados in *Siglo Veintiuno*, March 12, 1991.

62. Bruce Calder, "The Response of the Catholic Church to the Growth of Protestantism in Guatemala," (manuscript), Forthcoming in *Historia General de Guatemala*, No. 5.

63. For an early history of evangelicalism in Guatemala see Virginia Garrard Burnett, "Positivismo, liberalismo e impulso misionero: misiones protestantes en Guatemala, 1880-1920," *Mesoamerica* (19), June 1990.

64. CAM was the creation of the Dallas Theological Seminary, home of dispensationalist theology and the Scofield Reference Bible.

65. The departments of El Progreso, a part of Zacapa, Suchitepéquez, Retalhuleu, and Quetzaltenango were granted to the Presbyterians; Quiché and Totonicapán to the Primitive Methodists; Escuintla, Santa Rosa, Jutiapa, Huehuetenango, Sacatepéquez, Jalapa, San Marcos, and Sololá to the Central American Mission; a part of Zacapa, Izabal, and Chiquimula to the

Quakers; and Petén, Alta Verapaz, and Baja Verapaz to the Nazarenes. The Presbyterians and Central American Mission were to share the department of Guatemala.

66. Virginia Garrard Burnett, "Protestantism in Rural Guatemala: 1872-1954," *Latin American Research Review* 24, No. 1, 1989.

67. Roy Wingegard, "Primer Reporte General del Crecimiento y Distribución de la Iglesia Evangélica de Guatemala," January 1988.

68. Donna Eberwine, "To Ríos Montt with Love Lift," *The Nation*, February 26, 1983.

69. Smith, "Coming of Age."

70. Ibid.; David Stoll, *Is Latin America Turning Protestant? The Politics of Evangelical Growth* (Berkeley: University of California Press, 1990), p. 50.

71. For a valuable analysis of the foreign role in evangelical education and media see: Susan Rose and Quentin Schultze, "The Evangelical Awakening in Guatemala: Fundamentalist Impact on Education and Media," (Fundamentalism Project of the American Academy of Arts and Sciences, 1990).

72. Smith, "Coming of Age."

73. Enrique Ortego, "La mística del poder," *Siglo Veintiuno*, February, 24, 1991.

74. Dr. Jorge Serrano Elías, *La participación del cristiano en la vida pública* (Miami: Unilit, 1990).

75. Larmer, "Religious Row Endangers Guatemala."

76. As of 1990 there were 380 registered Guatemalan refugees in Honduras, 1,200 in Belize, and 400 in Nicaragua. According to the U.S. Committee on Refugees, political violence forced at least one million Guatemalans to abandon their homes in the early 1980s. U.S. Committee on Refugees, *World Refugee Survey: 1988 in Review* (New York: 1989), p. 34.

77. Sexual abuse of Central American women passing through Mexico is thought to be as high as 50 percent. American Friends Service Committee, *In the Shadow of Liberty: Central American Refugees in the United States* (Philadelphia: September 1988).

78. Arthur C. Helton article in U.S. Committee on Refugees, *World Refugee Survey*: 1988.

79. U.S. Immigration and Naturalization Service, "Enhancement Plan for Southern Border" (Washington), February 16, 1989, p. 19.

80. United Nations Economic Commission for Latin America, *Remesas, y economía familiar en El Salvador, Guatemala y Nicaragua* (New York: June 1991).

81. Louise Edwards, "Guatemala: Voices for Silent Refuge," *NACLA Report on the Americas*, Vol XXV (No. 1), July 1991.

82. Luis Raul Salvado, *The Other Refugees: A Study of Nonrecognized Guatemalan Refugees in Chiapas, Mexico* (Washington, DC: Center for Immigration Policy and Refugee Assistance, Georgetown University, 1988), pp. 1-7.

83. A valuable source of information on the circumstances facing repatriating refugees and the internally displaced is Beatriz Manz, *Refugees of a Hidden War: The Aftermath of Counterinsurgency in Guatemala* (Albany: State University of New York Press, 1988).

84. Edgar Gutiérrez, "La diáspora guatemalteca," *Siglo Veintiuno*, September 29, 1991.

85. By early 1992, of the 42,700 registered refugees (excluding children born in Mexico), 7,700 were living in four camps in Quintana Roo, 11,000 in four camps in Campeche, and about 24,000 were scattered among 128 camps in Chiapas along the border.

86. Fonapaz' council of directors includes the president, the vice-president (in his capacity as the head of CEAR), two presidential advisers, the secretary general of the government planning agency SEGEPLAN, and the ministers of Finance and Development.

87. This zone includes the departments of Sololá, Chimaltenango, Huehuetenango, Quiché, the northern reaches of San Marcos and Alta Verapaz, and a 50-kilometer-wide strip along the Usumacinta River in the Petén. As delineated by Fonapaz, Zonapaz comprises 102 municipalities and 652 villages.

88. Rachel Garst, "Fondo de inversión social a cargo de Fonapaz," *Siglo Veintiuno*, April 5, 1992.

89. See, for example, Brook Larmer, "Guatemalan Indians Become the Battlefield," *Christian Science Monitor*, September 4, 1990.

90. For a compilation of statements made by the CPR see: Guatemalan Church in Exile, *Offensive of the People: Campesino Against Campesino* (Managua: July 1989).

91. Communities of Population in Resistance, "Who We Are and Why We Resist," March 1989.

92. The 1989 Encuesta Nacional Sociodemográfica cited in UNICEF, *Situación de probreza: Guatemala* (Guatemala City: May 1991), p. 7.

93. AVANCSO, *Vonós a la capital* (Guatemala City: June 1991), p. 31. For information on fecundity rates in the departments of Jutiapa, Santa Rosa, and El Progreso see SEGEPLAN, *La fecundidad en Guatemala*, 1950-81 (Guatemala City: 1983).

94. These conclusions are drawn from AVANCSO, *Vonós a la capital*, pp. 1-5.

Part 6: Society and Ethnicity

1. See Alan Weisman, "The Real Indiana Jones and His Pyramids of Doom," *Los Angeles Times*, October 14, 1990.

2. *Los Angeles Times*, May 15, 1991.

3. Luisa Frank and Philip Wheaton, *Indian Guatemala: Path to Liberation* (EPICA, 1986).

4. Demetrio Cojtí Cuxil, "Sistemas colonialistas de definición del indio y de atribución de su nacionalidad," *Tradiciones de Guatemala* (magazine of the Centro de Estudios Folklóricos at San Carlos University), No. 32, 1989.

5. Kay B. Warren, *The Symbolism of Subordination: Indian Identity in a Guatemalan Town* (Austin: University of Texas Press, 1978), p. ix.

6. George Lowell, "Surviving the Conquest: The Maya of Guatemala in Historical Perspective," *Latin American Research Review* XXIII, No. 2, pp. 25-57.

7. Kenneth Freed, "Guatemalan Tribe Wears History Well," *Los Angeles Times*, August 7, 1990.

8. Carol A. Smith, "Maya Nationalism, " *NACLA Report on the Americas* XXV, No. 3, December 1991, p. 33.

9. These are Aguateco, Cakchiquel, Chortí, Chuj, Itzá, Ixil, Jacalteco (sometimes called Popotí), Kanjobal, Kekchí, Lacandón, Mam, Mopán, Pokomam (also Pocomám), Pokomchí, Quiché, Tzutuhil, Uspanteco, and Xinca. In addition, the Garífuna people speak a language by the same name (also known as Caribe or Araguaco). Dialects sometimes listed by anthropologists as languages include Acateco, Achí, Sacapulteco, Sipacapeño, and Teco. See, for example, William V. Davidson and Melanie A. Counce, "Mapping the Distribution of Indians in Central America," *Cultural Survival Quarterly* 13, No. 3, 1989.

10. AVANCSO, *Vonós a la capital* (Guatemala City: June 1991), p. 6.

11. Nancie L. Gonzalez, *Sojourners of the Caribbean: Ethnogenesis and Ethnohistory of the Garifuna* (Chicago: University of Illinois Press, 1988), pp. 17-21.

12. Melanie Counce and William Davidson, "Indians of Central America 1980's," *Cultural Survival Quarterly* 13, No. 3, 1989, pp. 38-9

13. Gonzalez, *Sojourners of the Caribbean*, p. 207.

14. Ejército Guerrillero de los Pobres, *Sebastián Guzmán: principal de principales* (mimeo), cited in Arturo Arias, "El movimiento indígena en Guatemala: 1970-1983," in Daniel Camacho and Rafael Menjivar, eds., *Movimientos populares en Centroamerica* (San José: DEI, 1985). The analysis of the early indian movement is drawn largely from this excellent account by Arias. Also see Arias, "Changing Indian Identity: Guatemala's Violent Transition to Modernity," in Carol Smith, ed., *Guatemalan Indians and the State, 1540 to 1988* (Austin: University of Texas, 1990).

15. "Los pueblos indígenas de Guatemala ante el mundo," *Cuicuilco*, No. 1 (Mexico City).

16. See Ricardo Falla, "El movimiento indígena," *Estudios Centroamericanos*, No. 351/352, 1978.

17. Severo Martínez Peláez, *La patria del criollo* (Guatemala City: Editorial Universitaria, 1971); Carlos Guzmán Bockler and Jean-Loup Herbert, *Guatemala: una interpretación histórica* (Mexico City: Siglo Veintiuno, 1970).

18. Indian Law Resource Center, *Question of the Violation of Human Rights and Fundamental Freedoms in Any Part of the World, with Particular Reference to Colonial and other Dependent Countries and Territories* (Presented in Geneva to UN Commission on Human Rights), November 12, 1982.

19. Sheldon Davis and Julie Hodson, *Witness to Political Violence in Guatemala: The Suppression of a Rural Development Movement* (Boston: Oxfam, June 1982). Also see Sheldon H. Davis, "Introduction: Sowing the Seeds of Violence," in Robert M. Carmack, ed., *Harvest of*

Violence: The Maya Indians and the Guatemalan Crisis (Norman: University of Oklahoma Press, 1988).

20. George Lovell, "From Conquest to Counterinsurgency," *Cultural Survival Quarterly*, Vol. 9, No. 2, 1985; Neil Boothby, "Uprooted Mayan Children," *Cultural Survival Quarterly*, Vol. 10, No. 4, 1986.

21. "Operación Ixil," *Revista Militar*, September-December 1982; Chris Krueger, "Re-education and Relocation in Guatemala," *Cultural Survival Quarterly*, Vol. 10, No. 4, 1986.

22. Michael Willis, "500 Years of Indigenous and Popular Resistance: Report on the Second Continental Meeting," *Report on Guatemala* 12, No. 2, Winter 1991.

23. Alex Michael, "Indigenous Peoples in the Guatemalan Struggle," *Report on Guatemala*, January-March 1989.

24. A statement by Jason Clay writing in *Cultural Survival Quarterly* as cited in *Report on Guatemala*, January-March 1989.

25. Interview with Carlos Guzmán Bockler, April 30, 1987. See Carlos Guzmán Bockler, *Donde enmudecen las conciencias: Crepúscula y aurora en Guatemala* (Mexico City: Secretaria de Educación Pública, 1986).

26. *Report on Guatemala*, September-October 1986.

27. Nora C. England and Stephen R. Elliott, eds., *Lecturas sobre la linquistica maya* (Antigua, Guatemala: CIRMA, 1990).

28. Cited in Diane M. Nelson, "The reconstruction of Mayan identity," *Report on Guatemala* 12, No. 2, Summer 1991.

29. Personal interviews with AMLG representatives, March 1992.

30. Interview with FAR commander Pablo Monsanto in *La Jornada* (Mexico City), July 22-5, 1991, reprinted in *Report on Guatemala* 12, No. 3, Fall 1991.

31. Mimeo declaration from EGP, 1985.

32. Domingo Hernández, "Elements in Understanding the Situation of the Guatemalan Indigenous Popular Movement" (Mexico City: mimeo, 1986).

33. Alex Michael, "Indigenous Peoples."

34. URNG, "For Peace with Justice and Democracy: Content of the Negotiations," May 1992.

Part 7: Nature and Environmentalism

1. The signification of Guatemala comes from José Ernesto Carrillo, "¿Tierra de Bosques?" in Ingemar Hedstrom, ed., *La situación ambiental en centroamérica y el caribe* (San José: DEI, 1989).

2. James Nations et al., *Biodiversity in Guatemala* (Guatemala City: AID, December 1988), p. 1.

3. Florence Gardner, Yaakov Garb, and Marta Williams, *Guatemala: A Political Ecology*, (Berkeley: The Environmental Project on Central America [EPOCA], October 1990). This 16-page report provides an overview of the country's environmental problems and their close association with structural economic issues.

4. Jim Burchfield, "Natural Resources Under Siege: The Environmental Costs of Counterinsurgency," *OSGUA Newsletter* (Chicago), Spring 1989.

5. The following description of the country's main environments is drawn largely from Nations et al., *Biodiversity in Guatemala*.

6. H. Jeffrey Leonard, *Natural Resources and Economic Development in Central America: A Regional Environmental Profile* (Washington, DC: International Institute for Environment and Development, 1987), p. 10.

7. Ibid, pp. 6-11.

8. Ibid.

9. *El plan de acción forestal para Guatemala* (Guatemala City: 1992).

10. UNICEF, *Situación de pobreza: Guatemala* (Guatemala City: March 1991); Nations et al., *Biodiversity in Guatemala*.

11. Burchfield, "Natural Resources Under Siege."

12. Nations et al., *Biodiversity in Guatemala*, p. 6.

13. Norman B. Schwartz, *Forest Society: A Social History of Petén, Guatemala* (Philadelphia: University of Pennsylvania Press, 1990), p. 242. Many of the Peteneros were *chicle* wage workers laboring under harsh conditions, but most were also independent farmers. The scarcity of labor and the immensity of the agricultural frontier as well as the wealth and beauty of the forest have fostered a less repressive and more democratic environment.

14. Ibid., p. 256.

15. Victor Perera, "A Forest Dies in Guatemala," *The Nation*, November 6, 1989.

16. Journalistic accounts of the extent of illegal timbering in Petén include Andres Oppenheimer, "Pirate Loggers Razing Guatemalan Rain Forest," *Miami Herald*, January 6, 1991, and Victor Perera, "The Last Preserve: Guatemala Guards its Rain Forests," *The Nation*, July 8, 1991.

17. Study cited in Schwartz, *Forest Society*, p. 287.

18. Leonard, *Natural Resources*, p. 94.

19. "Guatemala: Developing the Petroleum Industry," *Central America Report*, July 5, 1991, p. 197.

20. Ibid., p. 196.

21. The only refinery currently existing in the country is the Texaco refinery in Escuintla, which can only process about 20 percent of the oil extracted in Guatemala. Texaco, Exxon, and Shell all have marketing operations in the country.

22. Reported in Arturo Arias, "El movimiento indígena en Guatemala: 1970-83" in Daniel Camacho and Rafael Menjivar (eds.), *Movimientos populares en Centroamérica* (San José: DEI, 1985).

23. Leonard, *Natural Resources*, p. 119.

24. Ibid., p. 133.

25. Ibid., p. 136.

26. For an overview of the loss of rivers and lakes in Guatemala see Carrillo, "¿Tierra de Bosques?"

27. *Amigos del Lago* (Guatemala City), May 1991.

28. See Dr. Heriberto Arreaga et al., "Diagnóstico sobre el uso e impacto de los plaguicidas en America Central" (Guatemala City: October 1988).

29. Cited in Gardner et al., *Guatemala: A Political Ecology*. For an overview of pesticide-use problems in nontraditional export production see Polly Hoppin, "Pesticide Use by Growers of Non-Traditional Crops in Guatemala: Implications for Residues," Submitted to the Regional Office for Central America and Panama (ROCAP), April 15, 1989.

30. Interview with Dr. León Muniz, May 1984.

31. Pesticide Action Network, "Demise of the Dirty Dozen" (San Francisco: April 1991).

32. Guillermo Duarte, *Amatitlán y yo* (Guatemala City: Comité del Lago de Amatitlán, 1989).

33. Perera, "The Last Preserve."

Part 8: U.S. Influence

1. *New York Times*, August 22, 1982.

2. U.S. Agency for International Development, *Congressional Presentation Fiscal Year 1990*, Annex III (Washington: 1989), p. 88.

3. Between 1977 and 1982 Guatemala received $109.1 million in U.S. economic aid. For information concerning the levels of U.S. military assistance during the 1977-1986 period, see Allan Nairn, "The Guatemala Connection," *The Progressive*, May 1986.

4. For a discussion of U.S.-Guatemala relations during the Carter and Reagan administrations see: Robert Trudeau and Lars Schoultz, "Guatemala," in Morris Blachman et al., eds., *Confronting Revolution: Security through Diplomacy in Central America* (New York: Pantheon, 1986). In the 1982-85 period, Congress declined to grant the Reagan administration's request for direct military aid, but the administration did approve licenses for commercial sales of military equipment worth $769,800.

5. For a full discussion of "active neutrality" during the Cerezo administration see Edgar Gutiér-rez, "Política exterior y estabilidad estatal," in *Cuadernos de Investigación*, No. 5. (Guate-mala City: AVANCSO, 1989).

6. For a critique of pre-1989 U.S. State Department human rights reports on Guatemala see Jean-Marie Simon, *Eternal Spring, Eternal Tyranny* (New York: Norton, 1987), pp. 208, 225, 234. Also see Washington Office on Latin America, *Guatemala: A Test Case for Human Rights Policy in the Post-Cold War Era*, A WOLA Human Rights Brief (Washington: March 12, 1991).

7. *Latin America Weekly Report*, August 27, 1982.

8. Americas Watch, *Messengers of Death*, p. 78.

9. U.S. embassy, *Economic Trends: Guatemala* (Guatemala City, April 1992).

10. U.S. embassy, *Business Fact Sheets* (Guatemala City, November 1988).

11. Tom Barry and Debra Preusch, *The Central America Fact Book* (New York: Grove Press, 1986), pp. 245-8.

12. For more on *maquiladoras* in Guatemala see Kurt Peterson, *The Maquiladora Revolution in Guatemala* (New Haven: Orville Schell Junior Center for International Human Rights, 1992).

13. For an extensive treatment of AID support for counterinsurgency-related projects during this period see Tom Barry, *Guatemala: The Politics of Counterinsurgency* (Albuquerque: Re-source Center, 1986).

14. Tom Barry and Debra Preusch, *The Soft War: The Uses and Abuses of U.S. Economic Aid in Central America* (New York: Grove Press, 1988), pp. 107-44.

15. Ibid.

16. *New York Times*, November 22, 1954.

17. Embassy cable of July 21, 1954, cited in Charles D. Brockett, "Building a Showcase for De-mocracy: The U.S. in Guatemala, 1954-1960," Paper prepared for the XVI International Con-gress of Latin American Studies, Washington, DC, April 4-6, 1991.

18. Embassy cable of January 25, 1955, cited in Ibid.

19. State Department memorandum of November 14, 1957, cited in Ibid.

20. David Clark Scott, "Guatemalans Protest U.S. Funds for Army Think Tank," *Christian Sci-ence Monitor*, December 3, 1990.

21. For more on AFL-CIO's international institutes and their links with the National Endow-ment for Democracy see Beth Sims, *Workers of the World Undermined* (Boston: South End Press, 1992).

22. David Corn, "Foreign Aid for the Right," *The Nation*, December 18, 1989.

23. AID, *The Democracy Initiative* (Washington, DC: December 1990), p. 2.

24. U.S. Department of State, "Guatemala: Stopping Deliveries of Military Assistance," state-ment by Deputy Spokesman Richard Boucher, December 21, 1990. Devine, kidnapped from his home in Poptún, Petén, on June 8, 1990, was found decapitated twelve hours later. Devine, whose home bordered on an army base, had complained of receiving death threats shortly before his murder.

25. U.S. Department of Defense, *Congressional Presentation for Security Assistance Programs, FY1992* (Washington: 1991), p. 161.

26. U.S. Department of Defense, *Congressional Presentation for Security Assistance Programs, FY1993* (Washington: 1992), p. 180.

27. "U.S. Noose Around His Neck," *CERI-GUA Monthly Glance*, October-November 1989.

28. Washington Office on Latin America, *Guatemala: A Test Case for Human Rights Policy* .

29. These include the Criminal Investigations Training Assistance Program (ICITAP), Interna-tional Narcotics Matters (INM), and DEA programs. Although ICITAP, which like the INM program is managed by the State Department while administered directly by the Justice De-partment, does provide some training for judges, prosecutors, and investigators from the of-fice of the Human Rights Ombudsman, the bulk of the training and assistance is provided to the National Police, which, according to Americas Watch, "carry out gross violations of hu-man rights, including torture, murder, and disappearances." Americas Watch, *Messengers of Death*.

30. "U.S. Taking a New Tack in Guatemala," *Los Angeles Times*, May 7, 1990.

Bibliography

The following periodicals are useful sources of information and analysis on Guatemala:

Enfoprensa: Information on Guatemala (Chicago), weekly, English and Spanish.
Guatemala: Central America Report, Inforpress Centroamericana (Guatemala), weekly, English and Spanish.
NACLA Report on the Americas, North American Congress on Latin America (New York), bimonthly, English.
Pensamiento Propio, Coordinadora Regional de Investigaciones Económicas y Sociales (Managua), monthly, Spanish.
Report on Guatemala, Guatemala News and Information Bureau (Oakland), quarterly, English.
Update on Guatemala, Committee in Solidarity with the People of Guatemala (New York), bimonthly, English.

The following books and reports contain valuable background on many issues important to understanding Guatemala:

Tom Barry, *Guatemala: The Politics of Counterinsurgency* (Albuquerque: The Resource Center, 1986).
George Black, with Milton Jamail and Norma Stoltz Chinchilla, *Garrison Guatemala* (New York: Monthly Review Press, 1984).
Robert M. Carmack, ed., *Harvest of Violence: The Maya Indians and the Guatemalan Crisis* (Norman: University of Oklahoma Press, 1988).
Directory and Analysis: Private Organizations with U.S. Connections in Guatemala (Albuquerque: The Resource Center, 1988).

Jonathan Fried, Marvin E. Gettleman, Deborah T. Levenson, and Nancy Peckenham, eds., *Guatemala in Rebellion: Unfinished History* (New York: Grove Press, 1983).

James A. Goldston, *Shattered Hope: Guatemalan Workers and the Promise of Democracy* (Boulder, CO: Westview Press, 1989).

Guatemala: Security, Development, and Democracy (Managua: Guatemalan Church in Exile, 1989).

Jim Handy, *Gift of the Devil: A History of Guatemala* (Boston: South End Press, 1984).

Susanne Jonas, *The Battle for Guatemala: Rebels, Death Squads, and U.S. Power* (Boulder: Westview Press, 1991).

Susanne Jonas and David Tobis, eds., *Guatemala* (New York: North American Congress on Latin America, 1981).

Beatriz Manz, *Refugees of a Hidden War: The Aftermath of Counterinsurgency in Guatemala* (Albany: State University of New York Press, 1988).

Michael McClintock, *The American Connection: Volume II. State Terror and Popular Resistance in Guatemala* (London: Zed Press, 1985).

Messengers of Death: Human Rights in Guatemala, November 1988—February 1990 (New York: Americas Watch, March 1990).

James Painter, *Guatemala: False Hope, False Freedom* (London: Catholic Institute for International Relations/Latin America Bureau, 1989).

La Política de Desarrollo del Estado Guatemalteca 1986-1987 (Guatemala City: AVANCSO, 1988).

Política Exterior y Estabilidad Estatal, AVANCSO Cuadernos de Investigación No. 5 (Guatemala City: AVANCSO, January 1989).

Stephen Schlesinger and Stephen Kinzer, *Bitter Fruit: The Untold Story of the American Coup in Guatemala* (Garden City, NY: Doubleday, 1982).

Jean-Marie Simon, *Guatemala: Eternal Spring, Eternal Tyranny* (New York: Norton, 1987).

Chronology

1676	Founding of University of San Carlos (USAC) in Guatemala City as first university in Central America.
1821	Central American region declares independence from Spain.
1822	Annexation to Mexico.
1823	Independence from Mexico as United Provinces of Central America.
	U.S. pronouncement of Monroe Doctrine.
1826	Outbreak of civil war.
1830	Morazán takes Guatemala City, becomes president of United Provinces of Central America.
1839	Central American federation disintegrates.
	Guatemala claims to have inherited sovereign rights over Belize from Spain.
1850	U.S.-British treaty; Britain agrees to refrain from occupying, fortifying, or colonizing any part of Central America. Britain claims treaty exempts Belize as a prior settlement. Guatemala claims it signed treaty because parties agreed to build road to Caribbean coast for Guatemala's use.
1859	Guatemala signs treaty, recognizes British sovereignty of Belize.
1871	Gen. Justo Rufino Barrios takes power from Conservatives and launches Liberal reforms; Catholic Church suffers loss of power and prestige.
1882	U.S. missionary founds first Protestant church which now stands in the shadow of National Palace.
1884	Guatemala threatens to repudiate treaty of 1859.
1885	Barrios assassinated.
1894	Formation of several worker associations.
1898	Estrada Cabrera takes power.
	First *Huelga de Dolores* demonstration by students during Holy Week. Becomes annual tradition continuing to present, except during Lucas García regime.

1901	First transnational corporation, United Fruit Company, arrives in Guatemala.
1918	Formation of Worker Federation for the Legal Protection of Labor (FOG) under influence of American Federation of Labor.
	U.S. President Wilson determines who will develop oil resources in Guatemala.
1920	Estrada Cabrera overthrown; United States intervenes militarily.
	Central America Unionist Party elected.
	Formation of University Student Association (AEU).
1921	With U.S. encouragement, coup installs military government.
1922	Workers Regional Federation of Guatemala (FROG) begins organizing at United Fruit.
1929	International Railways of Central America (United Fruit affiliate), connects railways between El Salvador and Guatemala.
1931	Jorge Ubico takes over presidency; purge of leftists and repression of unions for next 13 years.
1936	Britain offers £50,000 to help build road to coast without admitting liability; Guatemala demands £400,000.
1944	Ubico overthrown in military coup; civilian/military "October Revolution" breaks out and victorious forces sponsor new elections.
1945	Reformist candidate Juan José Arévalo elected president.
	New democratic constitution promulgated; women granted suffrage; "Belice" defined as 23rd department.
1947	New labor code establishes right to organize and strike.
1948	Formation of Guatemalan Workers Party (PGT), although not legalized until 1951.
1949	Francisco Javier Arana, chief of armed forces, assassinated soon after announcing candidacy for president.
	Unsuccessful military coup attempt.
1950	Jacobo Arbenz Guzmán elected president.
1952	Agrarian reform law passed, opening way for expropriation of uncultivated estates and their redistribution to landless peasants.
	Communist Party legalized.
1953	United Fruit Company plantations and International Railways nationalized; 400,000 uncultivated acres redistributed to landless peasants.
1954	CIA's "Operation Success" topples Arbenz government in June; Carlos Castillo Armas of National Liberation Movement (MLN) takes power.
	Expropriated lands returned to former owners; all effective unions disbanded; thousands of people killed.
1955	Castillo Armas confirmed as president.
	Formation of Christian Democratic Party of Guatemala (DCG).
1956	New constitution promulgated.

	Formation of National Coordinator of Agricultural, Commercial, Industrial, and Financial Associations (CACIF).
1957	Castillo Armas assassinated; Vice-President Luis Arturo González named provisional president.
	Presidential elections turn into riots, military takes control of government and names Guillermo Flores Avendano as head of state.
	Formation of Revolutionary Party (PR).
1958	New elections won by conservative Miguel Ydígoras Fuentes.
1960	Failed U.S. invasion of Cuba launched from Guatemalan and Nicaraguan soil.
1961	Belize turns down offer to become "associate state" of Guatemala.
	Military rebellion against Ydígoras suppressed, forcing rebels to flee to mountains.
	Foundation of Rafael Landívar University.
	Formation of Conference of Religious Orders of Guatemala (CONFREGUA).
1962	Outbreak of major student and labor protests; Formation of M-13 and Rebel Armed Forces (FAR) guerrilla groups after failed coup attempt by group of reformist officers.
1963	Army removes Ydígoras and names Defense Minister Col. Alfredo Enrique Peralta Azurdia new president.
	Constitution replaced by Fundamental Charter of Government.
	Diplomatic relations with United Kingdom suspended due to dispute over Belize; Guatemala threatens war.
1964	Formation of Democratic Institutional Party (PID).
1965	New constitution promulgated.
	U.S. lawyer appointed by President Johnson mediates dispute with Belize. Proposal favors Guatemala and is rejected by all parties in Belize.
1966	Revolutionary Party (PR) candidate Julio César Méndez Montenegro elected president.
	U.S. Special Forces participate in "Operation Guatemala," a counterinsurgency campaign led by Col. Carlos Arana Osorio which kills more than 8,000 people.
	Appearance of White Hand and other rightwing death squads, believed to be responsible for more than 30,000 deaths over next seven years.
1968	U.S. Ambassador John Mein assassinated.
	Formation of National Confederation of Workers (CNT), affiliated with Christian-Democratic CLAT, as alternative to ORIT-backed organizations.
1969	Formation of Bank and Insurance Workers Federation (FESEBS).
1970	MLN candidate Carlos Arana Osorio elected president.
	West German Ambassador Karl von Spreti assassinated.
1971	Formation of Organization of People in Arms (ORPA).
	Foundation of Francisco Marroquín University.

1972	Negotiations with Britain break off; Guatemala threatens war by mobilizing troops at Belize border. Britain sends fleet and several thousand troops to Belize.
	Formation of Guerrilla Army of the Poor (EGP), which clandestinely begins organizing in Ixil triangle.
	Formation of Army Bank by Military Social Welfare Institute (IPM).
1974	Rightwing candidate Gen. Kjell Laugerud García elected president in fraudulent electoral contest against Ríos Montt.
1975	Tension with Belize prompts Britain to send squadron of Harrier jets to Belize.
	Belize takes territorial dispute to United Nations.
	EGP begins guerrilla violence.
1976	Earthquake leaves 22,000 dead, one million homeless, and Guatemala City partially destroyed.
	Formation of National Reconstruction Committee (CRN).
	Hunger protest and lockout at Coca-Cola precipitates formation of National Committee of Trade Union Unity (CNUS).
	U.S. Congress holds hearings on human rights situation in Guatemala, El Salvador, and Nicaragua.
1977	Massive march by Ixtahuacán, Huehuetenango, miners to Guatemala City.
	U.S. aid rejected by Guatemala because of human rights stipulations.
	Mexico and other Latin American countries begin to shift from siding with Guatemala to solidarity with Belize in the territorial dispute.
1978	Fraudulent national elections leave no candidate with clear majority; PR-PID-CAO candidate General Romeo Lucas García elected president by National Congress.
	Kekchí Indians protest land-grabbing by cattle growers; formation of Campesino Unity Committee (CUC), army massacres 100 Kekchí Indians at Panzós.
	Bus fare hikes prompt massive demonstrations.
	Government begins elimination of union leaders.
	Oliverio Casteñeda de León, a student, assassinated. Guatemalan University Student Association (AEU) changes its designation to include his name.
	Over 1,000 Guatemalans receive cooperative farming training in Israel.
	U.S. bans arms sales to Guatemala.
1979	ORPA launches first military operation.
	Formation of Democratic Front Against Repression (FDCR).
1980	Spanish embassy occupied by 39 protesters burned to ground by security forces; Spain breaks off diplomatic relations.
	Amigos del País and Guatemalan Freedom Fund hire U.S. public relations firms to launch campaign in United States praising Guatemalan government.

Guerrilla organizations, including ORPA, EGP, FAR, and leadership of Guatemalan Workers' Party, form alliance.

The United Nations passes resolution demanding secure independence of Belize before next UN session in 1981. No country votes against measure; Guatemala refuses to vote.

1981   Army carries out major counterinsurgency offensive in Chimaltenango; 1,500 Indian *campesinos* killed in two-month period.

CUC goes underground.

Formation of Enterprise Chamber (CAEM).

IMF agreement.

April   Negotiations with Guatemala provoke riots and state of emergency in Belize.

Sep.   Belize becomes fully independent member of Commonwealth of Nations (Great Britain), and joins United Nations. Guatemala refuses to recognize Belize's independence and impedes its entry into Organization of American States and other regional organizations.

1982   AID distributes $15.5 in economic aid.

Jan.   Foreign Ministers of Costa Rica, El Salvador, and Honduras form Central American Democratic Community. Guatemala and Nicaragua excluded.

Feb.   Formation of Guatemalan National Revolutionary Unity (URNG) by EGP, ORPA, FAR, and the PGT Nucleus.

March   PID candidate General Angel Aníbal Guevara wins fraudulent national elections; junta of army officers led by Efraín Ríos Montt seizes power before Aníbal is installed.

April   New junta unveils its National Development and Security Plan. Civil Affairs (S-5) division formed.

June   Junta disbanded and its leader, retired General Efraín Ríos Montt, takes power.

Ríos Montt's "Beans and Guns" counterinsurgency campaign escalates in Quiché, Alta Verapaz, Chimaltenango, San Marcos, and Baja Verapaz.

"Voluntary" Civilian Self-Defense Patrols formed; within two years there are 900,000 members.

July   State of siege declared.

Aug.   World Council of Churches reports government responsible for deaths of over 9,000 people in previous five months.

Sep.   Formation of Council of State.

1983   Ardent anticommunist Cardinal Casariego dies; new church leader Archbishop Próspero Penados del Barrio adopts more conciliatory tone.

Oil exports reach record high, but drop 70 percent by end of decade.

Formation of National Union Center (UCN).

Formation of Confederation of Guatemalan Trade Union Unity (CUSG).

Formation of Guatemalan Solidarista Union.

Jan.	Contadora group meets for first time to develop dialogue and negotiation in Central America; parties to peace accords include Costa Rica, El Salvador, Guatemala, Honduras, and Nicaragua.
	United States resumes sale of spare military parts.
March	State of siege lifted.
Aug.	Evangelical Ríos Montt alienates business, army, as well as Catholic Church; Defense Minister General Oscar Humberto Mejía Víctores seizes power in military coup.
	Mejía Víctores initiates "model villages" program, and army announces it will work to effect transition to civilian rule.
	Censorship, secret tribunals, and Council of State are abolished.
Sep.	Suspension of IMF agreement.
Nov.	Two AID employees killed by military; U.S. economic aid suspended.
1984	Constituent assembly convenes to formulate new constitution.
	Coca-Cola declares bankruptcy; workers occupy plant and eventually win ownership.
	World Council of Indigenous Peoples accuses military of systematic extermination of indian population.
	Kissinger Commission recommends $8 billion developmental aid to Central America and increased military assistance to Honduras, El Salvador, and Guatemala.
1985	Resumption of official U.S. economic and military aid.
	Reestablishment of Democratic Socialist Party (PSD).
	Formation of Union of Guatemalan Workers (UNSITRAGUA).
March	Coca-Cola plant in Guatemala City reopens after year-long occupation by workers and decisive international pressure.
Aug.	Week of massive demonstrations sparked by inflation and increased bus fares.
Oct.	Christian Democrat Marco Vinicio Cerezo Arévalo wins national elections.
1986	Cerezo installed as president in January.
	New constitution promulgated.
	Federal and municipal government employees granted right to organize.
	Department of Technical Investigations (DIT) "disbands;" many of its members join National Police.
	Padre Andrés Girón and Pro-Land Peasant Association lead 16,000 campesinos in march to National Palace to demand government distribute land to landless.
	A visiting UNICEF director says five Guatemalan children under age five die every hour from easily preventable diseases.
	Creation of Special Commission for the Assistance of Repatriates (CEAR).
	Germany gives over $175 million in bilateral assistance over next three years.

April	Formation of General Confederation of Guatemalan Workers (CGTG).
1987	Cotton production drops to 25-year low.
	AID distributes over $187 million in aid.
	Formation of Labor and Popular Action Unity (UASP), an alliance of popular and labor organizations.
Feb.	Representatives from El Salvador, Guatemala and Honduras meet in Esquipulas, Guatemala for peace talks.
July	SEPAL survey discovers 31.6 percent of Guatemalans are evangelical.
Aug.	Presidents of Costa Rica, El Salvador, Guatemala, Honduras, and Nicaragua sign Esquipulas II peace accord.
Sep.	Formation of National Reconciliation Commission (CNR), while army begins unsuccessful "Year's End" offensive to terminate guerrilla insurgency.
Nov.	Esquipulas Accords go into effect.
	Representatives from government and URNG meet in Madrid.
1988	Cardamom market becomes saturated, nearly half the country's producers unable to sell (or eat) their crop.
	Formation of Runujel Junam Council of Ethnic Communities (CERJ).
	Formation of National Coordinator of Guatemalan Widows (CONAVIGUA); Rigoberta Menchú becomes its well-known spokesperson.
	Catholic bishops release pastoral letter entitled "The Clamor for Land."
Jan.	Continued Esquipulas peace talks in San José, Costa Rica.
	U.S. INS reports that asylum applications from Guatemalans have risen 900 percent over previous year with arrests of Guatemalans rising 38 percent.
March	"Year's End" offensive canceled after major casualties incurred and failure to stamp out guerrillas becomes obvious.
	Costa Rican President Arias accuses countries of Guatemala, El Salvador, Honduras, and Nicaragua of not complying fully with Esquipulas Accords.
April	Government signs pact with UASP to increase wages and freeze prices.
	Five Central American vice-presidents meet in San José to discuss Central American Parliament and agree to present regional economic cooperation plan to United Nations.
May	Abortive military coup attempt.
	Government-UASP pact broken.
June	Offices of *La Epoca* firebombed.
	Guatemala accuses Costa Rica of noncompliance with Esquipulas Accords because it failed to ratify treaty to create Central American Parliament.
	Formation of Permanent Joint Commission with Belize.

Aug.	Another failed coup attempt.
	Regional peace talks postponed twice.
Nov.	Army massacres 22 peasants in Aguacate, blames guerrillas.
	Central American presidents agree to meet in January for peace talks.
1989	Emergence of "Jaguar of Justice," a new death squad.
	Colt Industries sells 16,000 M-16 assault rifles to army.
	URNG announces it inflicts seven casualties a day, hopes to raise to 15 per day by end of year.
	PGT formally incorporated into guerrilla coalition URNG.
Feb.	Kentucky National Guard participates in civic-action program near site of Aguacate massacre.
	Esquipulas peace talks held in El Salvador after four postponements; Guatemala, El Salvador, Honduras, and Nicaragua say they will go ahead with Central American Parliament without Costa Rica, whose Congress has not yet ratified plan.
March	URNG and National Reconciliation Commission (CNR) sign accord in Oslo to initiate three-step (political parties, social sectors, and government/military) dialogue over next several months.
May	Failed coup attempt.
1990	Guatemala becomes favored transshipment point for cocaine smugglers.
June	Accord signed at El Escorial, Spain between URNG and nine political parties commits participants to work toward political solutions to conflict.
Nov.	First round of presidential elections scheduled, with Jorge Carpio Nicole and Jorge Serrano emerging as two front runners.
Dec.	Massacre at Santiago Atitlán.
1991	Jorge Serrano wins runoff election in landslide victory over Jorge Carpio Nicole in January.
	"Framework agreement" on free trade signed with Washington.
	Wheat production shrinks to one-third of 1988 levels due to food aid and liberalized trade.
April	Peace negotiations begin between government and URNG.
Oct.	Massive conference and march to highlight 500 years of resistance by indigenous people.
Dec.	Serrano reshuffles military command.
1992	Army assigned to patrol Guatemala City streets alongisde police in order to control crime.
May	Serrano expels UN observer from peace talks.

SOURCES: *Encyclopedia of the Third World* (1987); *Conflict in Central America* (Longman Group Ltd, 1987); *Crisis in Central America: Regional Dynamics and U.S. Policy in the 1980s* (Westview Press, 1988); Gerald Greenfield and Sheldon Maran, eds., *Labor Organizations in Latin America* (Greenwood Press, 1987); and "Facts of the Matter" (Central America Education Project, Summer 1987).

For More Information

Resources

Centro Exterior de Reportes Informativos sobre Guatemala
(CERI-GUA)/Weekly Briefs, Monthly Glance, Special Reports
Apartado Postal 74206
Delegación Iztapalapa
México D.F. 09080
México

Enfoprensa/Information on Guatemala
4554 N. Broadway, Suite 204
Chicago, IL 60640

Guatemala News and Information Bureau/Report on Guatemala
P.O. Box 28594
Oakland, CA 94604

Inforpress Centroamericana/Infopress, Central America Report
9a Calle "A" 3-56, Zona 1
Ciudad de Guatemala, Guatemala

Latin America Bureau
1 Amwell Street
London, England EC1R 1UL

Peace and Justice

Central America Resource Center
P.O. Box 2327
Austin, TX 78768

Comité Pro Justicia y Paz de Guatemala
Apartado Postal 57-135
México D.F. 06500
México

Guatemalan Church in Exile
Apartado Postal 1395
Managua, Nicaragua

International Labor Rights Education and Research Fund
110 Maryland Avenue NE, Box 68
Washington, DC 20002

Network in Solidarity with the People of Guatemala (NISGUA)
1314 14th Street NW #17
Washington, DC 20005

Peace Brigades International
PO Box 1233
Cambridge, MA 02238

Human Rights

Americas Watch
1522 K Street NW, Suite 910
Washington DC 20005

Amnesty International
322 8th Avenue
New York, NY 10001

Comisión de Derechos Humanos en Guatemala/International
  Bulletin
Apartado Postal 5-582
México D.F. 06500
México

Guatemala Human Rights Commission, USA
3321 12th St NE
Washington, DC 20017

National Central America Health Rights Network/Links
P.O. Box 202
New York, NY 10276

Tours

Center for Global Education
Augsburg College
731 21st Avenue South
Minneapolis, MN 55454

Business/Official

Embassy of Guatemala
2220 R Street NW
Washington DC 20008

Embassy of the United States in Guatemala
APO Miami, FL 34024

Fundación para el Desarrollo de Guatemala (Fundesa)
Edificio Cámara de Industria, 9 Nivel
Ruta 6, 9-21, Zona 4
Ciudad de Guatemala, Guatemala

U.S./Guatemala Labor Education Project
c/o ACTWU-Chicago Joint Board
333 S. Ashland
Chicago, IL 60607

U.S. State Department
Citizen's Emergency Center/Travel Information
Main State Building
Washington DC 20520
(202) 647-5225

The Resource Center

The Inter-Hemispheric Education Resource Center is a private, non-profit, research and policy institute located in Albuquerque, New Mexico. Founded in 1979, the Resource Center produces books, policy reports, audiovisuals, and other educational materials about U.S. foreign policy, as well as sponsoring popular education projects. For more information and a catalog of publications, please write to the Resource Center, Box 4506, Albuquerque, New Mexico 87196.

Board of Directors

Toney Anaya, *Former Governor of New Mexico*; Tom Barry, *Resource Center;* Blase Bonpane, *Office Of the Americas*; Fred Bronkema, *National Council of the Churches of Christ*; Ann Mari Buitrago, *Institute for Public Access to Government Information*; Noam Chomsky, *Massachusetts Institute of Technology*; Dr. Charles Clements, *SatelLife*; Dr. Wallace Ford, *New Mexico Conference of Churches*; Antonio González, *Southwest Voter Research Institute*; Don Hancock, *Southwest Research and Information Center*; Patricia Hynds, *Maryknoll Lay Missioner*; Claudia Isaac, *University of New Mexico Community and Regional Planning Program*; Mary MacArthur, *Peace Brigades International*; Jennifer Manríquez, *Albuquerque Technical-Vocational Institute*; Carmen Alicia Nebot, *UCC / Disciples of Christ*; John Nichols, *Author*; Debra Preusch, *Resource Center*; Thomas E. Quigley, *U.S. Catholic Conference*; Margaret Randall, *Writer and Photographer*; Frank I. Sánchez, *Partnership for Democracy*; Peter Schey, *Center for Human Rights and Constitutional Law*; Beth Wood, *Community Activist*. (Organizations listed for identification purposes only.)

Central America Inside Out

By Tom Barry

Central America Inside Out, drawn largely from the Resource Center's Country Guide series, pulls readers deep inside the seven Central American countries, with description and analysis of what is happening today. The profiles of the seven nations allow readers to step inside the internal dynamics of most aspects of Central American society—from the labor movement to the elite business organizations, from the struggle to save the environment to the latest strategies to stabilize the economy.

Central America Inside Out
Grove-Weidenfeld Press, September 1991, 501 pages, paperback
ISBN 0-8021-3260-X
$16.95

Prepayment is required. Include $2.50 postage and handling for the first item you order; include 50¢ for each additional. Prices subject to change. Send check or money order made payable to:

Resource Center / Box 4506 / Albuquerque, NM 87196

Visa/MasterCard orders by phone!

(505) 842-8288